Black Masculinity and the Cinema of Policing

Jean-Michel Basquiat, Irony of a Negro Policeman (1981).
© The Estate of Jean-Michel Basquiat/ADAGP, Paris/ARS, New York 2017.

Jared Sexton

Black Masculinity and the Cinema of Policing

palgrave
macmillan

Jared Sexton
Department of African American Studies
University of California, Irvine
Irvine, CA, USA

ISBN 978-3-319-66169-8   ISBN 978-3-319-66170-4 (eBook)
DOI 10.1007/978-3-319-66170-4

Library of Congress Control Number: 2017950695

© The Editor(s) (if applicable) and The Author(s) 2017
This work is subject to copyright. All rights are solely and exclusively licensed by the Publisher, whether the whole or part of the material is concerned, specifically the rights of translation, reprinting, reuse of illustrations, recitation, broadcasting, reproduction on microfilms or in any other physical way, and transmission or information storage and retrieval, electronic adaptation, computer software, or by similar or dissimilar methodology now known or hereafter developed.
The use of general descriptive names, registered names, trademarks, service marks, etc. in this publication does not imply, even in the absence of a specific statement, that such names are exempt from the relevant protective laws and regulations and therefore free for general use.
The publisher, the authors and the editors are safe to assume that the advice and information in this book are believed to be true and accurate at the date of publication. Neither the publisher nor the authors or the editors give a warranty, express or implied, with respect to the material contained herein or for any errors or omissions that may have been made. The publisher remains neutral with regard to jurisdictional claims in published maps and institutional affiliations.

Cover design by Jenny Vong

Printed on acid-free paper

This Palgrave Macmillan imprint is published by Springer Nature
The registered company is Springer International Publishing AG
The registered company address is: Gewerbestrasse 11, 6330 Cham, Switzerland

To CES,
For teaching us that patience and perseverance are the roots of possibility.

TO AJS,
For sharing an inherited love of movies and always appreciating a good line.

Preface: The Perfect Slave

Black Masculinity and the Cinema of Policing offers a critical survey of the contemporary field of images of black masculinity in early twenty-first-century United States.[1] It argues that popular representations of black masculine authority have become increasingly important to the cultural legitimization of executive power within the national security state and its leading role in the maintenance of an antiblack social order forged in the epoch of modern racial slavery. The projection of American Grand Strategy today navigates a domestic political terrain pulled taught between, on the one hand, official pronouncements of neoliberal multiculturalism and neoconservative colorblindness and, on the other, between progressive racial justice movements and newly resurgent right-wing white nationalism. While the second decade of the 2000s revealed these conflicts in stark relief, from the founding of the Tea Party in 2010 to the emergence of the Black Lives Matter movement in 2013 to the election of Donald Trump in 2016, the lineaments of the current political conjuncture can be traced with careful attention to recent work in the culture industry. This book provides, to that end, a series of close readings of Hollywood films released between 2001 and 2009—between President George W. Bush's announcement of the US-led War on Terror and President Barack Obama's acceptance of the Nobel Peace Prize—alongside discussion of several antecedent television series.

---

[1]Burgin (1996) distinguishes "the contemporary field of images" from "the field of contemporary images" where the former allows for the persistence, recirculation, and reiteration of past images in present day visual culture (304–305).

Rather than offer a glancing look at a comprehensive filmography from this period, the approach employed here examines a constellation of representative samples to illuminate the complex and contradictory dynamics at work in the repeated attempts to reconcile the promotion of black male patriarchal empowerment and the recrudescence of gendered antiblackness within the narrative space of the film and television productions in question. This study suggests that Hollywood is of two minds about depicting a post-feminist patriarchal restoration through figures of black masculinity, whether military personnel or police officers, sports coaches or aspiring athletes. For the reassertion of patriarchal values so vital to the maintenance of an embattled American global hegemony—militarily, economically, politically—requires the simultaneous preservation of an antiblack matrix of value deeply rooted in American history and a cultural myth of racial equality and liberal democracy supposed to distinguish the USA from the rest of the world. If film and television are rightly regarded as aspects of an ideological state apparatus, then we should expect that the ambiguity and ambivalence of constituted power at home and abroad will play out in vivid detail on screens large and small, year after year, as the interpretive frame of public discourse shifts from post-civil rights to post-cold war to post-9/11 or, more recently, from to post-racial to post-truth (Althusser 2014; McDonald 2016).

The immanent critique pursued in the following chapters takes productions of the culture industry, no less than its independent offshoots and countercurrents, as privileged occasions for thinking again about how profoundly the global practice of racial differentiation, from slavery to segregation and beyond, structures the totality of state and civil society. This study questions to that end the very terms of the post-civil rights historical periodization in order to broaden and deepen the context for the particular readings presented below. Not only because there are other relevant and appropriate ways to understand the last half-century, but also because the very idea of a discrete "civil rights era" itself warrants greater scrutiny. Dubbed the "Second Reconstruction" by many within its ranks, the modern civil rights movement was meant to rejoin the collective efforts initiated in the aftermath of the US Civil War to pursue the effective abolition of racial slavery. But the permutation of such efforts over the subsequent hundred years alerts us to another and, I think, more adequate interpretative framework. Rather than approach the civil rights movement as a mid-century political moment spanning the 1950s and 60s, we are better served by thinking instead of a protracted black freedom struggle that encompasses the everyday resistance and episodic revolt of enslaved Africans from the fifteenth century onward; the petition, protest, and politics of abolitionism in the eighteenth and nineteenth centuries; the twentieth-century social movements organized under the headings of New Negro, Civil Rights and Black Power; and the range of ongoing campaigns to end police violence, to promote environmental protection and to ensure economic and reproductive justice, among others (Birnbaum and Taylor 2000; Cain 2016; Fairclough 2002; Lebron 2017; Robinson 1997; Ross and Solinger 2017). This more expansive historical view allows us to reconsider the prospects for abolition across the *longue durée* of the modern world and along at least two primary lines of stress.

First, there is a concern about the continuation of the political conditions of slavery *despite* the claim to emancipation enshrined in the Thirteenth Amendment to the US Constitution and similar legislation throughout the transatlantic region. Legal scholar Guyora Binder reminds us that emancipation, far from providing a remedy for slavery, is actually a component part of its form and function, so much so that "the institution of slavery could persist without any individual being lawfully held as a slave" in the usual meaning of the term (Binder 1996, 2064). Binder contends that, with respect to the USA as a principal case study, the legislative action and the preceding executive order of the mid-1860s served mainly to manumit slaves already effectively emancipated by the enormous dislocations of the Civil War. Thus emancipated, however, was the abolition of slavery a fait accompli? Binder finds to the contrary that "for reasons intrinsic to its subject… the Thirteenth Amendment confronts interpreters with multiple dimensions of ambiguity," most importantly "which of the deprivations imposed on slaves to regard as essential to slavery and which to legitimize as incidental to slavery" and "how the abolition of slavery redistributes the resources and power of the masters and what sort of historical narrative justifies those distributive consequences" (Binder 1996, 2070). Abolition would, accordingly, entail far more than universal manumission *ceteris paribus*, something we can only indicate here as the generalization, on a global scale, of the ex-slaves' demands for a radical reconstruction of society. Eric Foner's (2014) and Manisha Sinha's (2016) prodigious historical researches demonstrate exhaustively the chasm that separated the conceptions of freedom held by ex-slaves and those held by nearly everyone else in the nineteenth-century USA.

Where Binder seeks to "provoke uncertainty about the meaning of freedom and slavery, at least insofar as the alternative to such uncertainty is a reductive definition of slavery that places it at a safe distance from contemporary American society," he is all too right to claim that "when we speak of freedom and slavery we *do not* know 'what we are talking about' and *should not* speak with self-assurance" (Binder 1996, 2063). It is against that overwhelming tendency toward self-assurance that the second line of stress is expressed. It consists in a concern about a paradoxical "perfection of slavery" *through* emancipation and the ongoing struggle for black equality. Critical race theorist Anthony Farley (2004) has articulated this thinking most prominently, pulling together arguments regarding race, law, and society that he has developed since the early 1990s. Farley is not arguing that the basic elements of slavery persist *despite* emancipation under cover of a narrative of progress, though he surely would agree with Binder's insights to that effect. Neither is he at pains to track the cunning of political retrenchment and revanchist legal maneuvering *after* emancipation. Farley is not interested primarily in the machinations of the slave power as such or its functional surrogates. The perfection of slavery issues forth, rather, from *the slave's desire for equality* itself, from the dream-work aimed at participation in slave society. The more strident the demands for reform grow, in fact, the more perfect slavery, and the slave, becomes. "We are strangers to ourselves," Farley writes. "The dream of equality, of rights, is the disguised wish for hierarchy. The prayer for equal rights is the disguised desire for slavery" (Farley 2004, 224). He continues further along:

> It seems that after "a division of mental and manual labor appears" that the slave is assigned the latter and the master is assigned the former. All is not as it seems. The slave actually does the *mental* work that keeps the structure from falling apart. The slave dreams of rights and of equal justice under law. The production of dreams is the slave's true and secret function. The slave produces all of the equations that stabilize the system of death-over-life through its prayers for equal rights. The slave's prayer resolves all present contradictions into white-over-black, for white-over-black is all that equal rights or law can ever be or become. (Farley 2004, 227)

Emancipation, in this view, is a desire bound to the dream of equality, a palliative, an opiate of the enslaved masses, that wards against the true thought of freedom and the destruction of the terms of order of a global system of slavery it requires. Racial slavery does not simply persist in attenuated form as a legacy or aftermath demanding continued vigilance. Neither does it only persist in vacated institutional form post-emancipation, as slavery without slaves. Those are problems enough. Rather, it persists more fundamentally as a problem compounded by every effort to abolish it that fails to unravel the fabric of the modern world it brought into being, and not only its prevailing economic system. "To wake from slavery is to see that everything must go, every law room, every great house, every plantation, all of it, everything" (Farley 2004, 222–223). More to the point: "Without the dream-work of the slave, the many crises of the system of white-over-black blossom in revolution. The flames are wooed from their buds and continue to unfold until the entire plantation system is gone. The servile insurrection continues until it brings down the system of marks, the system of property, and the system of law. Slaves are trained to *not* think this way" (Farley 2004, 244).

But how, exactly, are slaves trained *not* to think this way? This is not an antiquated question for the historic instance of the chattel system alone, but also an urgent question of the present conjuncture. How are manumitted slaves, nominally free people of color—still, today—trained *not* to think critically about the system of marks, the system of property, and the system of law? How is that black radical thinking forestalled, preempted, disallowed? *Black Masculinity and the Cinema of Policing* is interested in tracing the contours of the sustained ideological labor dedicated to that sort of discipline and punishment in mass media representations of black masculinity during the years of Barack Obama's extraordinary political ascent, from the Illinois General Assembly in 1996 to the US Senate in 2004 to the White House in 2008. This chapter's title is drawn, in fact, from the high-profile figure of President Obama—not only a nominally free person of color, but also the proverbial leader of the free world—whose career and, more essentially, whose *character* is held up as a perverse ideal for so many urban black youth whose masculinity is said to be in acute crisis. My Brother's Keeper, a White House initiative meant to "bolster and reinforce our African-American boys… helping young African-American men feel that they're a full part of this society," was Obama's answer to George Zimmerman's acquittal for the killing of Trayvon Martin in the summer of 2013. The official response of the first black male president to the openly racist murder of a black male teenager was to redouble *ex officio* efforts among the rest of society to convince black male teenagers that they are educable and employable and therefore valued by the rest of society; as if the spectacular violence of a vigilante assault were a symptom of the victim's education level or employment status—a slave's prayer if ever there was one. Insofar as we endorse the above claim of a present-tense regime of racial slavery dependent upon the dream-work of "equal justice under law," the Obama Administration, rather than fulfilling the promise of freedom, presents us with the paradoxical achievements of the perfect slave.

This text speaks directly, then, to the convolution of slavery and freedom that informs the historic discourse on post-bellum black masculinity, from the heated 1865 congressional debate over "Negro manhood rights" to the infamous 1965 Moynihan Report on "the Negro family," from the fated 1890s anti-lynching crusade to the eclipsed 1990s campaign to end racial profiling. Vexation over the prospect of unbounded black masculinity, and the attendant worry about heteroclite black male sexuality, continues to animate current projections of racial uplift like the Open Society Foundations Campaign for Black Male Achievement (scaling previously local mentorship and job-training endeavors into a coordinated partnership of federal agencies, state and local governments, private foundations, and non-profit organizations) or the growing slate of single-sex charter schools aimed at the education of "underachieving" black boys (promoted and underwritten by the 2001 No Child Left Behind Act and renewed by the US Department of Education's 2009 Race to the Top grant program). It even shapes the controversy surrounding the 2016 release of *The Birth of a Nation*, writer-director-actor Nate Parker's film rendition of the 1831 Nat Turner insurrection (raising again the problematic of interracial sexual violence in relation to black male agency—real and imagined, material and symbolic). It is telling that Parker's *pièce de résistance* mutated into an uncanny swan song in the same immediate environment that consolidated authoritarian populism, both nationally and internationally, as a reverie of unreconstructed white supremacy and toxic masculinity. Whereas Parker sought, to a fault, to rewrite D.W. Griffith's reactionary paean to the Ku Klux Klan as a progressive homage to a twenty-first-century racial justice movement to come, Citizen Trump was far more intent upon, and far more capable of, updating the politics of Redemption for the age of Astroturf mobilization and social media marketing.

Black Masculinity and the Cinema of Policing examines the cycle of early twenty-first-century liberal filmmaking that helped to cultivate the ground both for Parker's flawed cinematic project and for Trump's successful seizure of executive power in the twilight of the Obama era. The half-dozen or so Hollywood productions under discussion include variations on the interracial buddy theme common to cop action films and sports films alike, as well as versions of the family drama and the (black) male coming-of-age story. And though the settings span the country from small town to mid-size city to major metropolis, and the configuration of characters is by turns inter-racial and intra-racial, inter-generational and near-peer, co-worker and cross-class, fraternal and gender diverse; the central focus of these conflict-driven narratives falls squarely upon the distributed virtues and vices of black boys and men. The operative question: What, if anything, can be done *with* them, given what has been done *to* them, that is, given their structural disinheritance? Some auxiliary questions: Can a proper morality be instilled in their hearts and minds? Can their bodies be adapted to the burdens and benefits of civilization? Can they be trusted to use the powers vested in them for good and not evil? Can a disciplined black masculinity become a figure of legitimate authority? Can it become a source of value or only a site for the destruction of value? Can it serve, finally, as a condition of possibility, individual and collective? Amid longstanding public consternation and private condemnation regarding the antagonism between black boys and men and nearly every major institution of US state and civil society—arts, athletics, education, employment, healthcare, family, law, military, news media, police, religion, transportation—this study delves into the cultural logic that, on this score, unites the platforms of our dueling political parties and, despite other important divergences, lends coherence to the wide swath of our political spectrum.

Irvine, USA   Jared Sexton

Acknowledgements

The author is grateful to the following publishers for permission to reprint these earlier articles and essays here in modified form: Johns Hopkins University Press for "The Ruse of Engagement: Black Masculinity and the Cinema of Policing." American Quarterly 6 (2009): 39–63 (Chap. 1); Rowman & Littlefield for "Life with No Hoop: Black Pride, State Power." Commodified and Criminalized: New Racism and African Americans in Contemporary Sports, 223–248. Edited by David J. Leonard and C. Richard King (2011) (Chap. 2); Peter Lang for "Fields of Fantasy and the Court of Appeal: On Friday Night Lights and Coach Carter." Visual Economies in/of Motion: Sport and Film, 103–120. Edited by C. Richard King and David J. Leonard (2006) (Chap. 3); Taylor & Francis for "Derelictum Ex Nihilo: On Origins and Beginnings in The Blind Side." Football, Culture and Power, 59–85. Edited by David J. Leonard, Kimberly B. George and Wade Davis (2016) (Chap. 4); and ABC-CLIO for "More Serious Than Money: On Diff'rent Strokes and Webster." African Americans on Television: Race-ing for Ratings, 82–113. Edited by David J. Leonard and Lisa A. Guerrero (2013) (Chap. 5).

Contents

1 Chaos and Opportunity: On *Training Day*   1

2 History and Power: On *Pride*   37

3 Fantasy and Desire: On *Friday Night Lights* and *Coach Carter*   67

4 Origins and Beginnings: On *The Blind Side*   89

5 Comedy and Romance: On *Diff'rent Strokes* and *Webster*   121

6 Shadow and Myth: On *Stranger Inside* and *Moonlight*   161

Index   195

List of Figures

Fig. 1.1	Detective Virgil Tibbs (Sidney Poitier) sits with Chief Bill Gillespie (Rod Steiger) at the train station in Norman Jewison's *In the Heat of the Night* (1967)	10
Fig. 1.2	Detective Alonzo Harris (Denzel Washington) leaves Office Jake Hoyt (Ethan Hawke) in the alley after terrorizing and releasing two homeless men suspected of sexual assault in Antoine Fuqua's *Training Day* (2001)	19
Fig. 1.3	Smiley (Cliff Curtis), Moreno (Noel Gugliemi), and Sniper (Raymond Cruz) find Letty's wallet while preparing to execute Jake	23
Fig. 1.4	Alonzo persuades Jake to finish the mission after they rob and murder Roger	24
Fig. 2.1	Coach Jim Ellis (Terrance Howard) considers the significance and difficulty of his task in Sunu Gonera's *Pride* (2007)	49
Fig. 2.2	Young Jim looks on as his white competitors refuse to swim in the same pool	53
Fig. 2.3	Coach Ellis confronts Coach Bink (Tom Arnold) for cheating and disrespecting the PDR swimmers	55
Fig. 2.4	Coach Ellis gives his swimmers a lesson on technique	59
Fig. 3.1	Coach Gary Gaines (Billy Bob Thornton) gives his team a halftime speech in Peter Berg's *Friday Night Lights* (2004)	70
Fig. 3.2	Coach Ken Carter (Samuel L. Jackson) disciplines his players during a practice session in Thomas Carter's *Coach Carter* (2005)	74

List of Figures

Fig. 3.3	Coach Carter explains the need for his players to prioritize academics over athletics	79
Fig. 3.4	The Richmond Oilers walk out of the locker room together to face their cross-town rivals	82
Fig. 3.5	The Permian Panthers line up against Dallas-Carter in the championship game	84
Fig. 4.1	Michael Oher (Quinton Aaron) walks through his old Memphis neighborhood in John Lee Hancock's *The Blind Side* (2009)	96
Fig. 4.2	Leigh Anne Tuohy (Sandra Bullock) reads to Michael and her son Sean (Jae Head)	101
Fig. 4.3	Leigh Anne inspires Michael to be more aggressive on the field	105
Fig. 4.4	Leigh Anne visits Michael's mother, Denise Oher (Adriane Lenox), to discuss the new arrangement	109
Fig. 5.1	Eddie Murphy plays "Buckwheat" on Lorne Michaels's *Saturday Night Live* circa 1982	126
Fig. 5.2	Billie Thomas plays "Buckwheat" in Gordon Douglass's *Glove Taps* (1937), part of Hal Roach's *Our Gang* series (1922–1944)	132
Fig. 5.3	Arnold Jackson (Gary Coleman) and his brother Willis (Todd Bridges) raise their concerns with Mr. Drummond (Conrad Bain) in Jeff Harris and Bernie Kukoff's *Diff'rent Strokes* circa 1979	144
Fig. 5.4	Gary Coleman poses for press pictures as "Arnold" on Diff'rent Strokes circa 1980	149
Fig. 5.5	Webster Long (Emmanuel Lewis) hugs George Papadapolis (Alex Karras) in Stu Silver's *Webster* circa 1983	153
Fig. 5.6	Webster talks with Katherine Calder-Young Papadapolis (Susan Clark) circa 1983	155
Fig. 5.7	Webster sits with his uncle Phillip Long (Ben Vareen) circa 1985	157
Fig. 6.1	Brownie (Davenia McFadden) comforts Treasure Lee (Yolonda Ross) in Cheryl Dunye's *Stranger Inside* (2001)	165
Fig. 6.2	The prisoners line up for roll call	167
Fig. 6.3	Treasure talks with Shadow (LaTonya 'T' Hagans) on the yard	169
Fig. 6.4	Little (Alex Hibbert) stands in the kitchen in Barry Jenkins's *Moonlight* (2016)	173

Fig. 6.5	Juan (Mahershala Ali) teaches Little (Alex Hibbert) how to swim in the ocean	176
Fig. 6.6	Naomie Harris as Chiron's mother Paula	179
Fig. 6.7	Chiron (Ashton Sanders) meets Kevin on the beach	182
Fig. 6.8	Black (Trevante Rhodes) drives to Kevin's place after their reunion at the diner	185
Fig. 6.9	Kevin (André Holland) stands in the kitchen and asks Black, "Who is you, Chiron?"	188
Fig. 6.10	Little looks out over the ocean at dusk	190

Summaries

Chapter 1 examines the place of commercial black filmmaking in the cultural politics of the post-civil rights era United States. It begins by situating what some consider a defining moment in black film history—the 2002 Academy Awards—with respect to widely-circulated images of black participation in projections of a "New American Century," with all of its intensified policing and militarism. I argue that a reassertion of antiblackness in popular culture has accompanied the clamor about "blacks in officialdom" that both neoliberal multiculturalism and neoconservative colorblindness have amplified over the last several decades, reaching fever pitch with the presidential election of Barack Obama in 2008. In this light, I consider whether setting this contradictory logic of representation alongside the continuing conditions of segregation that characterize black life in the United States over the same period undermines easy assertions about contemporary black inroads in state and civil society. More to the point, this chapter suggests that such convergence complicates the idea of an *institutionalized* black complicity with the structures of white supremacy, especially in the aftermath of 9/11. These various guises of black empowerment, particularly images of black masculinity as state-sanctioned authority, should not be contrasted with the associations of illegitimacy, dispossession, and violence that seem to otherwise monopolize the signification of racial blackness. Rather, the former should be understood as an extension of the latter. Antoine Fuqua's 2001 *Training Day* provides a case study for the discussion, and Fuqua's professional career articulates the structural conditions for a popular antiblack black visibility on a global scale.

Chapter 2 takes up Sunu Gonera's 2007 *Pride*, a 1970s era biopic about the life and labor of Philadelphia native Jim Ellis, a competitive swim coach whose unlikely program eventually produces the first black swimmers—and soon thereafter the first black medalists—for the US Olympic Team. The chapter situates the film's generally favorable portrayal of Ellis within the twentieth-century history of racially segregated municipal swimming and bathing, and the fairly complicated exploitation of African swimming and diving skills as an aspect of maritime slavery, in order to better comprehend the material and symbolic construction of the stereotype that "blacks can't swim." For Ellis, the introduction of ghettoized urban black youth to this supposedly quintessential white suburban middle-class pursuit will allow them not only to avoid the perils of their imminent recruitment to local street gangs, but also to contest the restrictive avenues of athletic excellence otherwise available to their neighborhood peers (i.e., football and basketball, to which we turn in the following chapter). And though Ellis, as surrogate father, challenges the inefficient and indifferent government bureaucracy represented by the black maternal figure to grant him the opportunity to make good on a promise to help his newly acquired charges, the bid for patriarchal protection requires him to call directly upon the police powers of the state in more ways than one. Ellis, not unlike his own white male coach before him, counsels young black men to seek liberation by soliciting the agents of their own repression and to stand up to racist assault by refusing to fight back in their own defense.

Chapter 3 presents a contrapuntal reading of two films in which high school sport serves as the ground for adjudicating the education of young men and the allegory for prospects of economic recovery, political deliberation, and social change in the contemporary United States: Peter Berg's 2004 *Friday Night Lights* and Thomas Carter's 2005 *Coach Carter*. The former is a cinematic adaptation of H.G. Bassinger's bestselling account of a small, predominantly white, working-class community in 1980s rural West Texas railing against prolonged economic crisis and investing all the more fervently in the success of their local high school football team. Importantly, the conditions of economic decline are exacerbated for residents by the seemingly imposing presence of distant urban black communities assumed to be in political ascendance in the post-civil rights era. The latter, in turn, is a retelling of the headline-grabbing intervention of the eponymous basketball coach in a predominantly black urban community in 1990s Northern California besieged by structural unemployment, concentrated poverty, unbridled policing, and an expanding underground economy. Both films feature narratives of individual salvation for the community's young men, tutored in the rites of passage by a tough-loving patriarch representing the values of an earlier day and age. Both films also pivot on stimulating the particularly masculine ambition to flee the horizon of dead-end lives and managing the peculiar pressures brought to bear when this mission is figured as a quest for proper manhood. However, these surface similarities are not evidence of an overarching project or underlying common ground. Not only are these two films *not* simply two versions of the same story, but also, more importantly, the success and possibility of *Friday Night Lights*, the efficacy of its symbolic universe, is premised on the failure and impossibility of the transcendent vision at the heart of *Coach Carter*.

Chapter 4 interprets John Lee Hancock's 2009 *The Blind Side*, the most successful sports drama in Hollywood history, as an indictment of the black family nearly a half-century after Senator Moynihan declared a crisis in need of national action in his infamous 1965 report. The film follows Michael Oher's improbable rise from the Memphis public housing and foster care systems to his 2013 Super Bowl victory with the Baltimore Ravens, and it is widely read as a feel-good story extolling the value of organized sports, in which the sad fate of a poor black urban youth is redirected by the intervention of an enterprising professional white woman and the institutional resources she affords. Yet, this work represents something more than an example of the patronage motif. Beyond the troubling reiteration of this longstanding narrative pattern, *The Blind Side* reveals that the NFL and the "Athletic Industrial Complex" that feeds it are essentially understood as aspects of the larger mission of public education in particular and of public services in general. Put somewhat differently, insofar as black football players—high school, college or professional—are assumed to serve at the pleasure of white benefactors—taxpayers, educators, coaches or team owners—we are led to examine the figure of the black male athlete in light of the figure of the black female welfare recipient and the question of reproductive justice raised by her predicament. This perspective not only interrupts the redemptive fantasy of racial capitalism promoted by Oher's rags-to-riches story, but also productively undermines the quest for hegemonic gender differentiation, even within the confines of mainstream narrative cinema.

Chapter 5 looks at some of the antecedent imagery of black youth in US visual culture and discusses the post-civil rights era television situation comedy as an oblique commentary on the racial politics of kinship in the afterlife of slavery. It takes Bernie Kukoff and Jeff Harris's *Diff'rent Strokes* (1978–1986) and Stu Silver's *Webster* (1983–1989) as case studies to that end. It traces the wildly popular black man-child characters that featured in primetime programming in the 1970s and 80s to earlier figures: the black "rascals" of the *Our Gang* film series of the 1920s, 30s and 40s (most notably Buckwheat) and, before that, young Topsy of Harriet Beecher Stowe's 1852 abolitionist novel *Uncle Tom's Cabin* and its subsequent stage productions. What we find across the great expanse is an indiscernibleness of both gender (male/female, masculine/feminine) and generation (adult/juvenile, parent/child) in the image repertoire of black juveniles. And these most pronounced forms of indiscernible difference are linked to an even more general crisis of categories therein, including autonomy/automaton, pleasure/pain, human/animal, organic/inorganic, and, of course, freedom/slavery. In the intervening years of the mid-twentieth century, the public witnessed sustained attempts by a new generation of black professionals and community advocates to politicize, yet again, the matter of black family preservation against ongoing attempts by state and civil society to shatter the bonds between black parents and children. It is argued here that this ongoing struggle is inscribed in the discourse of the television sitcom and returns symptomatically in its performance and reception.

Chapter 6 addresses Cheryl Dunye's 2001 *Stranger Inside*, a made-for-television film about a young black lesbian prisoner seeking to find her own incarcerated mother by deliberately transferring from her current unit to a higher security facility. It explores *Stranger* within the context of Dunye's early cinematic work, especially her 1996 *The Watermelon Woman*, in order to reconstruct her complex meditation on the psycho-politics of black kinship, and specifically of black maternity, as the disinherited matrix of gendering and ungendering as well as the orientation and disorientation of sexuality. Black female masculinity, under conditions of extremity, is the formation here that questions the relation between the psychic life of a state-sanctioned interdiction of black kinship and the willingness to suffer and/or inflict forms of physical, mental, and emotional violence to undo—or preserve or pervert—its effects. This racialized dislocation of embodiment, gender expression and sexual practice—where it is unclear in advance, and at various points along the way, who identifies with whom, who is related to whom, who is attracted to or involved with whom—serves also to upset the normative striving for a coherent social identity aligned with the dominant conceptions of filial love and loving affiliation. The chapter concludes by reviewing the critical itinerary travelled in our investigation of contemporary representations of black masculinity up to this point—from cop to prisoner, from coach to player, from parent to child, from (biological) father to (adopted) mother, from black man to white woman, from housing projects to high-rise penthouse, from post-civil rights retrenchment to antebellum abolitionism and back again—suggesting, finally, that independent films like Stephen Dest's 2017 *I Am Shakespeare: The Henry Green Story* and Barry Jenkins 2016 *Moonlight* represent a promising counter-cinema wherein a critical appraisal of black masculinity can be more fully developed. As such, an extended reading of *Moonlight* closes the book.

References

Adelman, Larry. 2008. *Unnatural Causes: Is Inequality Making Us Sick?* DVD. Directed by Llewellyn Smith, Tracy Heather Strain, Patricia Garcia Rios, Maria Teresa Rodriguez, James M. Fortier, Ellie Lee, Eric Strange, and James Rutenbeck. San Francisco: California Newsreel.

Althusser, Louis. 2014. *On the Reproduction of Capitalism: Ideology and Ideological State Apparatuses*, trans. G.M. Goshgarian. New York: Verso.

Binder, Guyora. 1996. "The Slavery of Emancipation." *Cardoza Law Review* 17: 2063–2102.

Birnbaum, Jonathan, and Clarence Taylor. 2000. *Civil Rights Since 1787: A Reader on the Black Struggle*. New York: NYU Press.

Burgin, Victor. 1996. *In/Different Spaces: Place and Memory in Visual Culture*. Berkeley, CA: University of California Press.

Cain, Cacildia. 2016. "The Necessity of Black Women's Standpoint and Intersectionality in Environmental Movements." *Medium*, April 14. Accessed May 28, 2017. https://medium.com/black-feminist-thought-2016/the-necessity-of-black-women-s-standpoint-and-intersectionality-in-environmental-movements-fc52d4277616.

Fairclough, Adam. 2002. *Better Day Coming: Blacks and Equality, 1890–2000*. New York: Penguin.

Farley, Anthony. 2004. "Perfecting Slavery." *Loyola University Chicago Law Journal* 36: 221–251.

Foner, Eric. 2014. *Reconstruction: America's Unfinished Revolution, 1863–1877*, Updated Edition. New York: HarperCollins.

Lebron, Christopher. 2017. *The Making of Black Lives Matter: A Brief History of an Idea*. New York: Oxford University Press.

McDonald, Kevin. 2016. *Film Theory: The Basics*. New York: Routledge.

Robinson, Cedric. 1997. *Black Movements in America*. New York: Routledge.

Ross, Loretta, and Ricky Solinger. 2017. *Reproductive Justice: An Introduction*. Berkeley, CA: University of California Press.

Satcher, David, George E. Fryer Jr., Jessica McCann, Adewale Troutman, Steven H. Woolf, and George Rust. 2005. "What If We Were Equal? A Comparison of The Black—White Mortality Gap in 1960 And 2000." *Health Affairs* 24: 459–464.

Sinha, Manisha. 2016. *The Slave's Cause: A History of Abolition*. New York: NYU Press.

1

Chaos and Opportunity: On *Training Day*

Introduction

The first generation of black (male) voters in the United States wondered aloud in the late 1860s whether the Civil War and the Emancipation Proclamation had achieved for them "nothing but freedom," as the movement to redeem white supremacy undermined even the best efforts of Radical Reconstruction (Foner 2007). Not only was the recently extended franchise and related bundle of political rights quickly rescinded, de facto and *de jure*; but the promised redistribution of material goods and services in reparation for several centuries of enslavement was also postponed indefinitely. The violent repression, political absorption and ideological cooptation of that Second Reconstruction otherwise known as the modern Civil Rights Movement of the mid-1900s, and the still widening "racial wealth gap" that ongoing backlash helped to preserve, gave similar pause to the black constituents of the first black head of state, President Barack Obama, some half-century later. When they gathered together in the nation's capital during the summer of 2013, on the fiftieth anniversary of the landmark 1963 March on Washington for Jobs and Freedom, they could not help but conclude that they had gained by the end of the post-civil rights era "a president… nothing else." The Supreme Court under Chief Justice John Roberts had, after all, effectively gutted the 1965 Voting Rights Act just two months earlier. Between the notorious Supreme Court decision in *Shelby County v. Holder* and the symbolic commemoration over which it cast a pall, the eponymous US Attorney General—Eric Holder, the first African American appointed to the position of federal "top cop"—announced to a meeting of the American Bar Association that the "tough on crime" zeitgeist that had driven a racist War on Drugs since the Nixon Administration and underwritten the largest prison buildup in the history of the world would now yield to a wiser "smart on crime initiative." Not, per President Obama, at the level of "some grand new federal program," but merely within the largely ineffectual discretionary parameters of the Department of Justice to establish federal sentencing guidelines. Smart cops compliments of the people who brought us smart bombs: all to reduce the "collateral damage" of civilian casualties at home and abroad.

Holder's press conference coincided with the general release of Ryan Coogler's award-winning film *Fruitvale Station*, which chronicles the last day in the life of Oscar Grant, a young black man shot and killed on an Oakland, California subway platform by a white Bay Area Rapid Transit police officer, Johannes Mehserle, on New Year's Day 2009. Mehserle was convicted of involuntary manslaughter and served just over eighteen months in jail, but was acquitted of more serious charges. It was also the season that witnessed the not-guilty verdict—widely expected, though no less enraging—in the trial of neighborhood watchman George Zimmerman for the 2012 murder of Trayvon Martin, a black male teenager, in Sanford, Florida. Less publicized was the contemporaneous trial of Officer Joseph Weekley in Michigan for the death of Aiyana Stanley-Jones, a seven-year-old black girl who was shot dead as she lay sleeping on her grandmother's couch during a midnight raid conducted by the Detroit Police Department's Special Response Team in 2010. Weekley returned to duty in 2015 after two consecutive mistrials. The deaths of Martin and Stanley-Jones, like Grant before them, reveal the same operative dynamic. In the rare instance that a police officer or surrogate is charged with a crime, or even subject to independent investigation, in the death of a black victim, the charges must, by definition, diminish or deflect or deny the *systematic* nature of the lethal violence at hand. Moreover, the charges must evacuate entirely the aggression inherent in the prosecution of openly declared domestic warfare. In the case of Weekley's trial, an effort to mitigate culpability ("I didn't mean to") quickly shifted toward a reversal of culpability altogether ("somebody grabbed my gun and it went off"). And in Zimmerman's case, his pursuit of the other morphed seamlessly into his protection of the self. Standard operating procedure ad infinitum: everything turns upside down—"Sentence first, verdict afterwards," the Red Queen insists in *Alice's Adventures in Wonderland*—and a false debate ensues. The question that can never be asked is, "What were armed and dangerous state-sanctioned shooters doing there in the first place?"

The Malcolm X Grassroots Movement (MXGM) reported in 2012 that, on average, someone directly employed or indirectly protected by the federal, state, or local government kills a black person in the United States nearly *every day*. We have since learned, thanks to international investigative journalism, that the number represents a gross undercount. The notorious "Stand Your Ground" laws—which, according to attorney Monte Frank, "empower ordinary citizens to act as vigilantes using lethal force"—have become emblems of a larger and more longstanding crisis, but their rollback, however welcome, would not save the day. We would still confront, among other things, the law's consistent rejection of black self-defense. What is at stake in documenting the casualties of "Operation Ghetto Storm" (to adopt MXGM's sardonic term) is neither the mission nor the morality of a Weekley or a Zimmerman or of the hundreds of other police officers, security guards, and vigilantes who take it upon themselves to end the lives of black people in the name of law and order. Nor should it be understood, whatever conservative pundits may insist, as a distraction from analyzing and intervening upon the extraordinary rates of (no less state-sanctioned) murder *between* civilians within many black communities. At stake is what enables *all* of this violence, and much more, to unfold as the normal state of affairs.[1] These general conditions moved Jamilah Lemieux (2013), writing for *Ebony* magazine, to declare that black folks are "BEING KILLED FOR EXISTING." Not for walking or driving or breaking the law; not for failing to work productively or for lacking proper documents; not for inhabiting valued land or possessing scarce resources; not for subscribing to a political ideology or adhering to a religious faith; not for doing any particular thing or being any particular place; but, rather, for being *at all*. In efforts to conceal or cancel this critical insight, which nonetheless suffuses the common sense of black communities across the country, a discourse of black male discipline and punishment has been disseminated throughout the contemporary political culture, requiring obeisance toward agents of state repression and identification with the hierarchical subordination of an antiblack capitalist patriarchy.

In this light, the present book examines of the role and function of commercial filmmaking in the cultural politics of the post-civil rights USA, and of the peculiar place therein of black masculinity inscribed in and as state-sanctioned authority. We begin by situating a watershed moment in US

---

[1] Gross health inequality, for instance, annually kills more black people than are lost to homicide in an entire decade (Satcher et al. 2005; Adelman 2008).

film history—the 2002 Academy Awards—with respect to widely circulated images of black participation in the imperial projections of a "New American Century," with all of its intensified policing and militarism.[2] We will see that a certain recrudescence of antiblackness in the culture industry has accompanied the growing clamor about "blacks in officialdom" that both neoliberal multiculturalism and neoconservative colorblindness have amplified over the last several decades. That clamor reached fever pitch with Barack Obama's 2008 election as the 44th President of the United States, becoming the first black person to hold the highest executive office. Setting this contradictory logic of representation alongside the continuing structural conditions of segregation that characterize black existence in the USA over the same period undermines easy assertions about contemporary black inroads in state and civil society. More to the point, such convergence complicates current thinking about an *institutionalized* black complicity with the structures of white supremacy, especially in the immediate aftermath of 9/11. These various guises of black empowerment should not be simply contrasted with the associations of violence, dispossession and illegitimacy that seem to otherwise monopolize the signification of racial blackness. Rather, the former should be understood as an extension of the latter. Antoine Fuqua's *Training Day* (2001) provides a case study for our discussion and the director's professional ascent more generally articulates some of the political, economic, and cultural conditions for a popular, and lucrative, antiblack black visibility on a global scale (Miller et al. 2005).

The (Black) Culture Industry

In the corporate media, the 74th Annual Academy Awards was unofficially dubbed "The Black Oscars." The selection of comedian Whoopi Goldberg as master of ceremonies and the collective honoring of Sidney Poitier, Halle Berry, and Denzel Washington prompted some commentators to wonder whether Hollywood had turned the proverbial corner with regard to its politics of racial exclusion and marginalization. Goldberg, enjoying a coveted

---

[2]I write "projections" here rather than "project" in order to distinguish the formal activities of the right-wing think tank that guided the Bush Administration (2001–2009), the Project for the New American Century, from the broader neoconservative political movement and the global hegemony of neoliberalism (Ryan 2010; Simon et al. 2016). The New American Century platform is not identical to the Trump Administration's efforts to "Make America Great Again"—owing principally to the latter's openly pronounced white nationalism—but there is, of course, significant overlap in their respective objectives and personnel.

invitation of her own, hosted the evening's events with her characteristic blend of sarcasm, wit, and panache. The gala began its run by handing down Sir Sidney Poitier the Academy's Lifetime Achievement Award, thereby canonizing the premier black actor of the postwar era. Halle Berry's wholly unprecedented Oscar for Performance by an Actress in a Leading Role— the first black woman to take home the trophy—for her lead as Leticia Musgrove in Marc Forster's *Monster's Ball* (2001) seemed to confirm the mood of the moment. Director Antoine Fuqua's otherwise unexceptional police action film, *Training Day* (2001), was touted by the critical establishment as a vehicle for one of Denzel Washington's most controversial and gripping roles since his eponymous lead in Spike Lee's *Malcolm X* (1992); and Washington's Oscar for Performance by an Actor in a Leading Role was termed a crowning achievement of an already stellar onscreen career. In fact, several critics suggested that the historic top prize, only the second to go to a black actor (the first went to Poitier nearly forty years earlier), provided a sort of belated vindication for a long-recognized talent whose efforts—most especially in Lee's biopic—were sorely unrewarded for no other apparent reason than that the business of filmmaking remains unrelentingly hostile to any "legitimate" or "respectable" black presence. As such, the official praise was marked as an awkward sign of overdue popular cultural redress, a small but richly symbolic instance of racial justice in the notoriously racist business of mass media entertainment (Bradshaw 2002; Samuels 2002).

Feting Washington and Berry together on the same stage (as Washington cracked, "Two birds in one night, huh?") suggested that both black men and black women would now enjoy a new day in Hollywood (as Berry claimed, "this door tonight has been opened"). Yet the gendered specificity of this watershed racial affair would not be lost on even the casual observer. Whereas Berry, upon receiving the award, notably remarked that her nod from the Academy came in the wake of a long and glaring *absence*,[3] Washington attempted to establish beneath his recognition a certain *lineage*, however slim or fragile. In his acceptance speech, Washington paid homage to Poitier as the latter looked on approvingly from the audience, saying: "I'll always be chasing you Sidney. I'll always be following in your footsteps. There's nothing I would rather do, sir. Nothing I would rather do." Yet, we must ask: what footsteps are these to follow? Who, or, moreover, what is Sidney Poitier for Denzel Washington to chase?

---

[3] Not surprisingly Berry's mode of expression received derisive sniping in the press, while the substance of her remarks about the cinema's exclusion of black female talents was only superficially acknowledged.

Of course, Poitier is a trailblazer: his Oscar for Best Actor as Homer Smith in Ralph Nelson *Lilies of the Field* (1963) interrupted the color bar on the position of Hollywood's leading man, the foremost site of cultural production for the fictions of racial whiteness and normative masculinity (though this brief hiatus cannot be said to subvert or challenge the force or function of either). More important to the current discussion is Poitier's role as Detective Virgil Tibbs in Norman Jewison's award-winning *In the Heat of the Night* (1967). In this capacity, Poitier, at the height of his powers, introduced to the big screen a bizarre figure whose prominence grew steadily in the following years and whose appearance proliferated wildly in the closing decades of the twentieth century. Mr. Tibbs is, of course, the first significant black male cop in US film history and, as such, predecessor to a considerable list of creatures whose careers can scarcely be labeled salutary.[4]

In this line, one thinks of William Roundtree's Detective John Shaft (*Shaft*), Billie Dee William's Detective Matthew Fox (*Nighthawks*), Eddie Murphy's Detective Axel Foley (*Beverly Hills Cop*), Danny Glover's Sergeant Roger Murtaugh (*Lethal Weapon*), Will Smith's Detective Mike Lowrey and Martin Lawrence's Detective Marcus Burnett (*Bad Boys*), Morgan Freeman's Detective Dr. Alex Cross (*Kiss the Girls*, *Along Came a Spider*) and Detective William Somerset (*Se7en*), Wesley Snipes's Detective Harlan Regis (*Murder at 1600*), Chris Tucker's Detective James Carter (*Rush Hour*), Samuel L. Jackson's Lieutenant Danny Roman (*The Negotiator*) and his year 2000 reincarnation of Detective John Shaft, Lawrence Fishburn's Officer Russell Stevens (*Deep Cover*) and Detective Whitey Powers, and, last but not least, Denzel Washington's Alonzo Harris. Or, before that, Washington's Officer Xavier Quinn (*The Mighty Quinn*), Officer Nick Styles (*Ricochet*), Lieutenant Parker Barnes (*Virtuosity*), Detective John Hobbes (*Fallen*), Detective Lincoln Rhyme (*The Bone Collector*), Special Agent

---

[4]Jewison's film won the Oscar for Best Picture. It was adapted to the screen by Stirling Silliphant (who also won the Academy Award for Best Adapted Screenplay) from John Ball's 1965 Edgar Award-winning novel of the same name. Ball went on to write six sequels to his debut novel between 1966 and 1986. As well, the film adaptation inspired two sequels starring Poitier—Gordon Douglas's *They Call Me MISTER Tibbs!* (1970) and Don Medford's *The Organization* (1971)—and served as the basis of a successful television series starring Academy Award-nominee Howard Rollins (Supporting Actor, *Ragtime*) as Tibbs and running a full eight seasons (1988–1995). This is all to say that the cultural production of the character of Virgil Tibbs, in print and onscreen, spanned more than two decades and met with great acclaim. Perhaps not coincidentally, Ball is also the author of much hawkish Cold War literature (the Tibbs series included), most famously *The First Team* (1971), in which the USA is invaded by the Soviet Union without firing a single shot because it has been weakened by a liberal President and the progressive and radical social movements of the day (civil rights, anti-war, etc.). Ball also served for a time as a Los Angeles County Sheriff. Dudziak (2002) explores at length the historical connections between racial liberalism and anti-communism in the United States.

Anthony Hubbard (*The Siege*), or even private investigator Easy Rawlins (*Devil in a Blue Dress*). Since the success of *Training Day*, we can include: Chief Matthias Whitlock (*Out of Time*), Agent John Creasy (*Man on Fire*), Detective Keith Frazier (*Inside Man*), Agent Doug Carlin (*Deju Vu*), Detective Zachary Garber (*The Taking of Pelham 1-2-3*), Agent Tobin Frost (*Safe House*), Agent Bobby Trench (*2 Guns*), Agent Robert McCall (*The Equalizer*), and Officer Sam Chisolm (*The Magnificent Seven*). As of this writing, Washington has been cast as an officer of the law sixteen times and, in related fashion, appeared as a current or former military officer another eight. To date, he has appeared in uniform in roughly half of the forty-odd films he has completed since his 1981 debut in Michael Schultz's *Carbon Copy*. As noted, nearly every noteworthy black male actor of the post-civil rights era has made this professional rite of passage as Officer, Detective, Sergeant, Lieutenant, or Chief. All have played roles as either a cop or a soldier and the lion's share have earned their reputations and their largest paydays in such roles, perhaps none more so than Washington.

What does this trend indicate about the conditions of labor and the politics of representation for black male performers in mainstream cinema post-civil rights? What does it imply about the shifting terrains of film culture and its relations to coordinates of race, gender, sexuality and the state? How is it involved in the image management of an emergent and uncertain black middle class or, rather, the profoundly convoluted focus on class stratification (i.e., distributions of education, employment and income) among the black population? How is the black male cop installed within the broad category of crime films (Rafter 2000), the genre of police films (Leitch 2002), or even the subgenre of police action films (King 1999); and how is this cultural politics related to the widespread vindication of "policing black people" in contemporary law and society (Cashmore and McLaughlin 1991; Parenti 2000; Wacquant 2002)?

James Baldwin penned the seminal reading of Mr. Tibbs more than a generation ago in his late essay, *The Devil Finds Work*. There we learn that, for all the dignity that Jewison affords the character and for all the grace and vitality and intelligence that Poitier contributes, Tibbs is nonetheless a terribly pitiful figure. Not only because the budding friendship between him and the otherwise typical white southern sheriff, Chief Bill Gillespie, is sentimental, misleading, and farcical. Of this Baldwin writes: "Black men know something about white sheriffs. They know, for one thing, that the sheriff is no freer to become friends with them than they are to become friends with the sheriff" (Baldwin 2000, 62). And again: "nothing, alas, had been made possible by this obligatory, fade-out kiss, this preposterous adventure: except that white Americans have been encouraged to continue dreaming, and black Americans have been alerted to the necessity of waking up" (Baldwin 2000, 59). Not only because Tibbs' tenure behind the badge (rather than simply before the barrel of a gun or locked in a cage) mandates the sort of immaculate pedigree and faultless demeanor, the model citizenship and shining patriotism, that newspaper mogul Matt Drayton requires of the saintly Dr. John Prentice before sanctimoniously granting his daughter's hand in marriage in Stanley Kramer's contemporaneous *Guess Who's Coming to Dinner?* Not only because *In the Heat of the Night* disables an incipient dramatization of white supremacy, capitalism, and the state, in both its southern patrician and northern industrialist aspects, by returning the murderous scandal to the banality of an accidental crime committed in desperation.[5]

Beyond all of this, to watch Mr. Tibbs pursue his cause is crushing—and confounding—because, in a film in which he is meant to presume, and the audience is meant to believe, that he is not, as it were, just a man (and nothing but a man), but also an effective social agent with unrivaled institutional power over life and death, we find this black male agent of the state nonetheless *unauthorized*, subjected entirely to the caprice of whites: men and women, young and old, rich and poor, liberal and conservative, northerner and southerner, officer and civilian, solitary soul and raging mob, present and absent, near and far. He is also, importantly, *unarmed*: a cop, alas, with no gun, no badge, and no jurisdiction. Even his title, Detective, which is all he is finally granted in the film, is useless. The sheriff acknowledges it only after it is confirmed by Mr. Tibbs' presumptively white captain in Philadelphia (who finally forces Tibbs, against his wishes, to take the case, on loan, into which Sheriff Gillespie is cornering him). The widow of the murdered industrialist, Mrs Leslie Colbert, insists that, in exchange for construction of the new factory to continue as planned, "the Negro detective" stay on the case when doubts arise regarding his suitability (on this note, Baldwin asks piercingly: "had the widow demanded the black man's blood as the price for the wealth she was bringing into the town… who, among the manly crew, would have resisted the widow's might?") (Baldwin 2000, 59). The several lynch mobs disregard Tibbs' word, given that they resent his very

---

[5]However, it is worth mentioning the film's oblique critical commentary on the gendered dynamics of shame and responsibility (i.e., the white boyfriend is under pressure to provide money to his girlfriend for the abortion of an unwanted pregnancy lest they wind up in a shotgun marriage; when he incidentally murders the propertied Northern white man that he robs to that end, he helps to scapegoat Tibbs for the crime) and the racialization of reproductive politics (i.e., the white woman's unplanned pregnancy is aborted illegally by a black woman from the other side of town in order to protect her public reputation and outsource the risk of prosecution).

existence. Even the pathetic waiter at the diner (whom Baldwin describes as "an utterly grotesque, hysterical creature"), ultimately revealed to be the culprit at the bottom of the whole mess, folds his arms and pays no heed to Tibbs' orders when asked to assist in the investigation.

Although Tibbs solves the crime, he does so not only under a tyrannical prerogative, but also in the custody of his small-minded, bungling, and impetuous white counterpart; custody in the place where otherwise there would be collaboration. Here I would modify Ed Guerrero's rich insight concerning the development of black—white buddy films in the period following Poitier's acme. Where Guerrero rightly identifies much of the dynamic in what he terms "protective custody," I depart from his arguments in one important way (Guerrero 1993b).[6] In my view, the black buddy or partner is shielded from harm by the white only after the black is dragged into danger by the white who will defend him, that is, only after he is positively imperiled, a situation not only initiated by the white but also usually involving him as a component of the larger threat as well. In the final analysis, the interracial relation of custody is not so much protective as it is punitive, less paternalistic than punishing, not only baldly aggrandizing for the white but also bluntly aggressive toward the black. Thus, the movement of magical bonding is not one that moves from an initial state of mutual distrust or dislike to one of eventual understanding and affection, but rather one in which the black is hauled in and knocked around and expected to smile about it, though the frenzy of image and narrative strives to convince the world that this encounter is somehow a problem that the white must endure with pursed lips, rolling eyes, and shaking head. The virtue of Poitier's role is that it produces no confusion on this front. Mr. Tibbs is just traveling home after visiting his dear old mother and, through an unfortunate turn of circumstances, which is to say as a result of his running into white folks, he has to spend the next twenty four walking the tightrope without a net, praying he'll live to see tomorrow (Fig. 1.1).

The sole redeeming moment of the film is, of course, the extraordinary exchange of blows between Mr. Tibbs and Mr. Endicott, the intransigent plantation owner and hardline conservative power broker (who may as well scream, "Get your cotton-pickin' hands off me, boy!"). Mr. Tibbs is

---

[6]On this score, it would be interesting to revisit Fiedler's contention: "We [white male Americans] continue to dream the female dead, and ourselves in the arms of our dusky male lovers" (Fiedler 1960, 29). In this light, the vexed interracial male bonding trope may appear as less a symbolic homoerotic resolution to a real political antagonism than a reiteration of that antagonism as a permuted form of homoerotic assault.

Fig. 1.1 Detective Virgil Tibbs (Sidney Poitier) sits with Chief Bill Gillespie (Rod Steiger) at the train station in Norman Jewison's *In the Heat of the Night* (1967). Image reproduced under terms of fair use

directed—I was going to say allowed—to strike a rich and powerful white man in the face, but only on condition that he is a very bad white man, the decaying symbol of a moribund Old South which is, quite naturally, yielding to the progressive movement of History (or at least begrudgingly acknowledging the virtue of Tibbs' diligence, charm, and good manners). In other words, Mr. Endicott is deposed so that the American nation, the souls of white folk, and the values of capitalist development may be redeemed by this maniacal tale emerging at the century's apex of black radicalism (Robinson 1997).

The subversive force of this dramatic reversal of racial violence—an image of black counterattack, a trace of black self-defense during an historical moment when the question is at fever pitch in the political field—is overwhelmed in the film by a diegetic milieu of helplessness. Sent on an official errand by his lords and masters, Tibbs is regarded by the white world as meddling and uppity (the black world, what little we see of it, regards him as unusual and perhaps a bit crazy), and were it not for the constant intervention of white authority and a countervailing white power, he would be dead several times over. He is, in a word, kept alive. It goes without saying that this triage is carried out not because he is sovereign, but because he is serviceable. A generation later, after the retrenchment and resurgence of the new Confederate spirit, does Washington's Detective Alonzo Harris find himself in so different a position? Is this the path along which the actor and the character is chasing? Is this what it means, in the end, to be following in the footsteps of the exalted?

These questions may elucidate the black press's considerably more circumspect celebration of the Berry—Goldberg—Poitier—Washington quartet. The wariness seems to have settled around two main concerns: First, the timing of this unprecedented heralding of black artistic achievement suggested a showcasing of racial liberalism and goodwill toward the nation's customary pariah, shoring the white majority against the loss of a mythic national unity and courting the sentiments of generally unsympathetic black communities for mounting military and police campaigns that were, at the time, roundly criticized for their blatant imperialism and unabashed authoritarianism (Wilson 2002). Second, black reviewers remarked that the particular performances prompting acknowledgment by the leading Hollywood institution of these giants of film history and popular culture held less than flattering implications about what an overwhelmingly white establishment (both the Academy of Motion Picture Arts and Sciences and the broader network of mainstream film critics) deems black cinematic work of accomplishment. Poitier, famously known for his casting as excessively wholesome characters, has long been a source of ambivalence for black audiences and his admission to the canon of Academy greats did not fail to reactivate varying degrees of disquiet, while Goldberg is considered for her antics, both on- and off-screen, a source of bewilderment as often as she articulates popular sentiment or generates political inspiration (Bogle 2016).

Regarding Washington and Berry, the apprehension was of another, related variety: while many were glad to have swept the Oscars, so to speak, and felt pride at the momentary rupture in Hollywood's ironclad omission of black actors and actresses, a pressing concern about the sort of message that their respective roles might deliver accompanied any pleasures of recognition.[7] After all, Berry is cast as a poor widowed black woman whose

---

[7]In seventy-four years and two hundred ninety-six possible Academy Awards, only four black actors—Sidney Poitier, Cuba Gooding Jr., Louis Gossett Jr., Denzel Washington—and two black actresses—Hattie McDaniel, Whoopi Goldberg—had won to that point. Since then, Jamie Foxx, (Best Actor, *Ray* [2004]), Morgan Freeman (Best Supporting Actor, *Million Dollar Baby* [2004]), Jennifer Hudson (Best Actress, *Dreamgirls* [2006]), Forest Whitaker (Best Actor, *The Last King of Scotland* [2006]), Mo'Nique (Best Supporting Actress, *Precious* [2009]), Octavia Spencer (Best Supporting Actress, *The Help* [2011]), Lupita Nyong'o (Best Supporting Actress, *12 Years a Slave* [2013]), Mahershala Ali (Best Supporting Actor, *Moonlight* [2016]), and Viola Davis (Best Supporting Actress, *Fences* [2016]) have taken home trophies—in other words, the number of black Oscar winners has doubled and achieved relative gender parity in the last fifteen years or so.

desire for the affections of an improbably reformed racist white prison guard is matched in intensity only by her ability, and perhaps willingness, to bracket out the fact that he is also her formerly imprisoned husband's executioner, a feat undertaken, moreover, while coping with the grief of her only son's recent accidental death.[8] Washington, for his part as Detective Alonzo Harris, veritably embodies the dark side of contemporary urban law enforcement, cast as an unscrupulous rogue cop whose singular ferociousness and ultimately incompetent scheming seems to absorb the corruption of the entire Los Angeles Police Department, highlighting and absolving a racist city power structure in one breathtaking gesture: in other words, living the nightmare of unchecked (white) police power and purging the (racial) terror that such impunity necessarily produces through his spectacularly violent death. Harris represents *par excellence* the fearsome black cop described by Baldwin a generation earlier:

> Blacks know something about black cops. […] They know that their presence on the force doesn't change the force or the judges or the lawyers or the bondsmen or the jails. […] They know how much the black cop has to prove, and how limited are his means of proving it: where I grew up, black cops were yet more terrifying than white ones. (Baldwin 2000, 63)

I will say more about Washington's performance below, but before doing so it is important to note that, for all the critical acclaim and financial success of *Training Day*, very little has been said about its director, one of the few black filmmakers—most of whom are men—to work soundly within mainstream Hollywood production channels and, until recently, the only one to direct an Oscar-winning film.[9] I am interested in reading his early works as points of condensation for two large historical trends: on the one hand, recent changes in the material and ideological bases of Hollywood cinema,

---

[8]Berry's role in the film is, of course, more complex than this pat judgment would suggest and I am glossing aspects of the black press's reception in pointed language only to emphasize divergence with the mainstream press. For a subtle reading of Berry's performance and the politics of race, gender, sexuality and death in *Monster's Ball*, see Holland (2006). For a detailed critique of Forster's film from another perspective, see Wilderson (2010).

[9]Spike Lee and John Singleton had been nominated previously, but neither of them won. Since 2002, Lee Daniels directed Mo'Nique's Oscar-winning performance in *Precious* (2009); Steve McQueen directed Lupita Nyong'o's Oscar-winning performance in *12 Years a Slave* (2013), which also won for Best Adapted Screenplay (John Ridley) and Best Picture; Denzel Washington directed Viola Davis's Oscar-winning performance in *Fences* (2016); and Barry Jenkins directed Mahershala Ali's Oscar-winning performance in *Moonlight* (2016), which also won for Best Adapted Screenplay (Tarell Alvin McCraney and Barry Jenkins) and Best Picture. Director Ezra Edleman also won an Academy Award for Best Documentary Feature for his *O.J.: Made in America* (2016).

including the emergence of virtual monopolies in the corporate mode of film production, the selective incorporation of black filmmaking talents over since the turn of the twenty-first century, and the rise of black celebrity personas across the whole mass media environment (Lewis 1998b; Gilroy 2000); on the other hand, the increasingly popular dissatisfaction with homegrown "structural adjustment programs" dictated by corporate globalization, the symbolic centrality of right-leaning black public intellectuals to the growth of a counteracting multicultural conservatism, and the further consolidation of a decades-old domestic militarization to preempt and disrupt political resistance and social unrest, particularly within black communities (Dillard 2001; Gilmore 1993, 2007; Simpson 1998). It goes without saying that these facets of the social landscape have undergone new and ominous inflections since the formation of the Department of Homeland Security and the executive declaration of an infinite or enduring global War on Terror. However, I hasten to add that the symbolic economy under investigation is less inaugurated than it is augmented by developments post-9/11 (Sexton 2007).[10]

We can situate Fuqua's rise to prominence more narrowly within the dynamics of post-civil rights era black film history, drawing an arc from the unparalleled radical output of the well-known "black independent cinema movement" of the 1970s to the appropriation of this collective critical impulse in the largely white-directed genre of "Blaxploitation" to the emergence of black "guerrilla cinema" from the likes of Spike Lee and Robert Townsend in the 1980s to the "new black movie boom" of the early 1990s, during which "New Jack" directors consistently turned inordinate profits along the lower tiers and margins of Hollywood's regular production schedule (Diawara 1993; Guerrero 1998). All along the way, a steady stream of black independent filmmakers from Charles Burnett to Haile Gerima have maintained critical distance from Hollywood, by choice or by circumstance, sustaining a vital counter-cinema through black film festivals, alternative

---

[10]This is perhaps the place to say something about what I take to be the principle functions of images of blacks in officialdom after 9/11 and the launch of the War on Terror. Sure enough, flattering representations of black politicians, police, or military personnel (like black achievements in arts, entertainment, industry, etc.) can serve as foils to deflect criticism about the racist structure of US foreign policy (including the military invasion of Afghanistan since 2001 and Iraq since 2003) and the policing of the homeland (including the defense of racial profiling, indefinite detention, and torture). But it is important to emphasize that, in the historic instance, the racial coding of state power and/or capital as black is more profoundly a reactionary paranoia about inverted racial domination than a liberal delusion or even a cynical conservative insistence about racial equality. In that sense, it enjoys a genealogy reaching back to the Reconstruction era at least (Blight 2001).

distribution networks, and video outlets.[11] This has particularly been the case for black women filmmakers like Julie Dash, Cheryl Dunye, Ava DuVernay, Leslie Harris, and Darnell Martin, whose works remain, in many ways, obscured, even within black communities, except among the ranks of the more committed film aficionados. Guerrero noted of an earlier generation, "if the situation for black male independent filmmakers has proven difficult, then it has been almost impossible for black women" (Guerrero 1993a, 174).[12] Perhaps unsurprisingly, white men continue to direct over ninety percent and finance almost one hundred percent of yearly Hollywood output, and film distribution is a similarly exclusive province.

This suggests that, for the most part, black cinematic practice in the USA, especially if it is critical and/or independent, continues to take place beneath the radar of the major institutions of mass media and popular culture. When blacks do participate in the mainstream film industry as actors, they have been permitted access "only on the condition that they conform to whites' images of blacks." When black creative talents find themselves in positions behind the camera, they "have tended to act precisely as whites have in similar circumstances" (Cashmore 1997, 1). Such is the price of the ticket: "black film, white money" (Rhines 1996). Given this context, what might we expect from an aspiring black director like Fuqua, drafted from the minor leagues of music video production to put out standard-fare action films with the glamour and style of the Hip Hop Generation?[13] If Fuqua had a critical political sensibility, how would it find its way to the screen?[14] Put somewhat differently, if "when it comes to greenlighting film

---

[11] Examples include: the African Diaspora Film Festival, the Black Filmmakers Foundation, the Pan African Film and Arts Festival, Rainforest Films, and New Millennium Studios, among others.

[12] The situation for black women directors in Hollywood has been changing slowly, given contemporaneous productions by Neema Barnette (*All You've Got* [2006]), Sanaa Hamri (*Something New* [2006]), Kasi Lemmons (*Eve's Bayou* [1997]), Nnegest Likke (*Phat Girlz* [2006]), Darnell Martin (*Cadillac Records* [2008]), Gina Prince-Bythewood (*Love and Basketball* [2000], *The Secret Life of Bees* [2008]), Angela Robinson (*D.E.B.S* [2004]), and Alison Swan (*Mixing Nia* [1998]), among others. More recently, we can note productions by Ava Duverney (*Middle of Nowhere* [2013], *Selma* [2014]), Tanya Hamilton (*Night Catches Us* [2010]), Dee Rees (*Pariah* [2011], *Bessie* [2015]), among others. See, generally, Welbon (2003) and Reid (2005). On black women's considerable inroads in television, see Toby (2016).

[13] Like F. Gary Gray (*Friday, Set It Off*) before him, Fuqua was a highly successful music video director before making the transition to feature-length filmmaking, having directed videos for R&B and hip-hop artists the likes of Toni Braxton, Coolio, Chanté Moore, Ce Ce Peniston, Prince, Queen Latifah, Shanice, Usher, and Stevie Wonder.

[14] Fuqua and Washington were generally evasive in interviews regarding the issue of police power. The gist of their commentary, individually and collectively, was that the institution of the police is basically sound, but that certain rogue officers may participate in exceptional cases of corruption. Moreover, they offered that terrible and unjust things happen to members of black communities, but that similarly terrible things happen to anyone under the right circumstances. In one interview, Fuqua states: "I don't

scripts, building stars' careers, or investing large amounts of capital for short-term profit…control over decision-making in production and distribution remains firmly a white monopoly;" and if in the "relationship industry" of Hollywood "*blackness* bears little 'relationship' to 'business'," then what vision of the world is mandated as a condition of possibility for any black presence whatsoever (Guerrero 1998, 331)? Even more relevant to the present discussion, if the monopolistic trajectory of the new corporate Hollywood "foreground[s] an entertainment industry… controlled by two or three highly diversified companies that… may well have and be able to implement a cultural or political agenda," then what does commercial black cinema, or black images *in* commercial cinema, have to do with such an agenda (Lewis 1998a, 4)? Beyond the highly profitable marketing of the exceptional "A-list" black male actor like Denzel Washington or Samuel L. Jackson or Will Smith, what additional functions might a black directorial signature serve in this instance?[15]

With respect to the racialized political economy outlined above, to have a black director behind the camera makes no substantive difference to the conventions of Hollywood filmmaking, whether at the level of narrative structure, plot, characterization, or film form. Directors may call the shots, but film editors and financial underwriters with pending distribution deals and potential consumer markets in mind always have the first and final word. But if we do not see a qualitatively different kind of film from Fuqua,

---

think [the police] care what color you are anymore. I think if they are having a bad day, you've got a problem" (Dudek 2001). Notwithstanding the insipid colorblindness of the passage—which would deny the existence of racial profiling and the overwhelming racial dynamics of mass imprisonment—Fuqua disavows the absence of legal recourse against the state he describes here, the horror of a system in which "you've got a problem" simply because a cop is "having a bad day." Fuqua is half right, of course. It is true today that the law grants the police impunity against the entire civilian population. However, the police see to the difference that race makes in the street-level practice of racial profiling. Fuqua has since teamed up with director Cle 'Bone' Sloan, former member of the Athens Park Bloods in Los Angeles, to produce *Bastards of the Party* (2006), a documentary examining the social, political and economic history of black street gangs in the LA area since the 1960s. Sloan's film is more critical of the *systemic* nature of racist police violence—including its function as political repression—than *Training Day*. That Fuqua saw fit to produce *Bastards*, however, suggests that he is not so much ignorant of the history of black radicalism as he is *managing* its contemporary significance.

[15]There are, as yet, no "A-list" black women actors, Berry's once $10 million average salary notwithstanding. In fact, Berry ranked tenth at the time on a list of the ten highest paid women in Hollywood, behind Reese Witherspoon, Angelina Jolie, Cameron Diaz, Nicole Kidman, Julia Roberts, Renée Zellweger, Sandra Bullock, Drew Barrymore and Jodie Foster (Associated Press 2007). *Forbes* magazine's most recent data on the highest paid actresses in the world feature no black women (Robehmed 2016). More to the point, Kidman, Roberts and Witherspoon are the only women to date to have been listed on James Ulmer's famous "A+list" of the ten most bankable actors in Hollywood.

we do nonetheless find new dynamics at work. One such dynamic is an effect of the contradictory nature of the culture industry and it is heightened by the entirely symbolic contributions of black directorial control. Another is a distinct but related byproduct of this first development and points to a potential intensification of black spectators' alienating identification with the images of absolute dereliction that we find coded throughout Fuqua's work as the hallmark of blackness. What stands out is the fact that the "wrenching ambivalence" and "psychic conflict" (Snead 1994, 24) that might characterize the experience of black audiences in this cinema threatens to subsume the relations of Fuqua's productive labor, as the director too must participate in—indeed, must orchestrate—scenes of his own subjection, be party to his own deracination, and be forced (by hook or by crook) to "feed well off [his] own abjection" (Marriott 2000, 32).

The colossal financial reward supplied by service to the Hollywood machine may mitigate the lure of anguished identifications and provide considerable material prop for social distancing, yet the management of this precarious class distinction is haunted by the possibility of categorical collapse (psychically and politically) for the black professional culture worker. In this sense, we discover a homology between the positions of Fuqua as director and Harris as protagonist under the respective institutional protocols of Hollywood and the LAPD. Washington, as inheritor of Poitier's dubitable legacy, sits at the median of this linkage. It remains to be seen whether this structural vulnerability will produce politically enabling effects, including better quality films, or simply exacerbate the ambivalence of collective disavowal: living large and running scared.

The Racial Allocation of Guilt

Taken together, *Bait* (2000), *Training Day* (2001), and *Tears of the Sun* (2003) rehash at rising scales of organization an unrelenting suspicion, if not cynicism, about the possibility of a humane affective tie or social contract among blacks. From family to community to nation to continent, black sociality in this troika of Fuqua's cinematic imagination only follows from the most repressive state intervention and seems to require gratuitous loss of life in the process. If the white subject—embedded in the institution of family-as-nation, metonym of the universal—has understood itself in the historic instance to be, both onscreen and off, under the enabling cover of the police and military, safely behind the frontlines of their respective wars against enemies foreign and domestic; then the black subject (we must use the term advisedly, under erasure) is not only prototype of that threat against which civilization must defend, but also that animate figure which must aspire to the very forms of existence from which it is constitutively barred (Dyer 1997; Morrison 1992).

Antiblackness is best described here as a series of forced choices—we all know the imperative, "your money or your life"—but choices which brook no answer (Gordon 1995).[16] For instance: Do you want to serve an extended prison sentence or sacrifice yourself to a sting operation of the national security state (*Bait*)? Do you want to wither indefinitely in a miserable refugee camp or fall victim to a military-sponsored campaign of ethnic cleansing (*Tears*)? More simply: do you want go home or go to jail (*Training Day*)? And where, exactly, is home, we might ask, if you are black in the contemporary world? Do you want to take a trip to "the booty house" (as Detective Harris tauntingly refers to the county jail) or languish on the streets of Los Angeles's skid row, strung out by an addiction to crack cocaine? Or, would you rather take a knife in the eye, a bullet in the head? Or, would you prefer to bleed to death from the wounds of a vigilante attack, castrated and raped in a state-sanctioned lynching? In what follows we will see that, although a chilling impetus seems to lie in the heart of our protagonist and the ensuing hazards are borne by his unguarded partner, the moral arc of the universe is short and it bends toward whiteness.

The hydraulics of a lethal extortion are introduced early in *Training Day*, in a scene just after Alonzo sets in motion the initial phases of his central design. He seeks to embezzle one million dollars in monies seized from a staged drug bust in order to pay a debt incurred to the Russian mob after the inadvertent murder of one in their ranks during an altercation outside a Las Vegas casino. In order to execute the plan, Alonzo must manipulate the ambitions, exploit the trust, abuse the subordination, and, finally, sacrifice the body of his naïve and eager trainee, Jake Hoyt (Ethan Hawke). En route, the film rewrites the script of the well-known interracial buddy formula, hollowing out the coveted bonds of interracial fraternity and promoting instead the obligatory vigilance of whites toward the treachery of blacks (Alexander 1996; Wiegman 1995; Willis 1997). Among the various tactics of setup, Alonzo coerces Jake into ingesting drugs as both a palliative for the forthcoming ordeal and an insurance policy against Jake's predictable

---

[16]Elsewhere he writes: "The antiblack world is conditioned by what we can here describe as two principles of value: (1) it is best to be white but (2) above all, it is worst to be black. When one fails to achieve principle (1), it becomes vital to avoid embodying the group designated by principle (2). We can reformulate our two principles thus: (1*) be white but (2*) don't be black" (Gordon 1997, 124).

desire to inform the *proper* authorities about the irregularities and illegalities of his training day. However, though Jake becomes increasingly vulnerable to Alonzo's maneuvering, he is not entirely susceptible to his wiles; he is doped but not duped. This resilience is all the more compelling because it is, at least initially, unselfconscious. As Jake endures the confusion and languor of the pusher's cocktail, he manages nonetheless to seize opportunity for demonstrating his commitment to public safety, a display that emerges, as it must, spontaneously. A young woman is in danger and she calls out for help as a man attacks her in a desolate alleyway (Fig. 1.2).

The racial division of labor in the scene is quite stunning, but I submit we have within it the universe of the film, and perhaps all of Fuqua's early work, in microcosm. Jake is concerned to the point of recklessness with the defense of the light-skinned Chicana teenager, Letty, a Catholic schoolgirl whose incipient sexual assault at the hands of a deranged black man in the alley he apprehends in an instant—through the haze of a PCP high—almost by instinct. He runs to the scene of assault without backup, forgetting his blind spots and losing his firearm, but still forcibly halts the attack, handcuffs the suspects, and secures the situation. The racial and sexual economy of this rescue proves decisive to Jake's survival (and hence to the redemption of the badge that he ensures against Alonzo's apparent dishonor), since it is this pseudo-karmic act of selfless valor that later stays the gangland *coup de grâce* that Alonzo has arranged for him. The young girl, it turns out, is the cousin of the would-be executioner. Jake's defense of her is, then, also a deferred and unsuspecting form of self-defense: first, against the black man in the alley and, second, against Alonzo's elaborate scheme of seduction and betrayal. Alonzo's threat of contract execution is conflated, at this level, with the threat of murder by the black man in the alley. The double payoff of this rescue, for Letty and for Jake, is echoed in the subsequent "liberation" of Alonzo's wife Sara (Eva Mendez) from her sequestering in "the Jungle." (To that end, it proves vital that Jake effortlessly wins the trust of Sara and Alonzo's son, Alonzo Jr., in order to gain entry to the stronghold in the climactic confrontation.) It also recalls the establishing shots of white domesticity at the film's opening in which Jake's commitment to police work is shown to derive from his fidelity to wife and child, and his desire to provide them with a better life or at least a better house.

We might set "white" in scare quotes here because, though Jake is referred to contemptuously several times in the film as "white boy," it is hinted in the opening shots that, in point of fact, Jake's wife, like Alonzo's, is a Latina. A deleted scene included on the DVD supports this reading, in which Jake reveals that his wife, Lisa, is a "light-skinned Chicana" and, moreover, that

Fig. 1.2 Detective Alonzo Harris (Denzel Washington) leaves Office Jake Hoyt (Ethan Hawke) in the alley after terrorizing and releasing two homeless men suspected of sexual assault in Antoine Fuqua's *Training Day* (2001). Image reproduced under terms of fair use

he is, in his own words, "Italian, Irish, and Mexican" (Alonzo adds jestingly: "but not necessarily in that order"). Reading Jake as *mestizo* or light-skinned Latino, married to a Latina and raising a Latina daughter, rather than Anglo "white boy," puts significant stress on the racialized alignments of good and evil, threat and defense, strong and weak that otherwise structure the film's narrative—what Alonzo summarizes as the calibration of "wolves and sheep." In the world of *Training Day*, no less in the brutal real world of policing the film attempts to represent, Latinos are surely placed on the far side of the law, criminalized. However, they are *also* positioned as part of the community of sheep and those good wolves on the hunt for justice in ways that blacks are not. That is, unless and until blacks are tutored by way of spectacular state violence.[17]

---

[17]Latinos—here mainly Chicanos/Mexicans and Central Americans—not only represent the largest percentage, though not the largest proportion, of prisoners in Los Angeles County and the State of California, *Training Day*'s fictional setting, but also constitute a bulk of the victims at the center of the so-called Rampart Scandal of the late 1990s, upon which David Ayer's screenplay is based (Hayden 2000; Bailey 2001). It is important to note that the principal defendant in the prosecution, and the lightning rod for much of the public outrage, was Officer Rafael Pérez, a Puerto Rican Afro-Latino with alleged connections to the Bloods street gang. Along with three Bloods-affiliated African American

Latinos, if they are sufficiently light-skinned and/or do not seem African-derived, are positioned thereby as figures of *mediation*—points of transfer (if male) and objects of exchange (if female)—between, on the one hand, the elemental menace of black violence and sexuality that includes and features Alonzo and, on the other, the ruthless civic sensibilities of official law and order, embodied by the Three Wise Men and shadowed in their unwritten pact with the Russian mob. If Jake is not presumptively white, then we have on our hands not a replay of the typical white supremacist dichotomy between white cop and black criminal or, in this case, good white cop and bad black cop (which elements remain in either case as a code of *color*). Rather, this is a more specifically antiblack competition for the middle position of racial and class hierarchies: lord of the common folk and junior partner to the brokers of determinant social, economic, political, and military power. In this battle for hearts and minds, Jake emerges victorious because his unassuming moral posture artlessly elides the resentment that Alonzo accrues as an effect of his smalltime tyranny.

Alonzo, for his part, is merely amused by the squabble in the alley and seems downright indifferent to the wellbeing of the young girl. In fact, he proceeds to scold and dismiss her in the immediate aftermath. For him, the ordeal is only a serendipitous pretext to terrorize a couple of "monkey-strong crackheads" (part of the inherently criminal element he otherwise calls "maggots" and "garbage") and he is sure to address the full weight of his sexual taunts, death threats, and battery to that quintessential nightmare of everyday urban life, a dark-skinned homeless black man. Fortunately, the white and black pair of would-be rapists conveniently mouth off only to their respective racial counterparts, but when Jake is confronted with a similar opportunity to "protect and serve" he opts instead to take the high road and moralize about the youth of the victimized girl (as if the situation would have been less disturbing were the victim, say, twenty-four or thirty-four rather than fourteen). And though it may seem a small detail, it

---

LAPD officers—Gino Durden, Kevin Gaines, and David Mack—Pérez was indicted for, among other things, the attempted murder of Javier Ovando, former member of the largely Chicano/Mexican 18th Street gang. The character of Alonzo Harris is loosely based on Pérez, whose racialization as black rather than brown in the U.S. context is only highlighted by the casting of Washington for the role. The diversification of Harris's corrupt crew in the film—his partners in crime are both black and white—seems a half-hearted attempt to demonstrate that, as it were, evil has no color.

is not insignificant that the white attacker threatens Jake with the specific promise to "crack [his] head open" whereas the black attacker's insults are explicitly sexual ("I'm gonna fuck you too, cop," "Suck my dick, bitch"). If the criminalization of black community presents itself here as a political problem for polite society, we do well to remember an observation by the late cultural critic James Snead who remarks, "in *all* Hollywood film portrayals of blacks… the political is never far from the sexual, for it is both as a political and as a sexual threat that… black skin appears on screen" (Snead 1994, 8; cf. Courtney 2004).

This sexual threat is posed not only to white or light-skinned women (e.g., the college girl in the Volkswagen, Sara, Letty, and Lisa—Alonzo half-jokingly offers to Jake to "knock her up" after already making suggestive comments directly to her over the phone in the opening scene), but also to Jake and other white or light-skinned men (e.g., recall the threats of the "big boys at the booty house," gang rape by the "homies," a shot gun blast to the testicles, Jake's designation as "virgin" or "daisy fresh," etc.). Of course, black men in this scenario are not beyond posing threats to black women and to one another as well, but any questions of black wellbeing are pushed outside the film's sphere of concern. Predictably, they are subordinated as background for the ethical dilemmas of the police force itself, which is to say of the relation of the repressive state apparatus to a civil society that excludes blacks by definition, but that may consider, allow, or even promote the welfare of non-black people of color if it serves to maintain the structural isolation of blacks. Extending our earlier point, we can say that if *Training Day* adheres to aspects of Hollywood's interracial buddy formula, it does so only by suggesting the mortal dangers of cross-racial fraternity, not its typically reconciliatory or recuperative attributes, fixating instead on the gruesome risks to life and limb that issue forth from the negotiation of racial difference within the precincts of the homosocial (Sedgwick 1985).

It is through the twinning of the political and the sexual that we must read the strained oscillations of identification, desire, and aggression between Jake and Alonzo throughout the film. For instance:

ROGER (upon first meeting Jake): "You [Alonzo] were just like him [Jake], same silly-ass look and everything."

ALONZO (after Jake's back alley rescue): "[What you did] reminds me of when I was out there, chasing down bad guys."

ALONZO (after Roger's murder): "You [Jake] sound just like me, and I know what you're going through, I know what you're feeling."

Or, recurrently: "My nigga." But the most significant instance of this forced equivalence arises at Jake and Alonzo's first meeting during an early morning breakfast at the diner. After impatiently demanding from Jake an amusing story and curtly dismissing his subsequently overly satisfied account of routine police work, Alonzo cajoles Jake about his refusal to have sex with his (it is stated: attractive, heterosexual) female training officer. Alonzo rebukes Jake's flaccid moral defense—"I got a wife"—with a crass truism—"You got a dick." It is implied, "you got a dick, just like me." However, Jake never affirms this identification at the level of sex, which is to say sexual deviance (promiscuity, infidelity, impropriety), nor does he grant the implication of those other identifications that may follow from it. He begrudgingly concedes propinquity to Alonzo for an interval, but only eventually to declaim him vociferously, severing any association between himself and Alonzo and, again, between Alonzo and the black community (gangs and all) in a bid to render pathological the actions and energies of the former while recruiting the compliance of the latter. "You know what I realized today?" says Jake. "I'm not like you." The pronouncement comes only after the good officer asserts, peremptorily, that the ghetto captives whom Alonzo regularly savages, and who will remain Jake's assignment at any rate, are somehow free of corruption as well—a strange and incredible absolution, to say the least, given the LAPD party line and Jake's express desire to redeem the organization. The isolation of Alonzo as criminal *par excellence* does not hold, of course, simply because the wholesale criminalization of black community (and the alternating criminalization of the Latino community) must remain firmly in place if the police are to remain in business and the film is meant to cohere. The foregoing image-track of urban fear and loathing is not undone by the eleventh-hour nod to street ethics or an appropriated honor among thieves (Fig. 1.3).

Jake's disassociation is testament to his survival and it indicates a rejection of another, more anxious sort. Alonzo, we recall, arranged Jake's execution as a rational business calculation, but the impending event is narrated by the executioners, much like the litany of Alonzo's regular threats, as metaphoric rape ("Holmes, you ever had your shit pushed in?"). Stating his difference from Alonzo, then, is also an insistence on his own impenetrability and Alonzo's manifest breach in a scenario that imagines the rape of males strictly as acts of uninvited anal penetration. Not only does Jake survive Alonzo's ambush, he also returns the favor with prejudice and precision in the climactic midnight showdown: "You shot me in the ass!" exclaims Alonzo, writhing in pain from the first of dozens of bullets to come (first from Jake, later the Russian mob). The reversal of prerogative

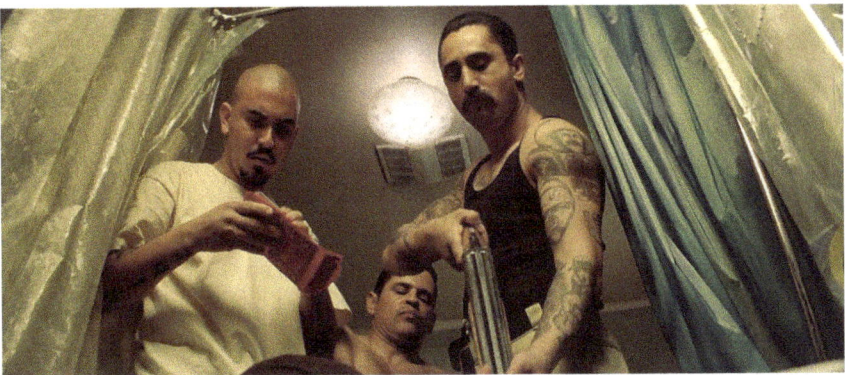

Fig. 1.3 Smiley (Cliff Curtis), Moreno (Noel Gugliemi), and Sniper (Raymond Cruz) find Letty's wallet while preparing to execute Jake. Image reproduced under terms of fair use

and the redirection of lethal violence are meant to reset the political order of things while regulating the sexual dynamics of activity and passivity. The real solidarity at work here is rather unambiguous, despite it being somewhat indirect in announcing itself. It is not the solidarity of the police or the good sheep, but that obtaining between white men across an array of social positions, national origins, and generations.

The "racial allocation of guilt" is increasingly discernible in the trajectory of Jake's disaffection and the jagged path to his eventual breaking point (Fanon 2006, 83). We can recall that the terrorizing of blacks is at the center of *Training Day*, both because it is the condition of possibility for Alonzo's daily bread (the residents of the Jungle are at his mercy—"I run shit around here! You just live here!") and the lynchpin of his pitiless enterprise. By these means he will secure the name of the intermediate drug supplier, Sandman, with the needed petty cash to purchase a search warrant for the big bust, the real payday. The shameless hard core of abuse against black women and men is couched within an ambivalence toward the welfare of Latinos, both women and men, and an entirely restricted relationship to the endangerment of whites, particularly white men. Jake responds to the situation according to these exact gradations of interest.

After being corralled by Alonzo into a bogus traffic stop, Jake skittishly complies in the petty harassment of several white suburban college kids. During this time, Jake exchanges the first of a series of lingering and ambiguous, perhaps premonitory, looks with white or light-skinned women: first, before leaving his home for the day, his wife; then, the white woman passenger of the stopped car, who bears uncanny resemblance to his wife; later,

Letty in the alleyway following his heroics; and, eventually, Sara as well, during his pair of visits to Alonzo's apartment. (By contrast, his exchange of looks with Sandman's wife, played by Grammy-winning vocalist Macy Gray, is hostile and untrusting.) After then being held at gunpoint by Alonzo and forced to smoke a PCP-laced joint, Jake balks momentarily, but ultimately takes the ordeal in stride. After Alonzo's beating of a handcuffed, homeless black man in the alley (and his disregard of the assaulted Latina whom Jake rescues), Jake does not put his foot down; he does not raise serious objection, even if he raises his eyebrow. After the street-side stalking and backroom violation of a disabled black man, Jake has only half-hearted reservations about the possibility of administrative sanction. After the armed invasion of a black woman's home and the looting of her stash (after which the duo is kindly escorted from the premises by a hail of gunfire from members of the resident gang set), Jake does not throw in the towel; he simply collects himself, since he has not yet reached the threshold of his intolerance. He loses his nerve entirely only in the wake of the murder of the drug-dealing white man, Roger (Scott Glenn), to which act he is unwillingly made party, at the dusk of this treacherous day (Fig. 1.4).

To counteract the unraveling of their tenuous bond, Alonzo deploys a careful balance of threats and incentives. Jake understands that he cannot

Fig. 1.4 Alonzo persuades Jake to finish the mission after they rob and murder Roger. Image reproduced under terms of fair use

prevail against the infamous blue wall of silence—four decorated officers will fabricate testimony naming Jake as the shooter—and the damning forensic evidence of narcotics that Alonzo has planted in his system. That much promises to keep him quiet for the time being. However, in order to ensure his permanent silence, Alonzo must again restore his trust and coax him into the last and final stage of execution. It is, in part, testament to Hawke's abilities that Jake's responsiveness does not simply tip over into the ridiculous; as he yields to Alonzo's entreaty, he manages to retain for the moment the look of ruin and disorientation. The remaining weight of this pivotal scene is carried, naturally, by Washington, whose facility in delivering the rousing passage breaks through with the particular force of revelation: beneath the streetwise *lingua franca* and armored bravado, the scorn and cynicism, beneath the ruthless micropolitics of close-quarters urban combat, beneath even the indefensible risks and compromises to which he has subjected his inexperienced trainee, Alonzo is, in fact, inspired by an ethical position that authorizes the wild plasticity of his moral code. The game of law enforcement is, we are told, "chess, not checkers." This recasting of the day's events as a complicated stratagem produces for Jake the crucial hesitation, holding out the possibility that the business of policing involves a grim sophistication greater than his immediate comprehension.

Indeed it does, although it appears that one dies by the sword only if one wields it for evil. Upon realizing within an inch of his life that Alonzo intends to have him killed in order to save his own hide, Jake proceeds to exact his own brand of justice, and in so doing does not so much beat Alonzo at his own game than demonstrate that Alonzo is playing in bad faith, which is only to say he is not really playing—or policing—at all. "You don't deserve this," Jake scoffs as he snatches Alonzo's badge from his neck. Yet the moralizing force of the film—the police are a self-regulating institution unrelated to the interference of public scrutiny and immune to calls for reform, much less abolition—hinges on a precise forgetting. Alonzo can be righteously defanged and defamed only if it is overlooked that he is, according to the official criteria, a highly successful career officer. To wit: "They build jails because of me." A hardnosed, self-vindicating efficiency in generating arrests, securing convictions, and accumulating "over fifteen thousand man-years of incarceration" is the ground not only for Alonzo's ascension through the ranks of the LAPD, but also for his recruitment to the station of henchman for the lieutenants of the ruling class. It is clear that contribution to mass imprisonment, despite the latitude it affords, is not thereby a guarantee of protection and it does nothing to offset his basic expendability when circumstances demand it. However, at no point has Alonzo done anything to offend the unwritten rules of the profession and, were it not for Jake, he would have continued in the good graces of the rich and powerful once he paid blood money to the criminal underworld. The film depicts plainly this system and it is a wonder how one might entertain the fraudulent merits of Jake's renegade grandstanding in this light. It is equally astounding that an audience could allow Alonzo to be the too-easy site of disposal that Jake declares him to be, whether this reproach is cause for relief or consternation.

The discrepancy is managed, in my view, through the racial coding of state violence as black and the combination of such black state violence with offenses in the register of conventional Christian morality (e.g., fornication, adultery, ostentation, profanity) and biopolitical panic over black population control. ("I got four sons," boasts Alonzo early in the film; in a deleted scene, he catcalls to another light-skinned Latina that he would give her "ten sons.") This bundling of issues enables, though it cannot secure, a reorientation of criticism away from the racial state, and the structures of white supremacy and antiblackness it articulates, toward more comfortable and familiar topics (e.g., the supposed black propensity toward violence and vice, the dangerous fecundity of black women, the predatory sexual appetites of black men), all while attempting clumsily to avoid suspicion that all blacks are indicted on the charges. Jake is juxtaposed to all such traits: he is loyal and loving, principled and pious, trustworthy and truthful, hardworking and honest. Within the moral economy of the film, it is this gross imbalance that motivates the otherwise inexplicable willingness of besieged black and Latino communities to assist the agents of their own repression, segregation, and disorganization in the public relations housecleaning known as internal affairs. As Smiley (Cliff Curtis), Jake's would-be executioner, disapprovingly states about Alonzo (even as he prepares to commit a contract killing!): "He don't believe in *nada*." The communal hatred of this particular black cop—the others in the film are no better—overrides a general and otherwise healthy skepticism toward the political functions of the police as such. This hatred runs so deep, in fact, as to encourage their active and reckless backing of a "whitened" cop who will return, as per job description, to violate many among their ranks in a scenario inadequately described as self-incrimination. This contrast and reversal makes possible the return of state violence to the site of the black body, again as *interracial* target, but now legitimized without the regular price of political capital.

In view of the revised racial schema, it is not insignificant that the Latinos who come to Jake's aid do so of their own accord (Smiley recognizes that Jake has defended the virtue of his teenaged cousin and deserves magnanimity in return), while those blacks who eventually step forward in arms against Alonzo do so only after witnessing the violent pedagogy of Jake's physical *coup*, that is, only after witnessing the spectacular example of Alonzo's badly beaten body, exhausted and prone. Force, rather than moral reciprocity, is the language of currency in the 'hood.' If Jake can defeat Alonzo, the tyrannical chief, the Head Negro in Charge, then perhaps all the Jungle residents should get while the getting is good. And is there really a choice? Could any one of the street soldiers at hand actually murder Jake in plain view and reasonably expect protection against the ensuing official onslaught from Alonzo, the ultimately clownish black henchman who cannot even protect his own ass? Latinos live in and work out of a house and they do the sort of business with Alonzo that can be rejected when and if they see fit. Blacks, in contrast, live and work outside, on the street, in the trees, on the roof with the pigeons and their *lebensraum* is wholly occupied by Alonzo's overbearing presence: he demands homage and tribute and sacrifice, but in a manner less Kurtz, the fallen soldier, than Kong, the Jungle emperor.

An Allegory of the Slave Trade

Washington was widely praised for his performance as Alonzo Harris, but it was the frantic and melancholic rage of his closing monologue that shocked moviegoers most and attracted the attention of so many establishment critics. After a brief shootout and brawl with a vengeful Jake, Alonzo finds himself cornered and out of options. Jake has foiled the plan by insinuating himself between Alonzo, the ransom, and the road to reprieve. As the witching hour approaches and time runs out on his earthly purgatory, Alonzo makes one final bid: pistols at ten paces as the bell tolls midnight. But as he makes his way to his gun, confident that Jake does not have the nerve to shoot him dead (though he has already put a bullet "in his ass"), Alonzo finds himself unsupported by his captive audience, his unlikely amen corner. Jake has converted them to his cause or at least opened for them a window of opportunity. Alonzo's erstwhile lackey draws a gun and trains it on his (Alonzo's) head: "Jake, go ahead and get outta here, homie. We got your back." Astonished at the mutiny, a turnabout meant to play the ghetto's liberation as a by-product of Alonzo's just deserts, Alonzo fulminates at length:

> **ALONZO**: Aww, you motherfuckers. Okay. Alright. I'm putting cases on all you bitches. Huh. You think you can do this shit… you think you can do

this to me? You motherfuckers will be playing basketball in Pelican Bay [State Prison] when I get finished with you. SHU [Security Housing Unit] program, nigga. Twenty-three hour lockdown. I'm the man up in this piece. You'll never see the light of… who the fuck do you think you fucking with? I'm the police, I run shit around here. You just live here. Yeah, that's right, you better walk away. Go on and walk away…'cause I'm gonna burn this motherfucker down. *King Kong ain't got shit on me!*

The infamy of this final exclamation is further established by a 2002 MTV Movie Award nomination for Best Line (Washington did take home the award for Best Villain). However, its rich symbolic cargo could stand to be unpacked. One could hardly anticipate that *any* director could get the most celebrated black actor of the late twentieth century—the perennial good guy—to compare himself onscreen to the archetypical figure of the "historical tendency [in Western culture] to identify blacks with ape-like creatures" (Snead 1994, 20). Yet a previously undistinguished Fuqua has managed to do so to great applause and thus, on a fundamental level, returns this pinnacle of black film history to the primal domain of its earliest and most problematic screen presence. The resurfacing of the image of the simian black reveals the tenacity of the visual, narrative, and characterological paradigm established in Hollywood cinema by films like *Birth of a Nation* (1915) and *King Kong* (1933) and the versatility of ideological appropriation in the realm of culture work more broadly.[18]

If Fuqua is, in part, drawing upon Francis Ford Coppola's film classic, *Apocalypse Now* (1979), which is, in turn, drawing upon Joseph Conrad's canonical *Heart of Darkness* (1899), which is, in turn, drawing upon the literature of travel writing and military dispatch in its meditation on the agonies and anxieties attendant to the European colonial adventure in

---

[18] I disagree on this point with Kellogg (2002), who overestimates the irony with which Washington is able to play the role of Harris by failing to consider fully the plot and the interrelationship of its central characters. Considering the broader resonance of the Kong reference in film culture, we note that the Great Ape has returned to the screen again in Peter Jackson's remake *King Kong* (2005) and Jordan Vogt-Roberts's reboot *Kong: Skull Island* (2017), recent entries in a long line, including Merian Cooper's original *King Kong* (1933) and John Guillermin's remake *King Kong* (1976), Ernest Schoedstack's *Mighty Joe Young* (1949) and Ron Underwood's remake *Mighty Joe Young* (1998). There have been remakes of other ape films of late, for instance, Frank Marshall's *Congo* (1995) and Tim Burton's remake *Planet of the Apes* (2001), the latter without the political critique of Franklin Schaffner's earlier *Planet of the Apes* (1968). The more recent *Planet* reboot series now features Rupert Wyatt's *Rise of the Planet of the Apes* (2011) and Matt Reeves's *Dawn of the Planet of the Apes* (2014) and *War for the Planet of the Apes* (2017).

Africa;[19] and if the mythology of Kong enters the sordid equation, bellowed in a manner otherwise superfluous to the narrative movement; then what are we to make of these eruptions of the history of the Euro-American invention of "the black"—its colonies, its plantations, its killing fields—in a tale preoccupied with exploring the racial and sexual orders of power in the present? In short, what does (the imagination of) the transatlantic history of racial slavery, and the wholesale colonization of Africa, have to do with (the imagination of) current contests about racial profiling, police violence, mass imprisonment—the collective terms of American Apartheid (Massey and Denton 1998)?

For film historian Thomas Cripps, the original *King Kong* "came to stand as an underground allegory for black experience," and was, in this sense, never an uncomplicated legend about a "mindless black brute." He recounts:

> The fifty-foot-high title role was the kidnapped king of an idyllic island lost in a prehistoric time-warp, ripped from ecological harmony, set down and chained on a New York stage to be gawked at by effete urbanites. "He has always been king of his world," says one of his tormentors, "but we'll teach him fear." He becomes a tragic figure, colonized, enslaved, cut from bucolic roots, destroyed by the city atop the empty engineering triumph, the Empire State Building, but to the end capable of love, cradling his miniature blond co-star aloft before his fall from the great tower. In the end Kong became an enduring mythic figure, part "bad nigger" and part universal victim of exploitation. (Cripps 1993, 278)

---

[19]Fuqua maintains that one of his primary influences in shooting *Training Day* was Francis Ford Coppola's *Apocalypse Now* (1979) and, by extension, Joseph Conrad's 1899 *Heart of Darkness*, though it is unclear whether Fuqua has read Conrad's novella or is at all versed in the contemporary debates it engendered (Conrad 1987). The stimulus is nonetheless apparent in the overarching organization of Alonzo's story and it is crystallized in the scene that introduces Jake/Marlow, and the audience, to Alonzo's/Kurtz's lair. Midway through the day's events, Alonzo informs Jake that they will be pausing so that Alonzo can visit his wife. Ostensibly, this pit stop is meant to give Jake the rest needed to continue the mission, but at the level of film image it paints the canvas of the jungle from which Alonzo hails and over which he continues to reign: wild, menacing, indecipherable. In order to establish this backdrop, Fuqua quotes Coppola's *mise-en-scène* and cinematography and he borrows liberally from narrative elements as well. However, *Training Day* suffers from contradictory effects as a result of the racial logic that girds the attempt, as Baldwin has it, "to bring black men into the white American nightmare." Because the violence of racial warfare is made flesh in a figure otherwise indistinguishable from the target population, the drama of "civilized man gone native" (pace Conrad and Coppola) plays out in Fuqua's rendition as oxymoron. Alonzo's adventurism serves as a stage for the film's largely counterfeit meditation on proper police conduct, yet the frightening image of the unchecked criminal cop is overshadowed, if not fueled, by a discourse of a priori black criminality. Hence the supposed outrage of the black rogue cop—which might otherwise provoke reappraisal about the reach of law—cannot avoid contamination by an extant culture of criminalization that takes blackness as its master sign (Miller 1996; Bhattacharjee 2002).

We should consider a key slippage in this passage in which Kong is described as both "a *universal* victim of exploitation" and "an underground allegory of *black* experience," where the latter aspect is best described, in Snead's words, as "an allegory of the slave trade" (Snead 1994, 17).[20] This critical specification leads us to ask whether, in constructing big screen stories about "man's inhumanity to man," there is not something about the singular terror of that "execrable trade" in human cargo that repeatedly intrudes upon Fuqua's work, a filmmaker blithely apolitical in his stated understanding of historical suffering. Why, for instance, the gratuitous, tragicomic references to towering figures of black political resistance: Malcolm X, Harriet Tubman, and Kunta Kinte (*Bait*)? Why the sardonic jokes about creating an entourage of "slaves in the afterlife" from the lost souls of civilians murdered by the police (*Training Day*)? Why the awkward evocation of kinship between a black US military operative and unspecified West Africans on *both* sides of a civil war drawn in primordial lines of ethnicity and religion (*Tears*)? What does it mean, finally, for a black man to declare an affiliation "beyond the law" with a mythological creature "neither beast nor man," stolen from its native land, the symbol of a "conglomerate blackness" that threatens the very borders of the human (Snead 1994, 20)? What does it mean to claim *that* allegory and to claim to improve on it, to endeavor to beat the giant ape at its own desperate, restricted game of riot and destruction? How does foreclosure from the realm of human species-being not only complicate, but radically undermine the Faustian bid for interracial arbitration on the grounds of masculinity, the quest for dominant male gender, most especially in its official capacities? If King Kong is an allegory of the

---

[20]I want to underscore as well the inaptness of the rubric of "exploitation," which I take to be a conceptual correlate to the misnomer "universal victim." See Wilderson (2003) for a generative discussion of the radical difference between exploitation and accumulation, the latter of which I take to be a more adequate explanatory framework for the structural position of the black. We should also note the connection here with Snead's earlier point regarding the political and sexual threat posed by black skin on screen. In a similar vein, Guerrero writes: "If nothing else, the huge, black, and fantastic King Kong climbing the Empire State Building while clutching his scantily clad, blonde object of desire presents us with a powerful, enduring metaphor for dominant society's barely repressed fears of black masculinity, sexuality, and miscegenation" (Guerrero 1995, 395). Again, it is not only the political threat of state repression that Alonzo symbolizes, but also, like the homeless black man in the alley, the sexual threats of rape, sexual coercion and miscegenation. The difference here is that the endangered are less white women in the old-fashioned, categorical sense as they are near white or light-skinned women (and men) on a color spectrum, most coded as Latina (i.e., Jake's wife Lisa, the schoolgirl Letty, Alonzo's wife Sara, etc.). What all of those women (and men) threatened by black male sexual violence have in common is, crucially, that they are *non-black*.

enslaved, then what sort of allegory is Alonzo Harris? Part "bad nigger" and part what?

"We'll teach him fear": what enjoyment does the reworking of this spectacle of command and control produce for contemporary audiences in a moment of renewed debate about *reparations* for slavery long after the debate about black *repatriation* has been discounted? Where King Kong is a tragic figure, "to the end capable of love, cradling his miniature blond co-star aloft before his fall from the great tower," Alonzo Harris—subject to the same fatal lesson, his body shredded by automatic weapons fire—is granted no majesty. He seems incapable of love and, though he is survived by his wife and son, he is not mourned by anyone within the film. Do we not have here a retreat from even the paternalistic, liberal racism of its cinematic forerunner, something *worse* than *King Kong*? The answer, I suggest, is that while *Training Day* disseminates images of black primitiveness and savagery, casting Harris (and the other black characters) as both fearsome and pathetic, rapacious and impotent, forbidding and wretched, its ungainly inscription of the King Kong trope nonetheless indicates a subtext of *ongoing* black captivity that Fuqua's work can neither transcend nor do without; a trope whose inarticulate demand for redress is not accommodated by a cinema that flirts with historical antagonism but fails to move beyond unmistakably inadequate resolutions, whether community policing schemes or individual escape attempts.

At the borders of an uninhabitable social incarceration—from prison to ghetto to refugee camp—the firing squad awaits and no degree of consent can adjourn its execution. In this world, the "yes or no" of the black has no objective value, whatever her employ. But if something is going to burn in response, as the walking dead man insists in his loneliest moment, then what and where and when? If someone must die to settle accounts, then who shall be the victim and by whose hand? Somewhere in this tangle of inquiries, we may yet discern an alternative impulse toward the formation of a critical black public sphere, a multidimensional and revisable bond forged on the move rather than on the run. As for Washington's historic Academy Award and the distinction afforded Fuqua in the process, it appears to be something more than Pyrrhic victory. It betrays the scent of a con, a black cinematic event released into custody, produced and distributed under conditions of cultural parole. Taking a final cue from the archive of prisoner testimonial and the corroborating statistical data (Mauer 2006), we may conclude that *parole* names not the release from prison into unalloyed freedom—if only the prison house of Hollywood's dream work—but rather continued regulation amid the foreboding sense of recapture.

References

Adelman, Larry. 2008. *Unnatural Causes: Is Inequality Making Us Sick?* DVD. Directed by Llewellyn Smith, Tracy Heather Strain, Patricia Garcia Rios, Maria Teresa Rodriguez, James M. Fortier, Ellie Lee, Eric Strange, and James Rutenbeck. San Francisco: California Newsreel.

Alexander, Elizabeth. 1996. 'We're Gonna Deconstruct Your Life!': The Making and Un-Making of the Black Bourgeois Patriarch in *Ricochet*. In *Representing Black Men*, ed. Marcellus Blount and George P. Cunningham, 157–172. New York: Routledge.

Associated Press. 2007. Reese Witherspoon Highest-Paid Actress. *Washington Post*, December 1. Accessed May 28, 2017. http://www.washingtonpost.com/wp-dyn/content/article/2007/11/30/AR2007113000445.html.

Bailey, Sam. 2001. *L.A.P.D. Blues*. DVD. Directed by Michael Kirk. Boston: Frontline.

Baldwin, James. 2000. *The Devil Finds Work: An Essay*. New York: Delta.

Bhattacharjee, Anannya (ed.). 2002. *Policing the National Body: Race, Gender, and Criminalization*. Boston: South End.

Blight, David. 2001. *Race and Reunion: The Civil War in American Memory*. Cambridge, MA: Harvard University Press.

Bogle, Donald. 2016. *Toms, Coons, Mulattoes, Mammies, and Bucks: An Interpretive History of Blacks in American Films*, 5th ed. New York: Bloomsbury.

Bradshaw, Peter. 2002. The Invisibility of Black Actors Has Long Been a Scandal. *The Guardian*, March 26. Accessed May 28, 2017. https://www.theguardian.com/culture/2002/mar/26/artsfeatures.awardsandprizes.

Cashmore, Ellis. 1997. *The Black Culture Industry*. New York: Routledge.

Cashmore, Ellis, and Eugene McLaughlin (eds.). 1991. *Out of Order? Policing Black People*. New York: Routledge.

Conrad, Joseph. 1987. *Heart of Darkness: An Authoritative Text, Background and Sources, Criticism*, ed. Robert Kimbrough. New York: W.W. Norton & Company.

Courtney, Susan. 2004. *Hollywood Fantasies of Miscegenation: Spectacular Narratives of Gender and Race, 1903–1967*. Princeton, NJ: Princeton University Press.

Cripps, Thomas. 1993. *Slow Fade to Black: The Negro in American Film, 1900–1942*. New York: Oxford University Press.

Diawara, Manthia (ed.). 1993. *Black American Cinema*. New York: Routledge.

Dillard, Angela. 2001. *Guess Who's Coming to Dinner Now? Multicultural Conservatism in America*. New York: NYU Press.

Dudek, Duane. 2001. Washington Takes on His First Role as Bad Guy in Cop Film, *Journal Sentinel*, October 3.

Dudziak, Mary. 2002. *Cold War Civil Rights: Race and the Image of American Democracy*. Princeton, NJ: Princeton University Press.

Dyer, Richard. 1997. *White*. New York: Routledge.
Fanon, Frantz. 2006. *Black Skin, White Masks*, trans. Richard Philcox. New York: Grove Press.
Fiedler, Leslie. 1960. *Love and Death in the American Novel*. New York: Criterion.
Foner, Eric. 2007. *Nothing But Freedom: Emancipation and Its Legacy*. Baton Rouge, LA: LSU Press.
Fuqua, Antoine. 2006. *Bastards of the Party*. DVD. Directed by Cle Sloan. New York: HBO Films.
Gilmore, Ruth Wilson. 1993. Terror Austerity Race Gender Excess Theater. In *Reading Rodney King/Reading Urban Uprising*, ed. Robert Gooding-Williams, 23–37. New York: Routledge.
Gilmore, Ruth Wilson. 2007. *Golden Gulag: Prison, Surplus, Crisis, and Opposition in Globalizing California*. Berkeley, CA: University of California Press.
Gilroy, Paul. 2000. *Against Race: Imagining Political Culture Beyond the Color Line*. Cambridge, MA: Belknap.
Gordon, Lewis. 1995. *Bad Faith and Antiblack Racism*. Amherst, NY: Humanity Books.
Gordon, Lewis. 1997. Race, Sex, and Matrices of Desire in an Antiblack World. In *Race/Sex: Their Sameness, Difference, and Interplay*, ed. Naomi Zack, 119–132. New York: Routledge.
Guerrero, Ed. 1993a. *Framing Blackness: The African American Image in Film*. Philadelphia: Temple University Press.
Guerrero, Ed. 1993b. The Black Image in Protective Custody: Hollywood's Biracial Buddy Films of the Eighties. In *Black American Cinema*, ed. Manthia Diawara, 237–246. New York: Routledge.
Guerrero, Ed. 1995. The Black Man on Our Screens and the Empty Space in Representation. *Callaloo* 18: 395–400.
Guerrero, Ed. 1998. A Circus of Dreams and Lies: The Black Film Wave at Middle Age. In *The New American Cinema*, ed. Jon Lewis, 328–352. Durham, NC: Duke University Press.
Hayden, Tom. 2000. LAPD: Law and Disorder, *The Nation*, April 10. Accessed May 28, 2017. https://www.thenation.com/article/lapd-law-and-disorder/.
Holland, Sharon. 2006. Death in Black and White: A Reading of Marc Forster's *Monster's Ball*. *Signs* 31: 785–813.
Kellogg, Alex. 2002. "Agh, a Negro! Denzel Washington Avoids the Racial Pitfalls of Hollywood and Redefines the Black Antihero." In *Colorlines Magazine: Race, Action, Culture*, Spring. Accessed May 28, 2017. http://www.highbeam.com/doc/1G1-83457956.html.
King, Neal. 1999. *Heroes in Hard Times: Cop Action Movies in the US*. Philadelphia: Temple University Press.
Leitch, Thomas. 2002. *Crime Films*. New York: Cambridge University Press.
Lemieux, Jamilah. 2013. "Jonathan Ferrell: Supposed to Die?" *Ebony*, September 16. Accessed May 28, 2017. http://www.ebony.com/news-views/jonathan-ferrell-supposed-to-die-304#axzz4ugDTuw7S.

Lewis, Jon. 1998a. Introduction. In *The New American Cinema*, ed. Jon Lewis, 1–10. Durham, NC: Duke University Press.

Lewis, Jon (ed.). 1998b. *The New American Cinema*. Durham, NC: Duke University Press.

Marriot, David. 2000. *On Black Men*. New York: Columbia University Press.

Massey, Douglas, and Nancy Denton. 1998. *American Apartheid: Segregation and the Making of the Underclass*. Cambridge, MA: Harvard University Press.

Mauer, Marc. 2006. *The Race to Incarcerate*. New York: New Press.

Miller, Jerome. 1996. *Search and Destroy: African American Males in the Criminal Justice System*. New York: Cambridge University Press.

Miller, Toby, Nitin Govil, John McMurria, Richard Maxwell, and Ting Wang. 2005. *Global Hollywood 2*. London: British Film Institute.

Morrison, Toni. 1992. *Playing in the Dark: Whiteness and the Literary Imagination*. Cambridge, MA: Harvard University Press.

Parenti, Christian. 2000. *Lockdown America: Police and Prisons in the Age of Crisis*. New York: Verso.

Rafter, Nicole. 2000. *Shots in the Mirror: Crime Films and Society*. New York: Oxford University Press.

Reid, Mark. 2005. *Black Lenses, Black Voices: African American Film Now*. New York: Rowman & Littlefield.

Rhines, Jesse Algeron. 1996. *Black Film, White Money*. New Brunswick, NJ: Rutgers University Press.

Robehmed, Natalie. 2016. The World's Highest-Paid Actresses 2016. *Forbes*, August 23. Accessed May 28, 2017. https://www.forbes.com/sites/natalierobehmed/2016/08/23/the-worlds-highest-paid-actresses-2016-jennifer-lawrence-banks-46-million-payday-ahead-of-melissa-mccarthy/#522f63ec5625.

Robinson, Cedric. 1997. *Black Movements in America*. New York: Routledge.

Ryan, Maria. 2010. *Neoconservatism and the New American Century*. New York: Palgrave Macmillan.

Samuels, Allison. 2002. Will It Be Denzel's Day? *Newsweek*, Febraury 25.

Satcher, David, George E. Fryer Jr., Jessica McCann, Adewale Troutman, Steven H. Woolf and George Rust. 2005. "What if We Were Equal? A Comparison of the Black-White Mortality Gap in 1960 and 2000." *Health Affairs* 24: 459–464.

Sedgwick, Eve. 1985. *Between Men: English Literature and Male Homosocial Desire*. New York: Columbia University Press.

Sexton, Jared. 2007. Racial Profiling and the Societies of Control. In *Warfare in the American Homeland: Policing and Prison in a Penal Democracy*, ed. Joy James, 197–218. Durham, NC: Duke University Press.

Silver, Jeffrey. 2001. *Training Day*. DVD. Directed by Antoine Fuqua. Burbank: Warner Bros.

Simpson, Andrea Y. 1998. *The Tie that Binds: Identity and Political Attitudes in the Post-Civil Rights Generation*. New York: NYU Press.

Snead, James. 1994. *White Screens, Black Images*. New York: Routledge.

Springer, Simon, Kean Birch, and Julie MacLeavy (eds.). 2016. *The Handbook of Neoliberalism*. New York: Routledge.
Toby, Mekeisha Madden. 2016. Who Runs the World? Black Women Showrunners, Of Course. *Essence*, November 15. Accessed May 28, 2017. http://www.essence.com/culture/black-women-showrunners-changing-television.
Wacquant, Loïc. 2002. From Slavery to Mass Incarceration: Rethinking the 'Race Question' in the US. *New Left Review* 13: 41–60.
Welbon, Yvonne. 2003. *Sisters in Cinema*. DVD. Directed by Yvonne Welbon. Chicago: Our Film Works.
Wiegman, Robyn. 1995. *American Anatomies: Theorizing Race and Gender*. Durham, NC: Duke University Press.
Wilderson, Frank B., III. 2003. Gramsci's Black Marx: Whither the Slave in Civil Society. *Social Identities* 9: 225–240.
Wilderson, Frank B., III. 2010. *Red, White, and Black: Cinema and the Structure of US Antagonisms*. Durham, NC: Duke University Press.
Willis, Sharon. 1997. *High Contrast: Race and Gender in Contemporary Hollywood Film*. Durham, NC: Duke University Press.
Wilson, Cintra. 2002. Oscars 2002: Somebody Make It Stop! *Salon*, March 25. Accessed May 28, 2017. http://www.salon.com/2002/03/25/oscars_2002/.

2
History and Power: On *Pride*

Introduction

Midway through Walter Hill's 1982 interracial buddy film *48 Hours*, Reggie Hammond (Eddie Murphy) walks into the middle of an all-white country music bar and declares: "I'm your worst nightmare. I'm a nigga with a badge." In doing so, he is actually signifying several things at once. Most immediately he is commenting ironically for the audience on the fact that he was, in fact, a prisoner on furlough impersonating a police officer, a living, breathing representative of the black criminal figure already deeply inscribed in the minds of the surrounding patrons. (Martin Lawrence would reprise this comedic conceit some fifteen years later as Miles Logan in another interracial buddy film, Les Mayfield's 1999 *Blue Streak*.) He was also making a point about the reversal of the normative legal authority in relations between blacks and whites, and especially between black and white men. But in assuming the position of the black cop, Hammond was actually violating a more general principle in the antiblack world: exhibiting qualities and qualifications supposed in the racist imagination to be foreclosed to black people. In this respect, Alonzo Harris's fate in *Training Day* can be read as a cautionary tale about the extension of such badges of honor across the color line. The presence of black men in occupations and pastimes previously reserved for white men scandalizes the very idea of privilege, but more insidiously it suggests that these same sites and activities can be corrupted from within. Jake Hoyt does his best to redeem the badge from degradation by his black counterpart and, as we will see below, Coach Richard Binkowski (Tom Arnold) seeks in similar fashion to protect the purity of water against the threat of pollution posed by Coach Jim Ellis (Terrence Howard) and his team of black competitive swimmers. The nightmare of black infiltration in state and civil society is the flip side of the dream of racial equality, the slave power and the slave colluding unconsciously while engaged in conscious combat.

Maritime Slavery

Blacks can't swim. It's an old joke, at least in the United States, serving as a humorous rejoinder to the curious looks and often-querulous comments solicited by the rare black swimmer among a field predominated by white teammates and competitors. The late Nell Carter—singer, dancer, actress and card-carrying black Republican—retold the joke to former African National Congress leader Nelson Mandela on a hot June day at the Los Angeles Coliseum. It was 1990 and Mandela was near the end of an eight-city tour of the USA following his historic release from nearly three decades of political imprisonment on the notorious Robben Island, four miles off the turbulent Atlantic coast of Cape Town. Many among the largely black audience of over seventy thousand laughed knowingly: "If black people could swim, slavery would have been impossible. We all would've swum back to Africa!" If Mandela could have swum back to the mainland, they mused, maybe things would have been different for President de Klerk's apartheid regime as well.

Blacks can't swim: the punch line evokes a pernicious and, it turns out, fairly recent stereotype insofar as it suggests some innate incapacity to acquire knowledge or skill set, or some natural incompatibility with aquatic environs (Associated Press 2008a). No one assumed the worst of Carter at this welcome ceremony for an icon of the global black freedom struggle. By contrast, one cannot help but recall the infamous comments made by former Los Angeles Dodgers General Manager Al Campanis on a 1987 episode of ABC's *Nightline* with Ted Koppel. When asked, per the theme of the evening's program, why there were no blacks in managerial positions in professional baseball on this fortieth anniversary of Jackie Robinson's historic breaking of the color line, Campanis, in a process of apparent free association, rationalized the persistent white monopoly by wading into the murky waters of analogy. "Why are black men, or black people, not good swimmers?" he asked rhetorically. The short answer: "Because they don't have the buoyancy."[1] On this account, blacks can't manage for the same reasons blacks can't swim, because they "lack the necessities." Thinking and swimming are, of course, rational activities. In their absence, inertia wins out. The inimitable black comedian Paul Mooney signified on that old chestnut during his 2007 *Know Your History* performance at The Laugh Factory in L.A., offering that blacks had been barred from riding on the 1912 maiden voyage of the British-owned RMS *Titanic* because whites believed their "heavy nigger bones" would make them too much a liability. Membership has its privileges.

Surely, there is ample quantitative data demonstrating much lower rates of swimming proficiency and much higher rates of drowning deaths among blacks relative to whites in every age group and region of the country. According to a 2014 study prepared by the YMCA, for instance, nearly seventy percent of black children have not learned to swim (more than twice the figure for white children) and they are three times more likely than their white counterparts to die from drowning (the second leading cause of accidental injury-related death among youth) (Danielle 2015). Nearly three-quarters of all blacks report having never been involved in swimming, whereas the numbers are nearly the opposite for whites. But, given that some forty percent of black children have in fact learned to swim and nearly a quarter of all black people participate in some sort of swimming activity during their lifetimes, one must account for the remaining disparity. A child's likelihood of learning to swim is strongly correlated with a range of sociological factors, including family environment (i.e., education and income levels, swimming proficiency, encouragement, and exercise habits), access to swimming facilities, and admiration of a highly competitive swimmer. Not surprisingly, the factors that contribute to the development of swimming proficiency are also strongly correlated with being white (or Asian) (Irwin et al. 2009). Lest we think that this is solely an outcome of the massive and growing racial wealth gap, it is important to add that class indicators account for well less than half of the difference in question (Powell 2010). In fact, "being Black reduces the odds of participation in swimming by approximately 60%, even while adjusting for age, sex, and household income" (Hastings et al. 2006, 908).

Among variables studied by a research team led by University of Memphis Professor of Health and Sport Sciences Richard Irwin was fear of water, or,

---

[1] Koppel, not missing a beat, retorted: "I think it may just be that they don't have access to all the country clubs and the pools" (Johnson 2007).

more specifically, fear of injury and death. Children develop fear of water if adult caregivers express fear of water, and that fear acts as an inhibitor. But why should black people fear the water in some *characteristic* way? Here we run into a sort of vicious circle. Fear of water inhibits development of swimming proficiency and lack of swimming proficiency amplifies fear of water and so on. This vicious circle begs the question: which came first in the historic instance, black aquatic incapacity or black aquatic aversion? Is this dilemma connected to a longstanding and transatlantic phenomenon akin to an African-derived cultural transmission or is it a more local and contemporary development linked to specific political and economic conditions? Pioneering research on the history of swimming published in the last decade would strongly recommend the latter conclusion, demonstrating that the widespread fear of water and general lack of swimming proficiency among black people in the USA are the exclusionary achievements of twentieth-century social engineering (Sugrue 2009).

Between the 1920s and the 1940s, public swimming as state-sponsored *bathing* (hence the moniker for the "suits") for the boys and young men of the "unwashed" European immigrant and black migrant masses was in decline and public swimming as a popular recreational activity—and eventually as a major competitive sport—for white families emerged. As young white women entered the scene, and as laborers, professionals, and business owners of European descent intermingled with more frequency, even across generations, white communities systematically segregated blacks from municipal pools throughout the country, and perhaps nowhere more violently than in the North. The interwar years saw the increasing social and spatial incorporation of working-class European immigrant communities into the mainstream of white middle-class America, and this expansion of the social category of whiteness in the transition from industrial to modern society entailed a renewed policing of blackness at the water's edge. "Pools became emblems of a new, distinctly modern version of the good life that valued leisure, pleasure and beauty. They were, in short, an integral part of the kind of life Americans wanted to live" (Wiltse 2007, 5).

"Blacks can't swim" is, then, a deeply equivocal statement in light of recent scholarship, to say nothing of the living memory of black oral history. It signifies both that blacks are powerless to do so and that they are prohibited from doing so. In other words, the statement cannot decide whether the point is that blacks *cannot* swim (and therefore should be excluded from participation on the rational basis of public safety) or that they *must not* swim (and therefore should be excluded from participation on the irrational basis of public health). Or, rather, they must not swim *here*. The edict of segregation in this case is pulled taut between its descriptive and prescriptive registers, prompting us to wonder about the relationship between the racist pseudo-science of leaden black bodies unable to float and the racist social practice of quarantining black swimmers from dissolving into liquid contact with whites. Is there a common logic underlying the claim that blacks are at risk in the water and the claim that whites are at risk in the water *with blacks*? Put slightly differently, is there some consistency between the notion that blacks are inherently deficient and the notion that this deficiency is, nonetheless, somehow communicable?

Historian Kevin Dawson has permanently disabused us of the notion that the statement "blacks can't swim" holds water as an essentialist proposition. Of course, the power of a stereotype lies not in its status (i.e., is it true?) but in its function (i.e., what work does it do in a given discourse?). That being said, it never hurts to debunk a myth whenever one is able. In fact, "blacks can't swim" is better termed an urban legend, given its roots in the reconfiguration of the city, especially the urban metropolises that served as points of destination for the millions of The Great Migration in the first half of the twentieth century. What Dawson reveals in his seminal article in the *Journal of American History*, "Enslaved Swimmers and Divers in the Atlantic World" (2006) and the reader's digest of his scholarship for *Swimmer* magazine, "African Swimmers Made History" (2010), is an archive of the rich aquatic history found throughout the African Diaspora, including what would become the United States. For the better part of the modern period, European accounts recognize not only that most Africans were sound and proficient swimmers, but that they also often displayed abilities far superior to Europeans.[2]

Enslaved African swimmers and divers were used variously for the expansionist projects of the major metropolitan powers in Lisbon, Seville, Amsterdam, Paris and London—salvaging valued supplies and *matériel* from sunken cargo ships; rescuing drowning or stranded crewmembers overboard; mining the ocean floor for the lucrative international trade in pearls; clearing swamps and creeks and rivers for the development of agricultural enterprise and commercial transportation routes; and, last but not least, providing entertainment for the slave-owning classes in "blood sport"

---

[2]He writes: "From the age of discovery up through the nineteenth century, the swimming and underwater diving abilities of people of African descent often surpassed those of Europeans and their descendants" (Dawson 2006, 1327). Or again: "Over more than three centuries, western travelers to West Africa reported that Africans were sound swimmers; several noted that they generally swam better than Europeans and described their use of the freestyle" (Dawson 2006, 1331).

contests against alligators, rays, and sharks (Dawson 2006, 1341–1350).[3] In fact, Dawson avers that advanced swimming, including the use of what we now call freestyle, may have arrived and proliferated in the New World as "the corollary of skills slaveholders desired" (Dawson 2006, 1339).[4] Though many Africans (and many Asian and Native people as well) swam freestyle throughout the modern period, "demonstrating its speed and strength to them for centuries," Europeans and white Americans did not take up the form until after the 1912 Olympic Games where Duke Kahanamoku, a native Hawaiian with no formal training or competitive swimming experience, broke not one, but *two* world records using the stroke (Dawson 2006, 1134). The unparalleled talents of African swimmers and divers in the Atlantic world were so generally acknowledged that well-known French scientist and inventor Melchisédec Thevénot would opine in his 1696 *Art of Swimming*: "Swimming was in great esteem among the Ancients. But to come to our times, it is most certain that Negroes, excel all others in these Arts of Swimming and Diving" (quoted in Dawson 2010, 50). Thevénot was implicitly addressing the historical decline of European swimming as well, making a point that opens up a materialist explanation for why "whites can't swim" became a veritable truism spanning the better part of an epoch. However, the disparity in European and African swimming capabilities did not lead the authors of this collective *reportage* to question their superiority as such. The genius of race, "a *complicated* figure, or metaphoricity, that demonstrates the power and danger of difference, that signs and assigns difference as a way to situate social subjects" (Spillers 1996, 80), enabled the

---

[3]Regarding the latter role, Dawson writes: "Most westerners, however, probably did not believe that aquatic clashes demonstrated slaves' bravery. True, whites seemed impressed. But many presumably perceived slaves' ability to swim with ease while overpowering dreaded creatures as proof that they were animal-like savages. [...] In short, people of African descent were typically viewed not as brave, but as ferocious" (Dawson 2006, 1343–1344). Condescension notwithstanding, the specialized skills honed by enslaved swimmers and divers afforded them a circumscribed leverage: "Though the work was grueling, enslaved swimmers and divers welcomed the escape from the monotonous, backbreaking labor their enslaved brothers and sisters performed in the agricultural fields of the Americas. But slavery, no matter the occupation, was always hard work, and the privileges divers enjoyed were restricted by the fetters of bondage. Being a slave, even an enslaved diver, meant subjugation, harsh treatment, and never-ending toil. Still, enslaved swimmers and divers used skills of African origin to make slavery more bearable, sometimes winning existences of privileged exploitation" (Dawson 2006, 1354).

[4]"As Africans were taken to the New World, many of them carried swimming and underwater diving skills with them. From the early sixteenth century on, slaveholders realized that slaves' swimming and diving abilities could be profitably exploited. [...] Thus swimming may have come to the New World as the corollary of skills slaveholders desired" (Dawson 2006, 1339).

Eurocentric imagination to sustain itself in the face of all that was eminently controvertible.⁵

> When chroniclers noted that Africans were proficient swimmers, they may also have been signaling that such swimmers were animal-like. [...] The writings of swimming theorists indicate that many westerners believed that, whereas animals instinctively knew how to swim, it was unnatural for humans to swim without logical instruction. [...] Since swimming theorists argued that logic was required to enable humans to swim, whites could conceivably have thought that people of African descent swam because they had used reason to overcome their fear of water. Whites, however, asserted that blacks were incapable of logic and reason. [...] Since whites did not believe that people of African descent were capable of logic or reason, they implied that animal-like instincts enabled blacks to swim naturally. (Dawson 2006, 1332)

Consistent across these wildly divergent impressions of black aquatic facility—from supremacy to shortfall—is that the condition indexes for the wily observer the impossibility of a dynamic principle and the total determination of the permanent quality, a direct line from instinct to anatomy by which the latter supersedes and preserves the former in subsequent iterations.

Municipal Segregation

During the July 13, 2009 episode of National Public Radio's *Tell Me More*, host Michel Martin talked briefly with historian Jeff Wiltse, author of the 2007 book, *Contested Waters: A Social History of Swimming Pools in America*, and Jim Ellis, retired junior high school math teacher and, since 1971, founding coach of the venerable Philadelphia Department of Recreation Swim Team (PDR), the first black competitive swim team to gain genuine national attention.⁶ The segment's topic was the then widely publicized allegations of racism against The Valley Club in Huntingdon Valley, Pennsylvania, a now-defunct private swimming facility located in an affluent and exceedingly white suburban setting about ten miles northeast of PDR's

---

⁵Snead described racism as "a normative recipe for domination created by speakers using rhetorical tactics" (Snead 1986, x).
⁶Wiltse's book won the 2007 Author's Award from the International Swimming Hall of Fame. Ellis, for his life's work as coach and mentor to hundreds of Philadelphia-area swimmers, won the 2007 Presidential Honor Award, also from the International Swimming Hall of Fame.

impoverished North Philly headquarters.[7] The allegations against The Valley Club, which opened its tony doors in 1954 as the monumental *Brown v. Board of Education* was being argued, included harassment by club members and exclusion by club management of four or five dozen black youth who had arrived on June 29, 2009 as part of a planned activity paid for by a local non-profit day camp, Creative Steps, Inc. Adding insult to injury, Valley Club president John Duesler told the press when questioned about the campers' harassment and exclusion that there was "concern that a lot of kids would change the complexion… and the atmosphere of the club" (Martin 2009).

Wiltse and Ellis were invited to NPR's *Tell Me More* in order to provide historical context for an incident that was framed in the dominant media—and the community protests as well—as an anachronism. "Jim Crow swims here" read one of the signs held by the small multiracial group of Philadelphians picketing outside the gates of The Valley Club several days earlier. Evoking pre-civil rights legal practices and their attendant political culture to describe these post-civil rights era events put rhetorical pressure on the prevalent neoliberal narrative about a "post-racial America" consolidated by the landmark 2008 election of Barack Obama as President of the United States. Musings like this, wishful in the first and last instance about "the end of black politics" rather than the end of racial domination, were elevated to new levels of earnestness with indications of his candidacy's viability (Bai 2008).[8] Wiltse connected the Huntingdon Valley *faux pas* with a capsule history of the virulent (and ongoing) segregation of swimming facilities, a battle he argues was even more difficult and fated than that waged around public schools.

---

[7] Since the initial allegations levied in a suit filed by several campers' parents and the US Department of Justice, and an investigation by the Pennsylvania Human Relations Commission which found probable cause and issued a $50,000 fine for slurs against one child, The Valley Club filed bankruptcy and the property was sold at auction for roughly $1.5 m to the Philadelphia-based Congregation Beth Solomon Synagogue and Community Center (Nunnally 2010). Proceeds from the sale were distributed to creditors, to several local community organizations and to plaintiffs as damages (Roebuck 2012). The 2009 events at the Valley Club represent one of several recent high-profile incidents of antiblack racism at swimming facilities, including the 2011 Ohio Civil Rights Commission ruling against Jamie Hein, a white Cincinnati landlord who posted a "whites only" sign on the gate of an apartment complex swimming pool (Mandell 2012), and the 2015 police assault of 15-year-old Dajerria Becton in McKinney, Texas, a Dallas-Fort Worth suburb (Elizalde 2017).

[8] "For a lot of younger African-Americans, the resistance of the civil rights generation to Obama's candidacy signified the failure of their parents to come to terms, at the dusk of their lives, with the success of their own struggle—to embrace the idea that black politics might now be disappearing into American politics in the same way that the Irish and Italian machines long ago joined the political mainstream" (Bai 2008).

When black civil rights organizations began to score legal victories against their exclusion from municipal pools in the 1950s, white patrons and city officials began retreating to private neighborhood clubs and backyard pools, resorting to the dereliction or destruction of former recreation sites. Wiltse explained that white "suburbanites recognized that if they wanted to protect the social environment of their pools—in particular, if they wanted to exclude [blacks]—they had to create a private club [in] which they could then still legally exclude [blacks] whereas, if they opened up a public pool, they wouldn't be able to do so" (Martin 2009). So even though municipal pools were legally desegregated, swimming, whether recreational or competitive, has yet to be integrated in any meaningful way. Ellis corroborated Wiltse's broader history with examples from his local experience in Greater Philadelphia, relating that when his swimmers ventured out to suburban swim clubs for meets in the early 1970s, well after white flight had become entrenched, they were treated in much the same way as the Creative Steps campers described things in 2009.

Facing financial difficulty from diminished membership of late, The Valley Club had revised its policy to admit local day camps as part of a marketing campaign to enlarge the geographic base of its revenue stream. The strategy of subsidizing white middle-class families' segregated R&R with poor black families' meager fees-for-service would prove entirely self-defeating, as actionable discrimination against the unwelcomed guests was as likely there as humidity in the summer, and the ensuing legal fees and fines would push the struggling outfit into bankruptcy by year's end (Grant 2010). Creative Steps, for its part, was in search of new swimming facilities for its membership largely because the local municipal pools previously utilized were closed or out of service, many as casualties of the Great Recession of 2007 (Brenna 2009).[9] Another way of saying this would be: Creative Steps was sojourning to the precincts of The Valley Club as a direct outcome of the same political and economic processes that continue to divide the two zones asymmetrically one from the other. The latter needs a pretty penny

---

[9]Noted *Philadelphia Inquirer* architecture critic Inga Saffron wrote about the matter: "It is worth remembering why the summer camp, Creative Steps, Inc., contracted with the Huntington Valley Swim Club in the first place. The answer, of course, is that Philadelphia was only able to open a token number of its public pools this summer because of the nation's devastating financial crisis, which has hit cities especially hard. The reduction in pool operations is just one more example of how America's fifth biggest metropolis is unable to provide its citizens with the sort of quality-of-life amenities that suburban dwellers take for granted. Not that anyone would have ever confused Philadelphia's no-frill public pools with those lush suburban oases like Huntington Valley, where the Olympic-size basins are surrounded by lawns and shade trees" (Saffron 2009).

to maintain a lush suburban oasis "surrounded by lawns and shade trees" (Saffron 2009); the former needs respite from an urban desert featuring only a mirage of basic swimming infrastructure (Hastings et al. 2006).

In the same vein, Ellis's storied PDR Swim Team has been disbanded indefinitely because their home pool, a brand-new facility when it opened in 1980, now "needs two and a half million dollars' worth of repairs" and so remains "shutdown today to a whole community" (Martin 2009). The irony is that this facilities closure and team disbandment occurred *after* Ellis and PDR were made the subject of a major feature-length film distributed by Lionsgate Entertainment. *Pride*, directed by Zimbabwean newcomer Sunu Gonera in his Hollywood debut, opened in March 2007 to mixed reviews and a poor box office performance. The immediate effect of the biopic was not to catapult Ellis and his veteran program into the national limelight (though he has made small rounds on the national and international speaker's circuit) but to sharpen the blow of PDR's imminent demise and his own early retirement.[10]

It is no shock, given the general trends, that less than one percent of competitive swimmers in the USA are black, or that only a handful of black swimmers have attained positions of international prominence to date (Lloyd 2016). Simone Manuel was the latest to join this select group, when she became the first black woman to win Olympic *gold* in Rio 2016, as a rising junior at Stanford University. She also set an Olympic and American record en route, and earned another gold and a silver medal that summer. Cullen Jones preceded Manuel with his own gold medal performance in the men's 4 × 100 meter freestyle relay at the 2008 Beijing Olympic Games; and he took home another gold and two silvers at London 2012. Maritza Correia became the first black woman to make the US Olympic Team in swimming, winning silver in Athens 2004 for the women's 4 × 100 meter freestyle relay. She is also the first black *woman* to medal in Olympic

---

[10] Membership at PDR had been in decline for some time prior to disbanding, from a peak of 175 in the early 1990s to roughly 30 in 2007. Ellis reported in a 2008 article for the London *Times*: "The movie came out and still no one has come forward to offer us better facilities. Why, in this day and age, should we continue to work in these poor facilities? I guess somewhere the colour issue is still there" (Slot 2008). Ellis also mentions in a 2007 article for *Ebony* magazine that he had been passed over for coaching positions at the University of Maryland and the University of Pennsylvania, despite having sent scholarship swimmers to their respective programs (John-Hall 2007). More generally, it seems in retrospect that the most extensive and critical coverage of Jim Ellis and PDR Swimming is Phillip Hoose's 1990 *New York Times Magazine* article, "A New Pool of Talent." There was another round of short pieces about Ellis's life and legacy in outlets like the local *Philadelphia Inquirer* around the domestic release of *Pride* (Klein 2007), but none had the depth, complexity, and sensitivity of the earlier feature story.

swimming and only the second black swimmer to win Olympic medal for the USA. The first African American Olympic medalist—and first black US Olympic Swim Team member—was University of California, Berkeley alumni Anthony Ervin, who took gold in the men's 50 meter freestyle and silver in the men's 4 × 100 meter freestyle relay at the 2000 Olympic Games in Sydney. (More recently, Ervin won his second gold in the men's 50 meter freestyle in Rio 2016, at the age of 35(!)—though his accomplishment, like Manuel's, was overshadowed by Michael Phelps's return from retirement to reinforce his reputation as the greatest Olympian of all time.) Enith Brigitha's two bronzes for the Netherlands in the women's 100 and 200 meter freestyle in Montreal 1976 made her the first black swimmer *from any country* to win Olympic medal in the sport. Suriname's Anthony Nesty became the second in Seoul 1988 when he out-touched US swimming great Matt Biondi to win gold in the men's 100 meter butterfly. This is all to say that the emergence of high-visibility black competitive swimmers in both the national and international arenas is very much an early twenty-first-century phenomenon.

Jones and Correia, at least, are aware of their collective novelty and the urgency that underwrites their recent success. The urgency is due not only to the symbolic value of breaking color lines in sports considered non-traditional for black participants, but also to the fact that swimming, unlike baseball or basketball or football or track (or golf or tennis for that matter), involves critical life-saving skills.[11] Both Olympians have participated in the privately-funded Make a Splash Initiative, a partnership of the non-profit USA Swimming Foundation and the corporate oil giant ConocoPhillips, designed to offer low-cost swimming lessons for black and Latino children at one of over two hundred local partners nationwide and, thereby, to help reduce the number of preventable water-related injuries and deaths among that population. Jones and Correia's good works and good examples are highlighted in Joshua Waletzky's 2009 independent documentary *Parting the Waters*, which follows the lives of several black and Latino youth seeking their own path to Olympic glory from the ranks of the Boston Elite Swim Team. Producer Jenny Levison perhaps overstates

---

[11]As part of the lead-up to the domestic release of *Pride* in March 2007, AOL's *Black Voices* ran a tribute to "blacks in non-traditional sports." Among the featured athletes were Correia, bobsledder Vonetta Flowers, and speed skater Shani Davis, all recent Olympic medalists. But the inclusion in this list of tennis greats Venus and Serena Williams and golf legend Tiger Woods serves to blur the line between traditional and non-traditional sports, revealing how it is that, at one time or another and to greater or lesser degree, it was—and is—considered "non-traditional" for blacks to pursue and participate in *every* sport (Douglass 2007).

the case when she claims that in broaching the subject of race in swimming their film is "dealing with one of the *last* areas of segregation in our society." But, in so doing, the project does insist rightly that the gross inequality of public investment in swimming infrastructure is a question of social justice.

On this score, social entrepreneurism makes for good human interest reporting, but it cannot begin to address the social structures that give rise to injustice.[12] While it may be laudable that Jones and Correia use their popularity to promote charitable giving rather than simply to chase lucrative endorsement deals, it is important to note that they are not, by any stretch of the imagination, joining the ranks of political organizers forging a culture of resistance or building a progressive social movement, as have many other prominent black athletes in the historic instance, from Paul Robeson to Muhammad Ali (Zirin 2008). Jim Ellis is in more ways than one their patron saint, having helped to blaze the trail for their athletic exploits and, even more, for the warm public reception of their athletic exploits, including considerable underwriting for their outreach efforts. Ellis, after all, has been priming the pump of black swimming talent since before Jones and Correia were born. He sent former PDR students Michael Norment and Jason Webb to the 1992 US Olympic Trials as the first black swimmers to qualify for the event (though neither made the team that year); and he sent participants to every Olympic Swimming Trials since that watershed.[13] Dozens of his graduates went on to swimming scholarships at notable colleges and universities. And so on. That he did all of this with ruefully underfunded, eventually ramshackle facilities at his disposal, and against the grain of deeply segregated institutional arrangements—local, regional, and national—makes his accomplishments the perfect blend of personal crusade and quiet heroism. Perfect, that is, for corporate-sponsored Black History and Hollywood mythmaking (Fig. 2.1).

---

[12]The Make a Splash Initiative is easily the most extensive and capitalized effort of this sort, involving the national governing body for competitive swimming in the USA and a major multinational corporation regularly ranked in the Top 10 of the *Fortune* 500. Assuming that there are five million black children that do not swim (a conservative estimate), that this number will not increase in the future (which it likely will), and that at least half of the 100,000 children that Make a Splash claims to service each year went on to swimming proficiency (rather than taking a one-time lesson), it would still take *more than a century* for this national program to resolve the problem.

[13]Michael Norment, a college superstar and one of the top breaststrokers in the world throughout the 1990s, is also the son of Temple University Professor of African American Studies Nathaniel Norment, Jr. (Whitten 1998). Along with Sabir Muhammad and Byron Davis, Norment was one of the "great black hopes" to break the Olympic color line in that decade.

Fig. 2.1 Coach Jim Ellis (Terrance Howard) considers the significance and difficulty of his task in Sunu Gonera's *Pride* (2007). Image reproduced under terms of fair use

Making Waves

Boston Globe film critic Wesley Morris—to my knowledge, the only black reviewer to make the esteemed "Top Critics" list at the *Rotten Tomatoes* online clearinghouse—described *Pride* as a "public-service melodrama" (Morris 2007). Given the film's PG rating and its clearly intended family audience, the phrase is less a friendly jab in an otherwise sympathetic discussion than it is an apt description. Cynthia Fuchs, film and television editor for *PopMatters.com*, concurred, adding:

> *Pride* brings something else that makes the after-school-special silliness seem secondary. First, and importantly, this is an uplift-the-race film where [unlike James Gartner's 2006 *Glory Road* or Richard LaGravenese's 2007 *Freedom Writers*] the inspirational coach/teacher/mentor is black. As well-intentioned as characters played [respectively] by Josh Lucas and Hilary Swank may be, this image (lit and designed with its significance in mind) resonates. This is enhanced by the fact that the kids' very visible supporters at meets are the "community," mostly anonymous black faces (parents and church members) who, despite the conspicuous device, do something unusual: they make a worthy political point. (Fuchs 2007)

Just what this "worthy" political point is requires further discussion. From one angle, despite its formulaic plot, sentimental scoring, mediocre writing and direction, and unremarkable performances, the value of *Pride* is in what the film opens onto—on the one hand, the recent uptick in interest in black swimming history in academia, mass media, and independent arts; on the other, the fledging attempts to cultivate a contemporary tradition of black competitive swimming in the United States (Hersh 1998). Witness, for instance, the International Swimming Hall of Fame's 2008 exhibit, "Black Splash: The Amazing History of Swimming in Black and White," at the Old Dillard Museum in Fort Lauderdale, Florida; the Annual Black History Invitational Swim Meet sponsored since 1987 by the Washington, DC Department of Parks and Recreation; the Annual National Black Heritage Championship Swim Meet organized by the North Carolina Aquablazers Swim Team since 2003; or the Annual Chris Silva Championship Swim Meet hosted for nearly fifteen years by the City of Atlanta Dolphins Swim Team as a memorial to the former college great, first black American record-holder, and Director of Minority Programs at the International Swimming Hall of Fame (Borenstein and Robb 1990). These grassroots efforts represent the impulse of the early Jim Ellis, "the Afro-wearing, dashiki-clad firebrand who chose swimming as his method of community activism back in 1971" (John-Hall 2007, 66), when it reaches past the individual to the collective.

From another angle, however, the political point of the film is disquieting. To the extent that the pursuit of swimming by blacks, from the recreational to the competitive, involves not only awareness of a need to dispel a stereotype but also an attempt "to establish and defend [the] right to participate in the general community of America" (Judy 1994, 221), an adjudication in the order of morality. What this means in the case of Ellis and his fictionalization as "Jim," a character played deftly enough by Oscar Award-nominee Terrence Howard, is that the story must construct a foil to highlight the grandeur of our protagonist and his contribution to what will be called "our house… our community." The film opens with a scene set in Salisbury, North Carolina. The year is 1964 and young Jim is in town with his teammates from Cheyney State College for a regional swim meet at the Blue Ridge Aquatics Center. Ellis did swim for a year at Cheyney State, the historically black college now called Cheyney University where he earned his BS in Mathematics, before the coach resigned and the team was disbanded.[14] But the four Cheyney State Chargers that first enter the screen as Jim's teammates are all white. And when the team coach, who is also

---

[14]Cheyney University is the oldest historically black college or university in the country. It was established in 1837 by the bequest of Richard Humphries, a Quaker philanthropist, who was prompted by an 1829 antiblack race riot in his adopted hometown of Philadelphia—one of more than a half dozen to occur there between 1820 and 1850—to create the African Institute, or Institute for Colored Youth, "to

white, regretfully informs Jim in the hallway before the meet that the other presumptively all-white teams are threatening to cancel the event because "it seems somebody saw you get on the bus," it confirms the film's desire to rewrite Ellis's story as one that was always already integrated. The effect of this opening gambit is to project antiblackness into an exterior and marginal space that blacks living and working in otherwise integrated places sometimes encounter, rather than a structural condition that blacks must navigate constantly across an array of occupations and a range of stations.

In the world according to *Pride*, white swimmers and coaches at the height of the civil rights movement, amid the rapid *privatization* of aquatics, participate unselfconsciously with their black teammate; they do not cave into the enormous social pressures to maintain recreational segregation; and they do not fail to come to the physical defense of a black man accosted by racist police and enraged white mobs—all in the backyard of a young Jesse Helms, whose nightly newscasts and weekly editorials on WRAL-TV (now a CBS affiliate) for the Raleigh-based Capitol Broadcasting Company were spreading the ultraconservative gospel of the New Right throughout the Upper South (Associated Press 2008b).[15] Coach Logan passes down to Jim a gem of patriarchal wisdom before taking a principled and fated stand: "My daddy always used to tell me, it's a lot easier to ask for forgiveness than for permission." Forgive us our trespasses, in the good name of competition, but when the cohort of white competitors refuse *unanimously* to enter the pool with Jim, and the police arrive on cue to forcibly remove the intruder from the premises, though he violates no ordinance, the coach's sage advice changes abruptly. "Don't fight 'em, Jimmy!" he pleads.[16] We should underscore the fact that Jim's insistence

---

instruct the descendants of the African Race in school learning, in the various branches of the mechanic Arts, trades and Agriculture in order to prepare and fit and qualify them as instructors." That is, vocational training as response to racist violence, discipline as antidote to punishment (Coppin 1913).

[15]In addition to his well-known racist, sexist, homophobic, and anti-communist positions, recently declassified documents suggest that Helms may also have been a contact for the Federal Bureau of Investigation, offering the services of his station to the law enforcement agency in its counter-intelligence operations against the civil rights movement (Kane and Christensen 2010).

[16]More properly phrased, Coach Logan might exclaim "Don't YOU fight 'em, Jimmy!" or "Don't you FIGHT 'em, Jimmy!" since the problem contained in the sentence is neither the verb (fight) nor the subject (Jimmy) in isolation but the particular combination of the two. Fighting against segregation is acceptable if it is initiated and led by a white man, on the black man's behalf, and the black man is acceptable as long as he "works so hard to get here" and does not fight to get into the pool. This point dovetails nicely with the sage advice of that other paternalistic white man, Bink, the racist school principle and head coach of Main Line Academy Swim Team: "If you want respect in this game, then you're gonna have to earn it! I know they taught you that at Cheyney State." Coach Jim, now a college

here on the right to participate in a sanctioned athletics event and, moreover, the right to speak freely in complaint of a denial of participation is not *even* civil disobedience. Yet this modest proposal prompts the white father figure to intervene, first and foremost to keep Jim calm and then to announce to the crowd, "If they don't want *us* to swim here, its fine, we'll go home!" The police, as they are wont to do, shake down Jim in any case, and after a terse exchange of pleasantries Jim fights back, striking an officer or two before he is wrestled into submission. Jim is left at the close of the scene in extreme close-up, face down on the pool deck, a police officer's foot pinning his head to the tile, sobbing audibly: "I got rights. I got rights. I got wronged, right?"[17] (Fig. 2.2).

On first blush, the film appears agnostic in the face of Jim's plaintive query. Ten years later, the college graduate and veteran swim instructor is denied employment in a teaching and coaching position at the prestigious and lilywhite Main Line Academy for which he is surely qualified. Granted an interview on the strength of his *résumé*, Jim is summarily dismissed by Principal Richard "Bink" Binkowski (Tom Arnold) when the latter discovers the applicant in question is black. The rationalization is simple: "I don't think a person like yourself could communicate properly with our students." Bink doubles as Main Line's head swim coach, so the two will meet again, on the deck, in a displacement of the classical education that runs through the field of mathematics onto the tutelary mission proper to the domain

---

graduate and in charge of the PDR Swim Team counters this imperative with recourse to the reciprocal aspect of the social bond: "If you want respect, you give it." Bink is adamant: "You *earn* it." This is the final word and lesson. The triumph of the film hinges on Jim's ability to earn the respect of this other and better white father, and he is to do so by instilling in his charges the proper desire for work. The desire for work, "the productive labor of modern subjects," is the *sine qua non* of morality. In this scenario, confronting a derogation that associates blackness with amorality, "it is presupposed that authentic being derives from morality. That is, the nigger ['a commodity-thing'] becomes the negro ['a human identity'] through moral behavior, or good works, founded on morality as a governmental habit of thought (police as internalized control)" (Judy 1994, 230). More on this point below.

[17]The whitewashing of Jim Ellis's educational past, the insertion of white allies and mentors in the place where there were likely black companions and comrades is consistent with a key aspect of Gonera's directorial vision: "'In Africa, racism was legal for many years, so I grew up with it,' Gonera says. 'I married a white woman and I had to deal with racism on a very personal level—people throwing bricks through your house, things like that. So when I read the script, that element didn't surprise me. But I was determined to be authentic and to show different sides of people. I didn't want it to be that any white person is racist, because that's not true'" (Archer 2007). It might seem curious that anxiety about the depiction of *white* personality as homogenous would arise in a film centered on the efforts of *black* community to dispute its status as stereotype through its internal differentiation. However, the attempt to "set the world straight," as the tagline reads for Josh Waletzky's 2009 documentary *Parting the Waters*, and the redemption-through-differentiation of whites should be viewed as two sides of the same coin.

Fig. 2.2 Young Jim looks on as his white competitors refuse to swim in the same pool. Image reproduced under terms of fair use

of sportsmanship.[18] As it turns out, discrimination carries perquisites. The standard fare rejection forces Jim into the overcrowded unemployment office where he is finally paired with the menial labor that will provide the condition of possibility for his ascent and his community's inspiration. Sent to prepare the condemned Marcus Foster Recreation Center for closure by the City of Philadelphia, Jim finds a diamond in the rough: among the dilapidation, a salvageable junior Olympic swimming pool. He will have to invest his own time and energy into this forsaken public work, but he cannot avoid appropriating municipal resources to that end—hundreds of dollars in unauthorized wages from the Department of Recreation, hundreds of thousands unauthorized gallons from the Philadelphia Water Department.

As Jim pilfers from the uncaring city government, a group of five black male youth, school kids all, squeeze the last few days out of a basketball

---

[18] As notable is Ellis' coaching achievement, his success as a middle-school mathematics teacher is barely understood. We know that a good number of those who have participated in PDR Swimming have gone on to undergraduate training, but we can gain no real sense of the impact that Ellis has had for the academic and intellectual development of his students in the classroom. How mathematics might also be approached as a form of community activism is exemplified well by the Algebra Project, founded in 1982 by former civil rights leader Dr. Robert P. 'Bob' Moses (Moses and Cobb 2001).

court just outside the pool's graffiti-covered doors. Before the hoops are finally removed by a city maintenance worker (played by Jim Ellis in cameo), the boys are watched (and watched over) by a local pimp and drug dealer, Franklin (Gary Sturgis), whose crew circles like vultures in search of carrion. Franklin's parked car is framed in the introductory sequence as if it blocks the forward progress of the yellow school bus that becomes the PDR Swimming transport. A stray basketball breaks Franklin's radio, putting Reggie (Evan Ross)—weak, stuttering, un-athletic, slight-of-frame, light-skinned—in his debt. Franklin targets this Achilles' heel in a bid to recruit Andre (Kevin Phillips), the alpha male and eventual captain of Jim's aspiring team, to his own drug dealing crew. The recruitment (which is actually a re-commissioning since Andre worked previously as Franklin's lieutenant until a non-fatal gunshot wound retired him from the set) is ultimately unsuccessful because Jim intervenes with force against Franklin's designs in a street confrontation that is crucial to the story's unfolding. The battle over Andre's loyalties, or, rather, his *custody*, represents the Appomattox of this miniature civil war. Franklin is defeated morally in this moment, but his desperation drives him to commit a very unpopular act of vandalism against the Foster Center, after it has become a proper hub of neighborhood activity by dint of Jim's trademark "pride, determination, resilience." Now acting in defense of territorial waters, Jim is authorized in dispatching Franklin and his minions, nearly drowning him to death in the process. And though Jim offers the obligatory apology to his team for the poor example his violent reprisal sets, issuing a self-imposed suspension from the coveted Eastern Regional Finals at the University of Baltimore, it is critical that, unlike events in 1964, no charges are filed against him for these multiple counts of assault and battery.

The showdown with Franklin is the last of three pool deck fight scenes in the film, a count that warrants our borrowing Wiltse's title as leitmotif. The first contest, as noted, opens the dramatic action and establishes the ethical problem to be adjudicated. The problem is elusive, however. Nestled in the theatrics of humiliation and peril, the problem, in the final analysis, is not that of normative white racist hatred but that of the black man's response to being wronged. The third contest is definitive because it allows the young swimmers to leave collectively the fold of their surrogate domesticity, and Jim's marked absence enables Andre, in particular, to emerge as *protégé*. But it is the second clash that proves most transformative. To give the newly minted PDR Swim Team suitable perspective on the stakes of their training, Jim takes them across town to face the best talents in the area. They receive their foreseeable thrashing from Main Line Academy with a bit too much good humor and aplomb until the showdown between the two team captains, one black and one white, reveals that winners arrogate to themselves the right to cheat. Andre attempts to fight back, like young Jimmy in Salisbury, and the black and white teams clear the benches (Fig. 2.3).

Coach Jim and Coach Bink mediate, and in the heated altercation Jim is told flatly: this late-game infraction, like the pregame slights and taunts, does not matter because PDR was losing so badly in any case. We kicked you, in other words, *because* you were down. Your dismal performance bespeaks a general lack of discipline, a problem of the will, and that weakness earns you nothing but our contempt. Bink thus clarifies: "If you want respect in this game, you're gonna have to earn it." Earning respect from state-sanctioned white power is not related to the restricted economy of exchange. One does not simply give respect and receive it in return. That is, one is not respected for being respectful. One is respected for being strong, even if one is, like ghettoized black youth and their mentors circa 1974, in a position of relative powerlessness. This is an important elision because it redirects Jim's project from empowerment and organization to strength training and character building. It is a moderate inflection of the era's political term of art: self-determination. Those aspects of the Black Power era that might include alterations of public policy and mobilization of constituency

Fig. 2.3 Coach Ellis confronts Coach Bink (Tom Arnold) for cheating and disrespecting the PDR swimmers. Image reproduced under terms of fair use

are left to the behind-the-scenes lobbying of the dark-skinned head of maintenance, Elston (Bernie Mac), who serves throughout the film as "uncle" in an interracial tale of parthenogenetic inheritance between (white) fathers and (black) sons.

If Elston represents the activist impulse in caricature, *homo civilis*, then Franklin represents the domestic enemy in drag, *homo criminalis*. Jim and Elston collaborate on the renovation project, enjoining the responsible black city councilwoman, Ms. Sue Davis (Kimberly Elise), to give the "good black man" the support needed to reform the principles of black masculinity and thereby rescue the community from itself. A black woman's support in this instance means not only reversing the facilities closure and allocating permanent funding to the recreation center in her function as political delegate, but also, as is so often the case, non-interference with the organic development of the supposedly essential relation between black men and boys.[19] Sue's maternal guardianship obstructs that relation; Franklin's paternal imposition perverts it. Yet the supporting cast duo Elston/Franklin should not be thought in opposition to one another, but rather thought together in opposition to the third, exalted figure represented by Jim, what cultural theorist RA Judy (1994) terms ironically "*homo Africanus Americanus moralis*."

The three operative terms—civility, criminality, morality—triangulate Jim's passage between the Scylla of political radicalization, missing the mark by assuming paradoxically that blacks are rights-bearing and so have nothing to prove, and the Charybdis of lawlessness, "constituting a threat to the survival of the community by giving the police cause to attack" (Judy 1994, 226). Elston lives in a crypt of Black Power iconography, his advanced age reinforcing the obsolescence of all that is symbolized by the black fist and silhouetted African continent that adorn the dusty walls of the abandoned offices. Franklin, for his part, lives parasitically on the decomposing host neighborhood beyond the center's mold and mildew. So, despite the early foregrounding of Jim Crow's legacy, the battle that animates the film is an intramural one. Elston must be converted to Jim's program. Sue must come to see his worth. Franklin must yield to his proprietary claim. In fact, the anticipated payback, in which Andre defeats his rival Jake (Scott Reeves) at the climactic regional meet to the sounds of James Brown's famous anthem,

---

[19]Among the various attempts to speak to this dynamic in recent black Hollywood filmmaking, David Marriott's (2000) reading of John Singleton's *Boyz in the Hood* (1991) and Wahneema Lubiano's (1997) reading of Bill Duke's *Deep Cover* (1992) remain among the best published thus far. A locus classicus of critique on the myth of the black matriarch is Davis (1981). See also Spillers (2003).

is painfully deferred by Main Line's spurious cancellation of their regularly scheduled appearance at PDR. In place of Andre's home crowd vindication against Jake, who kicked him in the teeth at their first meeting, we have Jim beating Franklin to within an inch of his life.

Unpunished physical violence modulates heteroclite black masculinity, and the narrows of the PDR credo must eschew transgression against the rules, written and unwritten alike. It must be law-abiding and mindful of racial etiquette, however retrenched, which is to say it must be self-policing, "exposed to the discipline of self-pride." "Protest" is not in its vocabulary, nor is "disobedience," even, or "demand," and the pursuit of power must be pried loose from the expression of pride and put to one side. Black Power, in whatever formulation, is contiguous with, if not identical to, black criminality.[20] Jim may be a badman, with a stiff spine, a sharp tongue, and a lion's heart; but he is not a bad nigger.[21] This discernment is the lesson of the three father figures that guide Jim's journey of self-discovery in the context of disavowed political upheaval. The interracial paternal trinity consists

---

[20] This conflation is evident, for instance, in the scene of PDR's first meet at the Main Line Academy. When they enter the pool, one hears a background comment from a man in the all-white audience: 'Must be some kind of a protest march.' On the blocks before the final event, the 50 yard freestyle, Jake, Main Line's star swimmer, looks over at Andre, his counterpart, and says: 'Just be glad they took off the cuffs so you can swim, brother.' The two comments are understood to be seamless with the general atmosphere of hostility.

[21] See Judy (1994) for a discussion of attempts in black cultural studies to distinguish between these two figures in the wake of gangster rap. Judy spends considerable time examining the work of musicologist Jon Michael Spencer (now called Yahya Jongintaba), whose "argument for the heterogeneity of the badman and bad nigger is [meant] to establish rap's authenticity as an African American form by rescuing it from the 'genocidal' tendencies of the bad nigger" (Judy 1994, 220). For Spencer, the badman betrays a "strong sense of social propriety, [an] understanding that strict obedience to social codes is essential for collective survival. The badman is the self-consciously representative black, he is an instantiation of morality above the law" (220). He may, according to folklorist John Roberts, challenge "the unjustness of the law of the state," but he does so "while preserving the moral law of the community" (221). The bad nigger, by contrast, "doesn't obey the law and take moral responsibility for his actions" (227). Though a full discussion of this point is beyond the scope of this chapter, it can be said at least that the disassociation of the badman and the bad nigger is, for Judy, a decidedly postbellum project, having to do with the changed function of law in the assault on Radical Reconstruction and the formation of Jim Crow. He glosses Roberts' claim as follows: In the postbellum period, "maintaining internal harmony and solidarity within one's own community was a form of protection against the law of the state. In this understanding, the black community becomes the police in order to not give the police any reason or cause to violate it" (221). Saidiya Hartman (1997) has called this "the burdened individuality of freedom," a juridical vehicle for maintaining the "tragic continuities in antebellum and postbellum constitutions of blackness" (7). Judy is interested to understand how black collectivities manage circumstances in which, to bend the popular saying, the more things change, the worse they seem to get. What he finds is a measure of downward continuity from the jackboot of the state-authorized armed regulatory force to the striking fist and pointing finger of the teacher or coach in state employ. This is what Judy suggests in his identification of community with the police, that is, "police in the broader sense of governmentality" (Judy 1994, 226).

of Coach Logan, who trains young Jimmy and both emboldens and contains his will to fight; Coach Bink, who issues the challenge to which Jim must rise; and the late Marcus Foster, in whose memory PDR's home facility is named. Of course, the three fathers correspond with the three elementary terms of the endeavor: *determination* to overcome obstacles (Bink), *resilience* to recover from setbacks and losses (Logan), and *pride* to give worth and direction to the struggle (Foster).

Pooling Resources

We conclude with a brief discussion of the final father, who is also the first. Midway through the film, after Elston has successfully persuaded Sue to rescind her order for closure, Jim presents his newly-minted team with a policy update freighted with an existential proposition. After asking rhetorically, "Do y'all remember the first gift that you was given after you made it into this world? What was it?" And, again, "What's the last thing that's remembered about you when you leave this world?" Jim declares, finally, that the *name* is the alpha and omega. He announces: "You are now the official representatives of the Marcus Foster Recreational Center." Having established their collective namesake in this fashion, Jim draws what might seem a small detail into the story's center of gravity. But who was Marcus Foster and what are we to make of the enigmatic and spectral presence of his name? An alumnus of Cheyney State College like Jim Ellis, he earned a PhD from the University of Pennsylvania. Foster went on to become a local hero, a celebrated educator and administrator serving with distinction for nearly fifteen years as a teacher and, after 1968, as principal in Philadelphia's Simon Gratz High School. He recounted that experience at length in his book, *Making Schools Work: Strategies for Changing Education* (Foster 1971).[22] Winner of the 1968 Philadelphia Award, one of the city's highest honors, for contributions to education and community service, Foster was eventually recruited to California and appointed in 1970 as the Superintendent of the Oakland Unified School District, the first black person to attain the position (Fig. 2.4).

Foster was a liberal reformer who promoted ideas of community participation in the decision-making of educational bureaucracy in order

---

[22]For more on Foster's life and work, see McCorry (1978).

Fig. 2.4 Coach Ellis gives his swimmers a lesson on technique. Image reproduced under terms of fair use

to counteract what he saw as a generally dysfunctional and adversarial relation between contemporary public schools and their constituents. He spoke directly to the importance of providing quality education for all students, especially those in districts serving the poorest neighborhoods of black ghettos. Most of his measures were embraced by local residents, but what some took to be his gradualism and willingness to compromise with law and order tendencies in municipal government drew criticism from radical political formations like the Black Panther Party. The latter's criticism never lost sight of the distinction between Foster and the state-authorized regulatory force of the police against which they were occasionally fighting live-fire street battles. Other groups were not so circumspect. On the evening of November 6, 1973, Foster was assassinated while leaving a meeting of the Oakland school board, shot to death in the parking lot by Joseph Remiro and Russ Little. The gunmen were members of an unknown quantity called the Symbionese Liberation Army (SLA) (Taylor 2002).

The SLA would go on to achieve a bizarre sort of notoriety the following year, when they committed the well-known but little understood kidnapping of Patricia Hearst, heiress of the renowned west coast media dynasty. It was the most popular news story of the year and much has been written since about that period.[23] But while most of those born before, say, 1965 remember something of the Patty Hearst phenomenon, few know about the Foster assassination that preceded it. Nor are they aware of the fact that the SLA committed the act that would become their most infamous precisely in order to secure Remiro's and Little's release from custody. In short, without Marcus Foster, there is no Patty Hearst.

The SLA's actions were denounced nearly across the board by leftist organizations of the day. And though the outfit had fully appropriated the rhetoric and tactics of more legible revolutionary confrontations with state and capital, the SLA offered little in the way of program or platform. Even as an urban guerrilla faction, its connections, both practical and ideological, to the black liberation movement sometimes cited as impetus were tenuous at best. There were, save leader Donald DeFreeze (a.k.a. Cinque), no black members. And though they often took refuge there during the four-month period between the kidnapping and the fatal LAPD shootout, the SLA was *in* the ghetto but surely not *of* the ghetto. In *Slippery Characters*, literary critic Laura Browder describes the SLA membership as "ethnic impersonators" that functioned as "a parody of a black militant party." She continues: "the SLA members embodied stereotypes in their embrace of blackness and used their excursion into black identity to liberate themselves from the inhibitions they linked to their white selves. […] Their performance of race was a thoroughgoing, if unselfconscious, satire" (Browder 2000, 225). Foster, then, is killed—assassinated—by a group of whites in "postwar blackface," whose short-lived career embodied the nightmare scenario in which black radicalism converges with black criminality at the direct expense of black morality. But if there is a more poignant example of how that convergence requires not only white psychic projection, but also white political performance, I have yet to see it.

Gonera awkwardly insinuates the Foster story into the film, playing fast and loose with the chronology of historical events. As noted, Ellis founded PDR Swimming in 1971, but *Pride* locates this founding three years later in 1974. This revision makes sense if the fictional recreation center is to be named after Foster, who is killed a year earlier. But there is an additional wrinkle. The Marcus Foster Pool in the Nicetown section of North Philly was not built and named until 1980, and it was constructed as a replacement for

---

[23]The popular literature on the topic is too vast to cite, but see for example: Hearst and Moscow (1988), McLellan and Avery (1977), and Weed and Swanton (1976). For critical scholarly accounts, see Graebner (2008), Castiglia (1996), and Browder (2000). For award-winning fictional renderings of the affair, see Choi (2003) and Sorrentino (2006).

the failing Sayre Community Recreation Center in West Philadelphia, where Ellis had coached for almost two decades prior. So rather than depicting the Foster Pool as a site of renewal, the film transports it backward in time and introduces it as already in disrepair. Foster's legacy is thus refurbished or resurrected in *Pride* rather than commemorated and continued. There is something uncanny about this *faux pas*, both for the vision of school reform championed by Foster and for the vision of sports mentoring practiced by Ellis. We recall that the feature film, bestowing upon its audience gleaming facilities and crystal-clear waters, is released in the same year that the actual Foster Pool, on this side of the screen, is closed indefinitely, "shutdown today to a whole community." (The fact that Ellis also received the Presidential Honor Award from the International Swimming Hall of Fame that year is small consolation.)[24] So the image-track of a decrepit recreation center cut off from the support of public revenue is fully resonant with its referent. This is the wretched state of affairs that the fictional Jim Ellis called "*life* with no hoop": shooting baskets on a backboard with no achievable object, one's aim is returned to its source over and over again. Perhaps it is only fitting, then, that this commercial failure was meant to serve as a financial contribution to the regional economic recovery of the locations where it was produced in the wake of Hurricane Katrina: Shreveport, Baton Rouge, New Orleans.[25]

References

Archer, Greg. 2007. Passion Behind Lens in *Pride*. *San Francisco Examiner*, March 23. Accessed May 28, 2017. http://www.sfexaminer.com/passion-behind-lens-in-pride/.

Associated Press. 2008a. Nearly 60 Percent of Black Children Can't Swim. *MSNBC*, May 1. Accessed May 28, 2017. http://www.nbcnews.com/id/24411271/.

Associated Press. 2008b. Former Sen. Jesse Helms Dies at 86. *CBS News*, July 4. Accessed May 28, 2017. http://www.cbsnews.com/news/former-sen-jesse-helms-dies-at-86/.

---

[24]Ellis was forced to conclude his work at PDR as a result of the loss of public funding and he has since 2010 served as the coach of the Salvation Army Kroc Aquatics (SAKA) swim team, quickly building it into the premier competitive swim program in Greater Philadelphia (Ebony 2017).

[25]For extensive discussion of the grossly unequal post-Katrina social, political, and economic fortunes of the Gulf Coast region, and especially its poor and working-class black residents, see Haubert (2015), Huret and Sparks (2014) and Wailoo (2010).

Bai, Matt. 2008. Is Obama the End of Black Politics? *New York Times*, Auguest 6. Accessed May 28, 2017. http://www.nytimes.com/2008/08/10/magazine/10politics-t.html.

Borenstein, Seth, and Sharon Robb. 1990. A Dual Nature in a Swim Lane. *Sun Sentinel*, Auguest 21. Accessed May 28, 2017. http://articles.sun-sentinel.com/1990-08-21/news/9002090900_1_black-swimmer-chris-silva-princess-diana.

Brennan, Chris. 2009. Protesters at City Hall: Closing City Pools is Racist. *Philadelphia Daily News*, July 14. Accessed May 28, 2017. http://www.philly.com/philly/blogs/clout/50732102.html.

Browder, Laura. 2000. *Slippery Characters: Ethnic Impersonators and American Identities*. Chapel Hill, NC: University of North Carolina Press.

Castiglia, Christopher. 1996. *Bound and Determined: Captivity, Culture-Crossing, and White Womanhood from Mary Rowlandson to Patty Hearst*. Chicago: University of Chicago Press.

Choi, Susan. 2003. *American Woman: A Novel*. New York: HarperCollins.

Danielle, Britni. 2015. "There's Nothing Funny About 70 Percent of Black Americans Not Knowing How to Swim." *TakePart*, June 29. Accessed May 28, 2017. http://www.takepart.com/article/2015/06/29/nothing-funny-70-percent-black-americans-cant-swim.

Davis, Angela. 1981. *Women, Race, and Class*. New York: Random House.

Dawson, Kevin. 2006. Enslaved Swimmers and Divers in the Atlantic World. *Journal of American History* 92: 1327–1355.

Dawson, Kevin. 2010. African Swimmers Made History. *Swimmer*, January–February.

Douglass, William. 2007. *Pride* & Prejudice: Black People Can Swim. *AOL Black Voices*, January 18. Accessed May 28, 2017. https://groups.yahoo.com/neo/groups/Blacksurfing/conversations/messages/1450.

Ebony. 2017. Black Kids Swim Interviews Swim Legend Jim Ellis. *Black Kids Swim*, March 23. Accessed May 28, 2017. http://blackkidsswim.com/2017/03/23/black-kids-swim-interviews-swim-legend-jim-ellis/.

Elizalde, Elizabeth. 2017. Teen Slammed to the Ground at Pool Party Files $5 Million Lawsuit Against Texas Cop, City. *New York Daily News*, January 3. Accessed May 28, 2017. http://www.nydailynews.com/news/crime/teen-slammed-ground-pool-party-files-5-million-lawsuit-article-1.2933569.

Foster, Marcus. 1971. *Making Schools Work: Strategies for Changing Education*. Philadelphia: Westminster Press.

Fuchs, Cynthia. 2007. A Person Like Yourself. *PopMatters*, March 27. Accessed May 28, 2017. http://www.popmatters.com/review/pride-2007/.

Graebner, William. 2008. *Patty's Got a Gun: Patricia Hearst in 1970s America*. Chicago: University of Chicago Press.

Grant, Joseph Karl. 2010. The Valley Club of Huntingdon Valley Discrimination Controversy: The Racial, Economic, and Legal Implications for African-Americans and Latinos. *Widener Journal of Law, Economics & Race* I: 1–8.

Hartman, Saidiya. 1997. *Scenes of Subjection: Terror, Slavery, and Self-Making in Nineteenth-Century America*. New York: Oxford University Press.

Hastings, Donald, Sammy Zahran, and Sherry Cable. 2006. Drowning in Inequalities: Swimming and Social Justice. *Journal of Black Studies* 36: 894–917.

Haubert, Jeannie (ed.). 2015. *Rethinking Disaster Recover: A Hurricane Katrina Retrospective*. Lanham, MD: Lexington Books.

Hearst, Patricia Campbell, and Alvin Moscow. 1988. *Patty Hearst: Her Own Story*. New York: HarperCollins.

Hersh, Philip. 1998. Black Swimmers Become a Growing Talent Pool. *Chicago Tribune*, December 3.

Hoose, Philip. 1990. A New Pool of Talent. *New York Times Magazine*, April 29.

Huret, Romain, and Randy Sparks (eds.). 2014. *Hurricane Katrina in Transatlantic Perspective*. Baton Rouge, LA: LSU Press.

Irwin, Carol, Richard Irwin, Timothy Ryan, and Joris Drayer. 2009. The Mythology of Swimming: Are Myths Impacting Minority Youth Participation? *International Journal of Aquatic Research and Education* 3: 10–23.

Jackson-Coppin, Fanny. 1913. *Reminiscences of School Life, and Hints on Teaching*. Philadelphia: A.M.E. Book Concern.

John-Hall, Annette. 2007. At the Pool with Jim Ellis. *Ebony*, April.

Johnson, Eric. 2007. *Nightline* Classic: Al Campanis. *ABC News/Nightline*, April 12. Accessed May 28, 2017. http://abcnews.go.com/Nightline/ESPNSports/story?id=3034914.

Judy, R.A.T. 1994. On the Question of Nigga Authenticity. *boundary 2* 21: 211–30.

Kane, Dan, and Rob Christensen. 2010. FBI Records Indicate N.C. Sen. Jesse Helms Was a 'Contact'. *McClatchyDC*, May 26. Accessed May 28, 2017. http://www.mcclatchydc.com/news/politics-government/article24583804.html.

Klein, Michael. 2007. Tough Swim Coach Inspires New Movie *Pride*. *PopMatters*, March 23. Accessed May 28, 2017. http://www.popmatters.com/article/tough-swim-coach-inspires-the-new-movie-pride/.

Mandell, Nina. 2012. Ohio Landlady Appeals to Keep 'White Only' Sign at Pool, State Panel to Make Final Ruling. *New York Daily News*, January 12. Accessed May 28, 2017. http://www.nydailynews.com/news/national/ohio-landlady-appeals-white-sign-pool-article-1.1005038.

Marriott, David. 2000. *On Black Men*. New York: Columbia University Press.

Martin, Michel. 2009. "Philly-Area Pool Rejects Black Swimmers, Stirs Anger." *National Public Radio*, July 13. Accessed May 28, 2017. http://www.npr.org/templates/story/story.php?storyId=106538011.

McCorry, Jesse. 1978. *Marcus Foster and the Oakland Public Schools*. Berkeley, CA: University of California Press.

McLellan, Vin and Paul Avery. 1977. *The Voices of Guns: The Definitive and Dramatic Story of the Twenty-Two Month Career of the Symbionese Liberation

Army, One of the Most Bizarre Chapters in the History of the American Left. New York: Putnam.

Morris, Wesley. 2007. The Coach: As Inner-City Swim Coach, Terrence Howard Mentors Black Youth in *Pride*. *Boston Globe*, March 23. Accessed May 28, 2017. http://archive.boston.com/ae/movies/articles/2007/03/23/the_coach/.

Moses, Robert, and Charles Cobb. 2001. *Radical Equations: Civil Rights from Mississippi to the Algebra Project*. Boston: Beacon Press.

Nunnally, Derrick. 2010. Synagogue to Use Swim Club for Members' Recreation. *Philadelphia Inquirer*, May 15.

Powell, Michael. 2010. Wealth, Race and the Great Recession. *New York Times*, May 17. Accessed May 28, 2017. https://economix.blogs.nytimes.com/2010/05/17/wealth-race-and-the-great-recession/.

Roebuck, Jeremy. 2012. For campers, $1.1M Accord in Swim-Club Bias Case is Bittersweet. *Philadelphia Inquirer*, Aug 18. Accessed May 28, 2017. http://www.philly.com/philly/hp/news_update/20120818_For_campers___1_1M_accord_in_swim-club_bias_case_is_bittersweet.html.

Saffron, Inga. 2009. Out of the pool. *Skyline Online*, July 10. Accessed May 28, 2017. http://changingskyline.blogspot.com/2009/07/out-of-pool-its-not-just-about-race.html.

Slot, Owen. 2008. Jim Ellis Takes Pride in Making Waves and Shattering Myths. *Times Online*, April 22. Accessed May 28, 2017. https://www.thetimes.co.uk/article/jim-ellis-takes-pride-in-making-waves-and-shattering-myths-3h3dt-wd7zmz.

Snead, James. 1986. *Figures of Division: William Faulkner's Major Novels*. New York: Routledge.

Sorrentino, Christopher. 2006. *Trance*. New York: Macmillan.

Spillers, Hortense. 1996. All the Things You Could be by Now, If Sigmund Freud's Wife Was Your Mother: Psychoanalysis and Race. *Boundary 2* 23: 75–141.

Spillers, Hortense. 2003. *Black, White, and In Color: Essays on American Literature and Culture*. Chicago: University of Chicago Press.

Sugrue, Thomas. 2009. *Sweet Land of Liberty: The Forgotten Struggle for Civil Rights in the North*. New York: Random House.

Swanton, Scott., and Steven Weed. 1976. *My Search for Patty Hearst*. New York: Crown Publishers.

Taylor, Michael. 2002.Forgotten Footnote: Before Hearst, SLA Killed Educator. *San Francisco Chronicle*. November14. Accessed May 28, 2017. http://www.sfgate.com/bayarea/article/FORGOTTEN-FOOTNOTE-Before-Hearst-SLA-killed-2754621.php.

Wailoo, Keith (ed.). 2010. *Katrina's Imprint: Race and Vulnerability in America*. New Brunswick, NJ: Rutgers University Press.

Whitten, Phillip. 1998. Stormin' Norment. *Swimming World and Junior Swimmer*, April.

Wiltse, Jeff. 2007. *Contested Waters: A Social History of Swimming Pools in America*. Chapel Hill, NC: UNC Press.

Zirin, Dave. 2008. *A People's History of Sports in the United States: 250 Years of Politics, Protest, People, and Play*. New York: New Press.

3

Fantasy and Desire: On *Friday Night Lights* and *Coach Carter*

Introduction

This chapter presents a contrapuntal reading of two additional Hollywood films in which high school sport serves as a practical ground for adjudicating the education of young black men and an allegory of prospects for economic development, political engagement, and social change toward greater racial equality in the contemporary United States. Here we move from the swimming pools of the Northeast Corridor to the football fields of the Deep South and the basketball courts of the West Coast. Many of the themes addressed along the way will be familiar from the previous two chapters; however, the particular ideological twists taken by these now familiar narrative structures, dramatic tropes, and visual clichés in the works discussed below warrant special attention.

Peter Berg's *Friday Night Lights* (2004) adapts H.G. Bissinger's bestselling journalistic account of the City of Odessa in the late 1980s: a predominantly white, working-class oil town in rural West Texas racked by the stagnation of its local industry in amid the restructuring of Reaganomics. The residents' struggle against unforeseen *economic* crisis is seemingly exacerbated by the paradoxically imposing presence of distant black communities in the Dallas-Fort Worth metroplex some 350 miles away, communities supposed to be in *political* ascendance in the post-civil rights era but that are symbolized, importantly, by preternatural *physical* power. The gridiron is thus the site of their potential collective redemption because a political response is out of the question. Thomas Carter's *Coach Carter* (2005) is an original screenplay drawn from the brief national media attention cast on the city of Richmond, California in the late 1990s: a predominantly black, working-class oil town in the metropolitan San Francisco Bay Area likewise suffering from the decimation of its working-class job base. But residents also face the dire consequences of a state-sanctioned underground economy of drugs, guns, and prostitution, and the menace of racial profiling and mass imprisonment as expanded under the Clinton Administration. They address this quotidian catastrophe by refusing to countenance the ongoing repression of black political organizing and forfeiting the public sphere whose emergence made possible the "hoop dreams" they maintain against all odds.[1]

Both films feature narratives of individual salvation for the community's young men, the rescue of its most suitable candidates enabled by uncompromising mentorship and firm tutelage in the rites of adult masculinity by a tough-loving patriarch representing the values of another day and age: Coach Gary Gaines (Billy Bob Thorton) in *Friday Night Lights* and Coach Ken Carter (Samuel L. Jackson) in *Coach Carter*. Both films, as well, pivot on stimulating the particularly masculine ambition to flee the horizon of dead-end lives, developing the will and the skill to actualize the escape plan, and managing the peculiar pressures brought to bear when this mission—which, again, displaces questions of political struggle and deceptively condenses multiple sources of social anguish—is figured as a matter of bestowing the rudiments of masculinity and inaugurating a quest for proper manhood (Baker 2003). However, these surface similarities should not lead the viewer to discover some overarching project or underlying common ground. Not only are these two films *not* simply two versions of the same story; more importantly, the *success* of the one is entirely dependent on the *failure* of the other. Put differently, the possibility of the former (*Friday Night Lights*), the efficacy of its symbolic universe, is premised on the impossibility of the latter (*Coach Carter*), its quarantine as a defensive fantasy without objective value. Race, specifically, is the fulcrum of this distribution, the organizing principle of its economy.[2]

---

[1] See Steve James's 1994 documentary *Hoop Dreams*, which follows the lives of two young black men, William Gates and Arthur Agee, who hope to turn successful high school basketball careers into high-paying professional contracts in the National Basketball Association (Gilbert and Marx 1994). It is also worth adding that the following discussion of the black-white racial dynamics of the two films is complicated, but not contradicted, by the demographic changes that have taken place in both locales over the last generation: Odessa, Texas and Richmond, California today have, according to 2010 census data, a clear Latino majority (51%) and plurality (40%), respectively.

[2] This racial bifurcation may account, in part, for the extended success of the *Friday Night Lights* franchise. Following the various runs of the film adaptation, a television series was developed by writer/director/producer Peter Berg. That series ran for five seasons (2006–2011) and garnered various critical plaudits, including a Peabody Award, a Humanitas Prize, and several Primetime Emmys.

The Artifice of Camaraderie

Within the precincts of this founding racial division, the *moral* victory of the young white Permian Panthers' valiant and narrow defeat at the hands of their black urban counterparts (whose mythic invincibility is dealt a symbolic blow) promises to redeem, though it cannot deliver, the entire community of Odessa, Texas (a potential converted in the actual the following year with the team's state championship win). In contrast, the young black Richmond Oilers' coming of age as college-minded student-athletes in their valiant and narrow defeat at the hands of their mostly white suburban counterparts (whose superiority is reaffirmed even as grudging respect is offered, not incidentally, by their single black "superstar") can be showered with the sentimentality of personal triumph only by reaffirming the dereliction of black life in Richmond, California and passionately heralding the exceptions that prove the rule—"a system," Coach Carter declares, "that's designed for you to fail."

In fact, the question of *exceptionality* is at the heart of these two films. Permian High School is, after all, no stranger to winning. Quite the contrary, the young men we encounter in *Friday Night Lights* inherit the burden, but also, crucially, the *opportunity*, of a notable athletic tradition, carrying the torch that has been passed to them with great expectations—from overbearing parents and anxious alumni concerned with protecting their good name and securing local bragging rights, from former players hoping to extend the twilight of their former glory, from admiring children in search of proper idols, and from adoring female peers soliciting the attention of small-town heroes with constant flattery and sexual favor. Of course, a distinction is drawn at points between the single-minded pursuit of "state"—the undisputed top prize in Texas high school football—and the supposed distractions of scholarly endeavor, but unlike in *Coach Carter* this tension is startlingly muted in the film (Fig. 3.1).

The point is underscored by the anomalous case of Boobie Miles, one of the few black players to pass through the Panther program (aside from Ivory "Preacher Man" Jackson who does anything but preach; he does not speak at all, in fact, until the climatic scenes of the championship game where he takes up the role of *vocal* leader in Boobie's absence) and the clear "heart and soul" of the 1988 squad. The issue of Boobie's academic life is preempted in the opening scenes, in which he flippantly asserts that he gets good grades—"of course"—*because* he is an athlete and not despite the demands of that role. The obvious implication is that his grades or, more pointedly, his *education* is immaterial, it lies beyond the sphere of concern inhabited by the

Fig. 3.1 Coach Gary Gaines (Billy Bob Thornton) gives his team a halftime speech in Peter Berg's *Friday Night Lights* (2004). Image reproduced under terms of fair use

coaching staff, the teaching faculty, and the larger Odessa community. It is unimportant to him as well and even to L.V. Miles (Grover Coulson), the father figure who adopts Boobie as his own son, removing him from the foster care system and arranging his attendance at a high school beyond the bounds of the black ghetto in which he was born and raised as a ward of the state. When a serious knee injury prematurely ends Boobie's high school career and effectively reduces his prospects for college football to ruin, he is left sobbing: "I can't do nothing else but play football."

For Boobie, football is not simply a means to facilitate admission to college or defray its otherwise prohibitive costs; it is also meant to be his subsequent career, his chance to save himself and his family. College, in other words, is supposed to function as the same hollow institutional affiliation as high school, merely a forum for athletic achievement en route to the unimaginable fortunes of the professional sports world. When this Faustian bid fails—as it almost always does—there is no gesture of dissent from any quarter, only a nod of regret: "tough break, kid." In any case, Boobie was to be a sacrifice for the team, for the school, and for the city in this precise sense: as the team transforms the substance of its internal bonds at his direct expense and in his name—all the better now as a non-competitive mascot—departing from the blind drive to win only to return to it more proficiently, his *subtraction* from the journey to maturity seems both permissible and *preferable*.

This preference becomes most evident at the denouement in which Mike Winchell (Lucas Black), Don Billingsley (Garrett Hedlund), and Brian "Chavo" Chavez (Jay Hernandez) reflect fondly on their accomplishments at Permian High and commence the properly nostalgic regard that those who came before them seem to relish and those to come will no doubt establish. This scene is only readable beyond the terms of pathos because the end of this chapter for the youthful trio is indemnified by the soft landings featured in the final still-frame sequence that announces their relatively bright futures. Each of their college experiences and subsequent professional achievements over the last decade are offered as palliative to the bittersweet runner-up finish. Awkwardly, Boobie is mentioned as well, off-screen, but it can only be stated about him that he does, in fact, still live somewhere and has somehow managed to father twin children in the meantime. He is held up, implicitly, as living proof that without your education you don't have *anything*. Yet, for all of the trials and tribulations faced by his white (or whitened) teammates, for all of the real material limitations of life in rural West Texas, they still manage, despite the odds, to come away with *something*.[3]

The artifice of camaraderie between the white and black players—not only the moments of locker room banter between Boobie and the three musketeers, but also the unique interracial friendship between Don Billingsley and Ivory Christian (Lee Jackson)—is suggested by the parallel montage of party scenes early in the film: whites party whites while blacks party with blacks. But it is only *confirmed* during the penultimate confrontation between the coaches of the Permian Panthers and the representatives of Dallas-Carter, the undefeated high school program against which Odessa must do battle in its quest for perfection. In negotiating the site of the

---

[3] This depressing point was underscored dramatically by the release of the 25th anniversary edition of Bissinger's *Friday Night Lights* in 2015. The three musketeers returned on this occasion to the Permian Panthers football field to reflect on their lives at middle age. While their stories are humble and there are pangs of nostalgia in their reflections upon high school greatness, it is suggested that they have each done well enough for themselves in the interim. Mike Winchell attended a local college and holds a stable career in the oil industry. He's a bachelor living in a small town outside Dallas near his extended family. Brian Chavez graduated from Harvard and took a law degree from Texas Tech. After practicing criminal law for years back in Odessa, he branched out into various small businesses and he now lives with his fiancé not far from his childhood home. Jerrod McDougal owns an excavation and construction company outside San Antonio. He's had his share of personal losses, including his younger brother to a car accident, and he lives alone after an engagement to be married fell through, but he's managed to keep his life together despite the tribulations. Boobie Miles, by contrast, is doing a ten-year prison term in the Mark Stiles Unit near Beaumont, following a parole violation. His legal troubles have been relatively minor but consistent enough to disrupt most of his adult life. He worked a series of menial jobs, struggled financially, and eventually lost custody of his children to his former girlfriend some years ago. He's become morbidly obese and battles a range of mental health issues (Bissinger 2015).

championship game, the possibility of the Carter team coming to Permian is ruled out reflexively and vociferously by the opposing coaches. The rationale is clear: Carter's team, we are reminded, is drawn from an "all-black" community and it is unsubtly understood that such constituency is anathema to the social environs of Odessa (although it is suggested, insidiously, that the problem is generated by the black side of the equation, its irrational dislike of the good people of Permian, and not the historically-grounded segregationist ethos of the white community).

On this score, Boobie finds an interesting counterpart in *Coach Carter*'s Ty Crane (Sidney Faison), the standout black *recruit* on an otherwise white basketball team in an otherwise white, private college preparatory school, St. Francis. In fact, Coach Carter's son, Damien (Robert Ri'chard), is initially enrolled at St. Francis, and would have played a similar role as Crane, though his attendance there would appear to be more organic, Damien having grown up with the tenuous material comforts and cultural capital of the black *petit bourgeois*. The function of Crane is, then, to both dissimulate the issue of persistent structures of segregation *and* lend an aura of street credibility to the elite private school rightly coded as white and affluent. But it is his *physical* talents—and his bodily stature—that connote the formidableness of the program more so than the cumulative economic, political, and social power its students, staff, and faculty mobilize. What this means is that, when the Richmond Oilers find themselves in the midst of a Cinderella season, the final frontier, as in *Friday Night Lights*, is figured as the body of an imposing young urban black male.

The problem here is that the Oilers themselves occupy the same symbolic position as Crane, one which is identical to that of Dallas-Carter in the narrative economy of *Friday Night Lights*—the mythical big black enemy—and they cannot recover or obtain the homegrown spiritual substance that Odessa claims for itself against the slick menace of black urban dwellers whose raw strength and bad attitudes betray the *illegitimacy* of their dominance in the athletic contest and, by extension, in the broader world. The bad black athletes may win the game, but they are a disgrace to the sport and, moreover, they fail to attain—and are likely even unaware—of the higher rewards it offers the true believer. Similarly, they may achieve proximity to political, economic, and social power but they will only ever gain access as interlopers. This is to say that the Richmond Oilers cannot *duplicate* the accomplishments of the Permian Panthers—beyond any record of wins and losses—and Coach Carter cannot assume the role of Coach Gaines. This is not simply because the tutelage of the former fails utterly to yield the results delivered by the latter (if graduation rates and college attendance at Permian are below average, they are absolutely abysmal at Richmond—quite literally, a 1 on an Academic Performance Index of 1 to 10), but also because the stakes and the significance of athletic and academic performance at these respective schools are marked by a *qualitative* difference. The stark divergence—young white men from Odessa go off to college or they stay in Odessa and work while young black men from Richmond go off to college or they go to prison or die young—indicates the enduring critical difference that race makes for such social determinations and conditions the functions of schooling for each. More importantly though, even if some unthinkable equity were achievable (in the public educational system, in the criminal justice system, in the whole array of social services and economic opportunities, etc.), the moral value that accrues to the *efforts* of the Permian Panthers does not translate to the players depicted in *Coach Carter*.

Political Moralism

"They're good kids": an opinion consistently offered about both sets of youth, white and black. But whereas it signals the ultimate *consistency* between the Panthers and the community of Odessa, in the case of the Oilers the statement is meant to *differentiate* the team—a dirty dozen— from the rest of their forsaken classmates and desolate neighbors. For black players, the very *possibility* for moral rectitude (which is a sham in any case, beholden as it is to the morality of a slave society) must be proven against an historically-structured suspicion; for white players, it is simply retrieved— regardless of their poor decisions, mistakes, failures, insecurities—which is to say that it is taken for granted, always already present, inherent even when nowhere apparent, permanently available for rehabilitation.

There is reason to believe that Coach Carter not only understands this bifurcation, but actually embraces it as well. It presents itself in the film as a forced choice, no doubt, but it is still one that could have been refused, that has been refused elsewhere, and is, in fact, refused to this day by others inside and outside the diegetic universe. Or perhaps it is better to say that if the choice itself cannot be refused, it can at least be rephrased. Instead, Carter insists on the transparency and the inevitability of the choice and indeed the film figures most prominently as a story about *choice*—a choice, as noted, between prison and college; a choice mediated by the universal challenge of discipline, the decisive quality instilled or cultivated by the paternal mentor. (One cannot help but hear a kinder, gentler iteration of Alonzo Harris's iron-fisted ultimatum in *Training Day*: "You wanna go home or

Fig. 3.2 Coach Ken Carter (Samuel L. Jackson) disciplines his players during a practice session in Thomas Carter's *Coach Carter* (2005). Image reproduced under terms of fair use

go to jail?") The disciplinary project is pursued, symptomatically, through the conservative transposition of Martin Luther King, Jr.'s moral example detached entirely from the tradition of civil disobedience and radical political struggle that lends the example its moral weight in the first place. A portrait photograph of King's deeply contemplative profile hangs prominently above Coach Carter's desk and the familiar image of the civil rights movement's central icon is framed in more than one shot parallel to Coach Carter's visage (Fig. 3.2).

The visual proposition of Carter's inhabitation of an explicitly political legacy is buttressed by a second dissimulation of black radicalism, one prompted deliberately by Carter's repeated question to Timo Cruz (Rick Gonzalez), his most wayward player: "What is your greatest fear?" The question is an open invitation to recite what was thought at the time to be the most memorable lines from the most memorable public address of the most memorable black political leader beyond US borders, namely Nelson Mandela's 1994 Presidential Inaugural Address following the first "non-racial" elections in the history of the Republic of South Africa:

> **TIMO**: Our deepest fear is not that we are inadequate. Our deepest fear is that we are powerful beyond measure. It is our light, not our darkness, that

3 Fantasy and Desire: On *Friday Night Lights* and *Coach Carter*   75

most frightens us. [...] Your playing small doesn't serve the world. There's nothing enlightened about shrinking so that other people won't feel insecure around you. We are all meant to shine, as children do. [...] It's not just in some of us; it's in everyone. And as we let our own light shine, we unconsciously give other people permission to do the same. As we are liberated from our own fear, our presence automatically liberates others.

It might seem presumptuous for a high school basketball coach, a small business-owner moonlighting in an essentially volunteer capacity, to make recourse to such grand oratory amid the banalities of halftime pep talks and everyday lectures about hustle and focus. And it might seem gratuitous that MTV films, not known for the intellectual depth or political engagement of its productions, would seize on such incongruous gestures in what is otherwise a formulaic feel-good picture about an underdog that carries the day. As it turns out, Mandela, the Nobel Laureate and former political prisoner, never uttered the words in any public speech, and the inspirational passage was actually drawn from Marianne Williamson's 1992 *A Return to Love*. Internet-fueled urban legend was apparently to blame for the gross misattribution, a point that has since been clarified by the African National Congress, the Nelson Mandela Foundation, and Williamson herself (McNeff 2012).[4] Williamson has been described, rightly or wrongly, as a New Age guru, but her grounding in Helen Schucman's 1976 *A Course in Miracles* clearly sets her writing firmly within the self-help genre. And Christian spiritual self-help in particular, as the excised lines from the extended quotation read: "We ask ourselves, 'Who am I to be brilliant, gorgeous, talented, and fabulous?' Actually, who are you not to be? You are a child of God... We were born to manifest the glory of God that is within us." This is no liberation theology; this is the cause of an inner spiritual transformation unrelated to any progressive social change. Charitable work and civic engagement are acceptable in this framework, of course, but extra-parliamentary motion and community-based movement-building remain

---

[4]McNeff is the co-founder and president since 1978 of the Miracle Distribution Center, an educational nonprofit organization dedicated to promoting the study and dissemination of *A Course in Miracles*. In an earlier version of this chapter, I also unwittingly reproduced the urban legend that linked Williamson's passage to Mandela's inauguration, so I am happy to correct that mistake here.

beyond the pale.⁵ The crucial passage is, then, perhaps fitting after all. *Coach Carter* is, in this way, hardly more than an unimaginative remake of David Anspaugh's *Hoosiers* (1986), walking the tightrope between homage and plagiarism, not only in its comforting story but also in its plot, its *mise-en-scène*, and its direction as well.

Yet where *Hoosiers* successfully constructs an aesthetic of *renaissance* in the conservative bastions of rural Middle America and the ruthlessly conformist "back to basics" vision of Coach Norman Dale (Gene Hackman) can be celebrated by the community of Hickory, Indiana; Coach Carter can function only as a political *disservice* to the black urban community to which he returns (as a perversion of the fabled prodigal son) and in which he intervenes (as the representative of higher education and private-sector business interests). His neoliberal entrepreneurialism—which brings market philosophy to bear on all aspects of living—is a blatant *betrayal* of the progressive platforms, radical spirit, and living legacies of the civil rights and anti-apartheid movements that resentfully frame the moral force of his onscreen presence and whose animating demands—"freedom, justice, and equality"—continue to circulate confusedly in the common sense of those unprincipled black folks he must assiduously reprimand. Much like Coach Dale in *Hoosiers* and Coach Gaines in *Friday Night Lights*, to return to our present comparison, Coach Carter embeds a conservative ideology of individual achievement as the pathway to the players' rescue within his larger promotion of team spirit. Achievement becomes available to any and all that demonstrate the requisite traits: work ethic, respect for authority, obedience, lawful behavior, and self-discipline. Discipline, as we have seen, is the key issue and its constant repetition across all of the films mentioned thus far is telling. The boys must be brought under control wherever we find them, but it is only in the case of *Coach Carter* that the force of law—the police, the prison—is a real and present danger, immediate and omnipresent.

In each instance, the coach must reproduce writ small the social contract between himself and his players; an agreement must be forged upfront and in advance. The boys must submit *wholly* to the terms he establishes, without negotiation. But again, the situation mutates in Richmond. The minia-

---

⁵Williamson, a noted Los Angeles philanthropist, is also founder of Project Angel Food, a meals-on-wheels program for people living with life-threatening illnesses, and The Peace Alliance, a national policy initiative promoting non-violent conflict resolution. Her work has been celebrated by the likes of Oprah Winfrey, Charlie Rose, and Bill Maher, and she was recognized by *Newsweek* magazine as one of the fifty most influential Baby Boomers. She has sold over three million copies of her various books to date (Aron 2014). For a critical discussion of Schucman's *magnum opus* in the broad context of Western esotericism, see Hanegraaff (1996).

ture contract must be *written*, literalized not spoken ("parole," we'll recall, signifies the bond of one's *word*), and in this case supersedes the public authority in its minimal requirements—as adjudicated at the level of local governance, however ineffectual—and tightens the reigns of control, now with a self-arrogated authority, an authority grounded in the rights of an un-failed patriarch: formally educated, professionally employed, financially solvent, properly conjugal, dutifully paternal, morally grounded, exceedingly athletic, demonstrably streetwise, physically and mentally tough. It is the latter few qualities, and toughness in particular, that found the reformatory mission. In the identical scenes of first encounter—the coach meets the ragtag group of players—Coach Dale simply eliminates the mouthiest from the team roster, but Coach Carter must physically accost Timo Cruz, slamming him up against the wall like an arresting officer, truly *throwing him out*, before doing the same. Not so much the power of *formal* exclusion is exercised (attached to his legal position) as the power of *physical* confrontation (attached to his brute force). This racially coded and specifically working-class masculinity signifies here as "the best of both worlds"—*proletarian* and *bourgeois*—and points toward that which makes Carter the proper object of respect for the young black males he must train. Retaining all of the manly attributes of streetwise youth and combining it, or, better, *parlaying* it as voucher to college and viable business ventures, Carter avoids the twin pitfalls of a quintessentially black unmanliness—the effete *bourgeois* bureaucrat, the province of the "new black middle class," and the futureless *lumpen* thug, the plight of the black "underclass." Both are failing the community, as it were, the one by disseminating disastrously low expectations to black students and the other by distracting these same students with the lure of quick money and endangering them with illicit, often deadly forms of labor.

Despite clear evidence that the troubles Carter finds at Richmond High are institutional and ordered unambiguously by broader political, economic, and social contexts, questions of systemic change encouraged by collective political struggle—the *sine qua non* of his inspirational figures, King and Mandela—are mercilessly crowded out. The situation as such is reified and militancy (which operates diffusely in the "wildness" of his players before being discharged in a patronizing joke against his sister, Linda, who is "radical" and sports "a big Afro") is countered with sober resignation. Carter declares, in response to the likelihood that his players will be imprisoned rather than graduate high school and attend college: "those are the numbers; those are some statistics for your ass." On this point, the rhetoric of black "community" thrown about in the film effaces the history and politics of the black "ghetto" and the advent of mass imprisonment over the last generation or two, an effacement marked by the revealing slippage between the narrative of continuity (Carter says that his players face "the same story" in the late 1990s as he and his cohort faced in the early 1970s) and the narrative of discontinuity (Carter says also that "things are different now" by which he means *worse*) that guides his approach. However, the conclusion, he insists, is not to think critically about how or why things have gotten to this point, much less to act in concert to contest the present state of affairs, but simply to avoid being one of the statistics, that is, to be one of the exceptions.

Father Knows… Nothing

In this dim light, Coach Carter's is a success story, if by that we mean one featuring negligible impact for short-term labor: the depressed Academic Performance Index (API) at Richmond High is undisturbed, as are the dismal rates of graduation and college attendance; the majority even of his own players during the distinguished season were unable to make good on his advice (two college graduates emerged from a team of fifteen, or a rate of 13 percent) and the basketball program remains a shambles to date.[6] (This record might be contrasted with the rise of Carter's own career as a motivational speaker and multifaceted media personality, including his being the subject of a commercially successful mainstream film.)[7] In sum, the players, the school, and the city are left only with "that ever-elusive inner victory." If this seems an unfair evaluation—what, after all, could one person do in so dire a context?—we can only reply that what is put forward as a heartwarming tale of accomplishment is, in fact, a pernicious defense of depoliticization in a moment of neoconservative ascendance (Fig. 3.3).

---

[6]Richmond High School has continued to struggle academically by every standard measure since Coach Carter's departure in 2002. The only major change has been to the demographics of the student body. Whereas the school served, through the 1990s, predominantly black students in the vicinity, it is now over 80% Latino and black students represent less than 10% as of this writing. This shift is part of a much larger trend, especially in California, of displacement and depopulation in historically black neighborhoods, a complex process of gentrification in which low-income Latinos and Asians often pave the way for the arrival of more affluent middle and upper class white residents to return to previously avoided black ghettos (Hwang 2016). This gentrification is strongly correlated with a re-segregation of public schools nationally (Brown 2016).

[7]Carter has, since his tenure at Richmond High School, served as the coach of the Los Angeles Rumble, one of six teams in the international SlamBall League. SlamBall is a form of novelty basketball played on trampolines while wearing protective gear. Slam Dunks are the eponymous means of scoring.

Fig. 3.3 Coach Carter explains the need for his players to prioritize academics over athletics. Image reproduced under terms of fair use

It is the particularly destructive form of depoliticization that invests the recovery of black urban communities in the resuscitation of its fathers in the most conventional sense, which is to say as patriarchs. And, in fact, the only way that a black patriarchy could be established would be in and as the form of depoliticization. Through Coach Carter's eyes we see that the old ways are not working (i.e., the ineptitude of the elder Coach White, played by Mel Winkler); that the women cannot handle the task at hand (i.e., the lassitude of Principal Garrison, played by Denise Dowse); that the male educators are too bookish and overly concerned with their jurisdiction to get the job done (i.e., the wheedling teacher, played by Marcus Woodswelch); and that the strict, young, energetic patriarch must return to assume the mantle, to serve not only as father figure, but as father *surrogate* for a representative sample of a whole generation of fatherless sons.

This is no metaphor, as it is in *Friday Night Lights* where Coach Gaines is simply fatherly toward his players. There are, in fact, no fathers in *Coach Carter*—the only direct mention of a player's father finds him already in prison. There are only mothers and maternal figures and they either provide *support* (actively or passively, vocally or silently, as cheerleaders, wives, girlfriends or muses) or they present *obstacles* (irrational attachments to teenage parenthood, sorry excuses for poor administrative leadership, injurious derangements of priorities, or the distractions of sex and drugs). The boys, it seems, have not been spared the interference of women, have not yet been allowed to forge the relationships *among themselves* that would give them a chance in the world. This is why the consummation of the coaching mission is captured so poignantly in the clichéd image of the pregame team entrance: a small group consisting exclusively of uniformed men, organized around a common goal, passionately attached to both the corporate objective *and* to one another within the corporate form, a band of brothers, inspired by the motto: "all for one and one for all." Most importantly, the fates of women and girls in both films are settled in advance: the *question* of their transcendence, literal or figurative, of debilitating local conditions is strictly precluded. However, it is not simply unfortunate that these entirely incommensurable appeals—on the one hand, to the revival of pastoral virtue, coded racially white, against the predations of modern urban life, coded racially black, and, on the other, to the ameliorative effects of redoubled educational efforts, coded racially black, against the predations of gross and concentrated material inequality, coded, again, racially *black*—take the form of such politically regressive characterizations of women and men, and, along the way, analogize the sports arena to the battlefield, the team to the fraternal military unit. The sporting enterprise, not unlike professional policing, is a paramilitary undertaking.

Rather, we encounter here most acutely the dramatic limitations of *any* recuperation of patriarchal deliverance for "black strivings in a twilight civilization" (Gates and West 1996) and not only owing to serious problems *inherent* to commandeering the bravado of street culture for upward mobility *qua* athletic accomplishment, academic excellence, and professional success. Something similar can be said, ultimately, for the material fortunes of the white rural working class as well; however, the symbolic order of white supremacy, its libidinal economy, makes possible an effective imaginative capture yielding significant dividends for whites, even those of humble means, while the economies—symbolic and material—of antiblackness preclude the alliances necessary for such a project to become anything more than a reactionary dream quarantined in and as internecine warfare, on scales large and small, in spaces public and private. The anachronistic strongman—whose mettle is tested repeatedly, often by misguided and unreasonably demanding women or by desperate, emasculated men—betrays the rightward lean of the *entire* ensemble of questions pursued by this cinema of sport, the whole range of its machinations. This is why we are well served to think of the cinema of sport as a cinema of policing in the broader sense.

We have long struggled with the mythology, noted above, that the salvation of black communities lies with black men's arrival within, rather than their struggle against or departure from, dominant formations of gender and sexuality and their concomitant ascension to, rather than their struggle against, the middle and upper classes. *Coach Carter* participates in this cinematic "politics of respectability" with a vengeance (White 2001). Not only for the ways it systematically writes off the mass of black youth as the statistical casualties of urban life, or even its unconcealed recasting of progressive political movements as personal aggrandizement. Not only for its single-minded meditation on the welfare of men and boys, its clear relegation of female gender to the margins of narrative movement, sequestered to spectacle and sideshow, the non-viable options of support or obstruction for male fortunes. But also, a point that might be made more often, because it sells a lie even, perhaps especially, to those young black men whose identification it solicits in such evident bad faith. For the uniformed black male—here in the sports arena, other times among the troops or behind the "thin blue line"—the game is rigged against him (Wilderson 2010) (Fig. 3.4).

This last point is made plainly in the closing scenes of the film, following the buzzer-beater defeat of the Richmond Oilers by their well-heeled cross-town rivals. Coach Carter offers what is meant to be a capstone speech, but that comes across as a warmed-over collection of platitudes: "I came here to coach basketball players and you became students. I came here to work with boys and you became men." Interesting, at one level, that manhood is here aligned with academic engagement—interesting, that is, because the men in question are black—but it should not escape attention that the sort of schoolwork promoted by Carter is instrumental, almost perfunctory. Neither critical intellectual activity, nor even the mind-numbing "basic skills training" celebrated by earlier "blackboard jungle" films like John Avildsen's *Lean On Me* (1989) or John Smith's *Dangerous Minds* (1995), but rather the minimal grade point average and test scores necessary to gain college entrance and, hopefully, win athletic scholarship funding. In short, the young men of Richmond High—halfway across the country, a decade later—are pushed to pursue the pipe dream of Boobie Miles, the dream, perhaps, of their sports nemesis, Ty Crane, as well. What is being asked of them, in other words, is that they put forth extraordinary efforts to accomplish what are considered from the dominant vantage to be below-average results and, most importantly, to take pride in so doing, to believe themselves role models, paragons of self-determination, beacons of hope for the entire community, a hope that the community can rid itself of its despair

Fig. 3.4 The Richmond Oilers walk out of the locker room together to face their cross-town rivals. Image reproduced under terms of fair use

and control its pathological manifestations in the meanwhile.[8] They offer proof positive that no *systemic* change, no *fundamental* social transformation is necessary, that the American Dream is alive and well in the places least likely to nourish it.

The Big and the Small

No such fallacy is propagated among the white players of rural Texas in *Friday Night Lights* or among their predecessors from rural Indiana in *Hoosiers*. Surely, high school sports stars are shown to be inspirations to young children and sources of vicarious triumph for local residents as well.[9] But they are not saddled with the additional symbolic freight of substantiating the viability of the communities from which they hail; they are not held up as the terri-

---

[8]Gordon (1997) speaks volumes about this perverse imperative. The black in the antiblack world, he maintains, is required to commit extraordinary efforts to the achievement of ordinary existence, while the latter is perpetually harassed, if not altogether foreclosed.

[9]Here the stars are all men, but there will be increasing numbers of Hollywood women's sports films like Karyn Kusama's *Girl Fight* (2000), John Stockwell's *Blue Crush* (2002), Clint Eastwood's *Million Dollar Baby* (2004), and Drew Barrymore's *Whip It* (2009); women's police films like Joel Coen's *Fargo*

tory upon which the *intrinsic* value of such communities is arbitrated, as is the case in *Coach Carter*. Quite the contrary, the threat to human viability in these instances is located *externally*, as an impingement or encroachment. The operative question is thus: Can the community muster the collective resolve to hold the line or turn the tide? This, then, is the crux: the overriding forces, however complexly their evocation, are marked most crudely and most prominently by the signs of racial blackness.

In *Hoosiers*, the "big city" is not only the mailing address of the favored team in the state championship basketball tournament, but also the center of the state's governance and its most vital economic activity. It is the place where the perpetual doldrums of rural life are diluted in the urban solution of historical change (what the students in the film innocently discuss as "modernization"), where learning moves beyond the vocational toward broader horizons, the hub of possibility in the postwar dawn of the American Century. It is the place where the strictures of parochialism are thrown off, but also where the endearing values of increasingly isolated small-town life (paradoxically: familiarity and privacy, austerity and security, insularity and wholesomeness, frustration and fulfillment) are corrupted. However, we never see the figures of "big government" and "big business," the movers and shakers of modern industrial society, the ruling class of the state of Indiana or even the decadent middle class of the city of Indianapolis, to say nothing of national or international developments of the time. Rather, what we see, in the film's climatic sequence, is an awesomely capacious sports arena (the 15,000-seat Hinkle Fieldhouse at Butler University) peopled by a black coaching staff, black cheerleaders, black fans, and a team of black players, most especially their indomitable standout guard: the first and last appearance of black characters in the film and all without speaking parts.

This formula is repeated with little modification in *Friday Night Lights*. Though there are numerous references to economic decline in Odessa, accompanied by the recurrent image-motif of unattended oil pumps, we never encounter onscreen the politicos of Austin or the corporate elite of Dallas. There is, moreover, no discussion of the means by which economic restructuring, or even political disempowerment, has unfolded throughout the state, or beyond. What we do see, at the emotional crescendo of the

---

(1996), Donald Petrie's *Miss Congeniality* (2000), Ridley Scott's *Hannibal* (2001), Gregory Hoblit's *Untraceable* (2008), and Paul Feig's *The Heat* (2013); and women's military films like Edward Zwick's *Courage Under Fire* (1996), Ridley Scott's *GI Jane* (1997), Rob Cohen's *Stealth* (2005), and Kathryn Bigelow's *Zero Dark Thirty* (2012); none of which will necessarily challenge generic conventions or offer visions of women or womanhood beyond that of, say, the Feminist Majority or the Democratic Party.

Fig. 3.5 The Permian Panthers line up against Dallas-Carter in the championship game. Image reproduced under terms of fair use

film's narrative development, is an overwhelmingly capacious sports arena (the 60,000-seat Houston Astrodome—just before it served as a notorious makeshift shelter for the displaced victims of Hurricane Katrina in 2005), peopled by a black coaching staff, black cheerleaders, black fans, and a team of undifferentiated black players; a team whose most notable quality is their size: "they're big" is repeated nearly a dozen times throughout the film before and during the championship contest, as is its correlate, "we're small." In fact, this *physical* disparity is the frame of the film's famous story, its source of dramatic tension, and size matters here on any number of levels. The black players from Dallas-Carter are other things as well: inhumanly fast, characteristically rude, prone to cheap shots and, unsurprisingly given the earlier portrayal of their head coach, "racist" as well. The sole indication of racist slur and one of the few pointed comments regarding racial difference in the entire script—for a film, recall, based in a predominantly-white community in West Texas in the late 1980s—is issued by a black player against one of the few non-white Permian Panthers: Chavez is taunted, mildly, as "Mexican" (Fig. 3.5).[10]

---

[10] There is an important elision here, as well, about Anglo-Latino conflict in and beyond Texas, one that not only obscures dimensions of the history of white supremacy and US imperialism, but also solicits—not least in the bond of the three musketeers—a racialized solidarity, against blacks, between white Anglos and their non-black Latino counterparts (Yancey 2003; Foley 2010).

Conclusion

White players defeat their black opponents in these two films, regardless of whether they win the contest. The moral victory is the coveted prize[11]—not, to repeat, because blacks could or should claim as much in relation to whites (a moral victory over what? There is, after all, no trace of white racism!), but because the white community as such is in desperate need of this test of character; a call to arms perhaps, a revival at the very least. The new black menace that everywhere personifies the troubles of contemporary white rural and suburban life in this post-civil rights image archive enjoys a public reputation as *insuperable*. We encounter, on this score, white communities in a weakened state, demoralized, stagnant, wrestling with doubt, seeking again—and finding—the will to believe. The marriage of this unhappy white rural community and the wandering, crestfallen white man, back from the urban wilds, that will lead it to greatness marks the reunion or, better, regrouping of an erstwhile imagined community now scattered and fragmented (Lipsitz 1998).

It is appropriate, then, that so quintessential a story from the Reagan–Bush era would return with success in the cultural milieu of Bush II, a pat adjunct to the resurrection of so many personnel from the former administration in the apparatus of the latter, a resurgence of its gloves-off schema to reorganize the globe, and its flirtation with the mobilizing thematic of race war (we see, in hindsight, that Clinton's neoliberalism truly authorized the panoply of racist code words in official political nomenclature and rendered them illegible as such) (Chomsky 2003; Mahajan 2003). Indeed, if we are to entertain or be entertained by the force of *Friday Night Lights* and consider *Coach Carter* to be its "other side of the tracks" equivalent as the critical establishment has done, it would appear that the struggle against this dark and dangerous figure of black masculinity is something that whites and blacks have in common.

---

[11]The moral victory, the reconsolidation of *character* becomes the primary focus, whereas the winning determined by the scoreboard operates as a byproduct of the more important development of *self*. The loss of the championship in *Friday Night Lights* is important, however, insofar as the moral victory is underscored by the loss of the brass ring. The fact that the featured team in *Hoosiers* actually wins might be taken as a sign of the times, both the Pax Americana of the 1950s (in which it is set) and the conservative restoration of the 1980s (in which it was released). The Permian Panther's loss seems more resonant with the contemporary period, well after the end of the short American Century, the era of diminished returns, the beleaguered post-9/11 USA, a nation that can suffer a traumatic loss and keep moving. We should note that, *Friday Night Lights* forecasts the win *next* season, the gathering storm on the horizon of the New American Century. *Coach Carter*, on the other hand, holds out no such promise.

This is why *Coach Carter* is by far the more disturbing film. In the history of Hollywood productions, it is at least anticipated—though no less injurious—that populist films about the redemption of the white American heartland deploy images of threatening blacks (Bernardi 2001; Vera & Gordon 2003). Yet, increasingly, we see that equally successful, nominally *black* films—written and directed by blacks, featuring mostly black casts, and/or aimed at a black or "blackened" youth audience—envision the revitalization of a putative black community through the same gambit: there is a hulking black male adversary in the distance and conflict is in the offing. The pain of this alienating identification—which black audiences today may enjoy widely nonetheless—is only compounded by the collapse of the critical boundary: the outside falls back inside; the trouble out there becomes suffocating and close; it is, in fact, internal and, moreover, *intimate*, inescapable and, ultimately, irrefutable. It is unopposable. That black specter is me. I am that thing.

References

Aron, Hillel. 2014. Marianne Williamson Aims to Defeat Henry Waxman and Save Washington's Soul. *LA Weekly*, January 16. Accessed May 28, 2017. http://www.laweekly.com/news/marianne-williamson-aims-to-defeat-henry-waxman-and-save-washingtons-soul-4316162.

Baker, Aaron. 2003. *Contesting Identities: Sports in American Film*. Chicago: University of Illinois Press.

Bernardi, Daniel (ed.). 2001. *Classic Hollywood, Classic Whiteness*. Minneapolis: University of Minnesota Press.

Bissinger, H.G. 2015. Stars of Friday Night Lights Reunite to Relive Their Story 25 Years Later. *Sports Illustrated*, August 3. Accessed May 28, 2017. https://www.si.com/high-school/2015/07/29/friday-night-lights-25th-anniversary-hg-bissinger-book-excerpt.

Brown, Emma. 2016. On the Anniversary of *Brown* v. *Board*, New Evidence that U.S. Schools are Resegregating. *Washington Post*, May 17. Accessed May 28, 2017. https://www.washingtonpost.com/news/education/wp/2016/05/17/on-the-anniversary-of-brown-v-board-new-evidence-that-u-s-schools-are-resegregating/?utm_term=.4b7865c3826d.

Chomsky, Noam. 2003. *Hegemony or Survival: America's Quest for Global Dominance*. New York: Metropolitan Books.

Foley, Neil. 2010. *Quest for Equality: The Failed Promise of Black-Brown Solidarity*. Cambridge, MA: Harvard University Press.

Gale, David. 2005. *Coach Carter*. DVD. Directed by Thomas Carter. Los Angeles: Paramount/MTV Films.

Gates, Henry Louis, Jr., and Cornel West. 1996. *The Future of the Race*. New York: Vintage.
Gilbert, Peter., and Frederick Marx. 1994. *Hoop Dreams*. DVD. Directed by Steve James.
Gordon, Lewis. 1997. *Her Majesty's Other Children: Sketches of Racism from a Neocolonial Age*. New York: Rowman and Littlefield.
Grazer, Brian. 2004. *Friday Night Lights*. DVD. Directed by Peter Berg. Universal City, CA: Universal Pictures.
Hanegraaff, Wouter. 1996. *New Age Religion and Western Culture: Esotericism in the Mirror of Secular Thought*. New York: Brill.
Hwang, Jackelyn. 2016. Pioneers of Gentrification: Transformation in Global Neighborhoods in Urban America in the Late Twentieth Century. *Demography* 53: 189–213.
Lipsitz, George. 1998. *Possessive Investment in Whiteness: How White People Profit from Identity Politics*. Philadelphia: Temple University Press.
Mahajan, Rahul. 2003. *Full Spectrum Dominance: US Power in Iraq and Beyond*. New York: Seven Stories Press.
McNeff, Beverly Hutchinson. 2012. *A Return to Love* in the Movies. *The Holy Encounter*, September/October.
Vera, Hernán., and Andrew Gordon. 2003. *Screen Saviors: Hollywood Fictions of Whiteness*. New York: Rowman and Littlefield.
White, E. Frances. 2001. *Dark Continent of Our Bodies: Black Feminism and the Politics of Respectability*. Philadelphia: Temple University Press.
Wilderson, Frank B., III. 2010. *Red, White, and Black: Cinema and the Structure of US Antagonisms*. Durham, NC: Duke University Press.
Yancey, George. 2003. *Who Is White? Latinos, Asians, and the New Black/Nonblack Divide*. Boulder, CO: Lynne Rienner.

4

Origins and Beginnings: On *The Blind Side*

Introduction

It will come as little surprise for most readers to learn that professional football is the most popular sport in the United States, and has been for at least the last thirty years. It is also by far the most lucrative. The dimensions of football's economic and cultural dominance, its centrality to public understandings of American society within and well beyond its fan base, is hard to overstate and easy to underestimate. More than a third (35%) of professional sports fans rank the National Football League as their favorite, over twice the percentage (14%) of the second-place vote, Major League Baseball, the country's erstwhile "national pass time." College football garners another 11% of the vote at present, putting nearly half of the self-identified viewing audience in the gridiron camp. Auto racing, hockey, college, and professional basketball each only score in the single digits. Live attendance numbers verify the trend. According to ESPN, the average attendance at NFL games (approximately 70,000) more than doubles that of the MLB (approximately 31,000) and almost quadruples the NBA (approximately 18,000) (Rovell 2014).

The numbers are even more skewed when approached as a matter of television market share, which is, after all, how the vast majority consume sports programming today. The fit between the contest and its principal medium of dissemination has been more than fortuitous. Dave Zirin (2008): "Pro football, a fringe sport for decades [before its ascent in the 1950s], was tailor-made for television like nothing else on the landscape" (127). Since 2010, Soven Bery (2013) reports, "NFL games have accounted for an amazing 55 percent of all TV shows averaging 20 million viewers, 70 percent of all TV shows averaging 30 million viewers and 92 percent of all TV shows averaging 40 million viewers." The Super Bowl is now the most-watched television event of the year and to date accounts for the twenty-two most-watched events in television history, dwarfing the numbers of the season finales of the most popular series.[1]

Football, then, is the quintessential sport of the postwar USA, highly adapted to and for its rapidly emerging television industry, its expanding consumer culture, its resurgent masculine anxiety, and its affinity with the militarism of the newly codified warfare state (Buttersworth 2017; Sparrow 2011), including varied attempts to displace racial antagonism through partial and hierarchical integration. The professionalization of football—with its lines of scrimmage, its bombs and blitzes, its offensive and defensive strategies, its dynamics of camaraderie and morale, its tests of strength and will—represents more than an apt metaphor of the force projection underwriting the American Century.

It has also become an important material element in the transformation of US capitalism, providing a forum for the increasingly central economic function of the "sales effort" as an instrument for addressing stagnation and stimulating effective demand as monopoly capital has evolved into monopoly-finance capital (Holleman et al. 2009). Bolstering declining rates of profit in this era has required a massive expansion of public and private debt and an elevation of the FIRE (finance, insurance, real estate) sector over manufacturing, since the attendant upward redistribution of income and wealth flattened real wages and decimated vital social services, undercutting the very purchasing power and relative financial stability of the middle and working classes required to absorb the economic surplus generated within production. The subsequent promotion, financing, and exploitation of debt has been at the center of recurrent economic crises since the 1980s—the Great Recession foremost—enlarging by an order of magnitude already ballooning private profits and public costs.

Given that US capitalism is *racial* capitalism,[2] this economic restructuring and its accompanying political culture have interacted powerfully

---

[1] It remains to be seen whether the NFL will incur any significant losses in light of challenges by players and medical researchers over the devastating consequences on players' health outcomes (McDonald 2015).

[2] Robinson writes: "The development, organization, and expansion of capitalist society pursued essentially racial directions, so too did social ideology. As a material force, then, it could be expected that racialism would inevitably permeate the social structures emergent from capitalism. I have used the term 'racial capitalism' to refer to this development and to the subsequent structure as an historical agency" (Robinson 2000, 2). Though they do not share a common theoretical orientation or conceptual

with the "historical trajectory of racial domination in the United States," especially the more recent of those "several 'peculiar institutions' [that] have successively operated to define, confine, and control African-Americans" (Wacquant 2002, 41). Loïc Wacquant's critical schema, drawing from the work of eminent black sociologists St. Clair Drake and Horace Cayton as well as the wave of revisionist historians that came of age during the era of the modern movements for civil rights and Black Power, tracks the permutations of racial domination from slavery, to Jim Crow segregation, to urban ghettoization, to the contemporary regime of mass incarceration. Spanning more than four centuries of Atlantic history (and referring to much longer historical developments), this conceptual outline, while in no ways exhaustive, provides a shorthand for addressing conjunctural concerns within, rather than despite, the longer view.

What Wacquant emphasizes in each historic instance is not only the varied political and economic functions of these institutions, but also the conditions of political and economic crisis that prompted their succession. Between slavery and Jim Crow, the cataclysm of the US Civil War; between Jim Crow and the ghetto, the Great Migration of nearly five million black people from the rural South to the urban North alongside a series of successful challenges to legal segregation; between the ghetto and the prison, the combined impact of mid-century black social movements and a decade of frequent urban uprisings in black ghettos from New York to Los Angeles. In each of the first three cases, the institutional form was no longer suited to its dual political and economic function and the underlying imperatives were carried forward otherwise. But if slavery and Jim Crow are understood—all too readily—as suffering fatal blows under the law, each having been ostensibly criminalized by the relevant legal decisions and legislative reforms, the ghetto and the prison have not so much succeeded one another as combined into an intensified, hybrid dispensation. Wacquant explains:

> As a new century dawns, it is up to the fourth "peculiar institution" born of the adjoining of the hyperghetto with the carceral system to remould the social meaning and significance of "race" in accordance with the dictates of

---

framework, a growing literature regarding the economic history of capitalism attributes a central role and function to racial slavery, throughout the Atlantic world and beyond, with lasting effects to the present and into foreseeable future. See, for example, Baptist (2014), Barrett (2013), Beckert (2014), Johnson (2013), and Schermerhorn (2015). John Carlos Rowe noted in the preface to Barrett's *Racial Blackness*: "Slavery was not an oversight of the Founding Fathers, subsequently corrected in that second revolution, the U.S. Civil War and abolition; *slavery remains an integral part of a capitalist system dependent on racial, sexual, and class hierarchies to maintain its power*" (Barrett 2013, xvii).

the deregulated economy and the post-Keynesian state. Now, the penal apparatus has long served as accessory to ethnoracial domination by helping to stabilize a regime under attack or bridge the hiatus between successive regimes... But the role of the carceral institution today is different in that, for the first time in US history, it has been elevated to the rank of main machine for "race making." Among the manifold effects of the wedding of ghetto and prison into an extended carceral mesh, perhaps the most consequential is the practical revivification and *official solidification of the centuries-old association of blackness within criminality and devious violence*. (Wacquant 2002, 55–56)

The new carceral mesh highlights a certain stalling out of the historical evolution of racial domination in response to novel challenges across the nineteenth and twentieth centuries. Jim Crow casts a net around the recently emancipated, generalizing the badge of slavery throughout the Southern region in the wake of Reconstruction. As black people migrate *en masse* beyond regional boundaries, the formation of the urban ghetto maintains, and in ways deepens, the fundamental relations they sought to escape. The prison then plays the role of fail-safe, as the strict confinement of the ghetto begins to reveal its limitations. Now, the regime of mass imprisonment itself, including especially the predations of antiblack police violence, has begun to suffer a crisis of legitimacy, posing again the question of what new institutional forms might rise to the occasion.

But the fourth peculiar institution also announces a departure from the previous three, "in accordance with the dictates of the deregulated economy and the post-Keynesian state." Whereas "America's first three 'peculiar institutions'… were all instruments for the conjoint *extraction of labor* and *social ostracization* of an outcast group deemed unassimilable" (42), the racial domination of today "does not carry out a positive economic mission of recruitment and disciplining of the workforce: it serves only to warehouse the precarious and deproletarianized fractions of the black working class" (53). Put somewhat differently, that warehousing is the predominant form that social ostracism now takes. Given that the positive economic function of the previous four centuries could fall away without dismantling the equally persistent reproduction of stigma—if anything it has enhanced it—demonstrates that the latter function is in fact most essential to this history; that is to say, the derivation of symbolic value from the condemnation of black social status. If that symbolic value coincides with windfalls of profit or the long-term accumulation of capital, so be it. At any rate, it appears that the dynamics of the capitalist system cannot proceed apace unless its symbolic economy of anti-blackness remains operative within a parameter.

This is no less true for the capitalist enterprise of professional football and its widespread representation in the multimedia culture industry.

John Lee Hancock's *The Blind Side* (2009) grossed over $300 million at the international box office on a modest $30 million budget and it garnered a host of awards, including the Oscar and the Golden Globe, for lead actress Sandra Bullock. In fact, *The Blind Side* became the most successful sports drama in Hollywood history. It follows Michael Oher's improbable rise from the Memphis public housing and foster care systems to his All-American football career at the nearby University of Mississippi to his professional employment for the Baltimore Ravens, with whom he went on to win a Super Bowl Championship. *The Blind Side* is often read as a feel-good story extolling the virtues of athletics-as-uplift, in which the likely fate of a poor black urban youth is redirected by the intervention of a professional white woman and the institutional resources she accesses and affords, including a pathway to organized sports. And yet this work represents something more than an example of the patronage motif analyzed at length in Matthew Hughey's *The White Savior Film* (2014).

Beyond the troubling reiteration of this longstanding narrative pattern, this cinematic production reveals that the NFL—the apotheosis of professional sports—and the "Athletic Industrial Complex" (Smith 2009) that feeds it are essentially understood as aspects of the larger mission of public education in particular and of public services in general, i.e., the welfare state. Put somewhat differently, insofar as black football players—whether high school, college or professional—are assumed to serve at the pleasure of white benefactors—whether taxpayers, educators, coaches, or team owners—we are led to examine the figure of the black male athlete in light of the figure of the black female welfare recipient and the question of reproductive justice raised by her predicament. This perspective not only interrupts the redemptive fantasy of racial capitalism but also productively undermines the quest for hegemonic gender differentiation.

Colorblind Origins

"White people are crazy" is the provocative first line spoken by *The Blind Side*'s lead actor Quinton Aaron. Aaron, who debuted as a tough guy with a soft heart in Michael Gondry's 2008 comedy-drama *Be Kind Rewind*, plays here the part of Michael "Big Mike" Oher, the central concern of this cinematic adaptation of journalist Michael Lewis's biographical account of the accomplished NFL offensive lineman. The film spends the balance of its running time attempting to disabuse the viewing audience of this notion, introduced to us, rather blatantly, in the first scene: not, we shall see, because the film pursues a genuine deconstruction of the idea of race or craziness or race-based craziness, but rather because it labors to disassociate craziness from the production and reproduction of racial whiteness and to reassign it elsewhere. In so doing, we learn that whiteness as such, proper bourgeois whiteness, is racially aware, but not racially obsessed. It is neither blithely nor bitterly colorblind, but rather pretentiously forgiving, as it were, of racial difference. And it defends itself against racialists of all stripes, those who harbor explicit beliefs that race *matters*.

The rub, however, is that the defense against black and white racialism is itself racially bifurcated. White racialism, on this account, is unseemly and bested by the moral persuasion of good words and good deeds; black racialism is life threatening and vanquished only by the state-sanctioned force of arms. This might appear a strange lesson to take away, given that most critics saw in the film a rags-to-riches tale of enlightened Southern hospitality transcending boundaries of race, class, and gender, all while artfully circumnavigating the longstanding taboo surrounding black–white interracial sexuality. Yet insofar as *The Blind Side* treats the game of football, or any other sporting venture, as a microcosm of the post-civil rights United States and declares on that basis, not unlike Will Smith a few years prior regarding his own bootstrap manifesto, that indeed "America works," it must, like the star of Gabriele Muccino's 2006 *The Pursuit of Happyness*, make recourse to a disavowed organized violence, marshaling it and managing it at once. To hear Smith tell it:

> This is the only country on the face of the earth that [the formerly homeless multimillionaire investment broker] Chris Gardner can exist. […] The hope for that doesn't even exist anywhere else on Earth. That you're homeless, you have $21, and without killing anybody, without oil, without an army, [but] strictly based on an idea that you have in your mind… you create a multimillion dollar empire. (Williams 2007)

Of course, that hope can and does exist all too widely across the contemporary world, well beyond the shifting boundaries of the USA, and it is no more reasonable—or ethical—here than it is anywhere else. What interests us, aside from the unremarkable exceptionalism of the comment, is Smith's unprompted evocation of killing, with the backing of formidable economic resources and deployable military force, as a precondition to accumulation as imperial pursuit. Smith, ever the apologist, pretends that Gardner achieved the latter without incrimination by the former.[3] But he does so only by mystifying the institutional arrangements and articulated systems of power that make it possible to generate and maintain classes of the rich and the poor, and therefore to make movement across that division compelling. Why aren't both figures—the homeless, destitute Gardner and the philanthropic, super-rich Gardner—or, rather, both conditions of material extremity, unacceptable? And why doesn't their juxtaposition over the short arc of the biopic inspire imagination of fundamental social change, or even simple downward redistribution, rather than hope for a miraculous individual change of circumstance?

These questions are perhaps even more pertinent to the case at hand, given that Michael Oher's homelessness in *The Blind Side* is explicitly linked to shared conditions of concentrated poverty and residential segregation and, however weakly, to the attendant social and political relations as well. In this sense, *The Blind Side*'s subplot of highly-skilled manual labor handsomely rewarded is the more tangible and proletarian counterpart to the immaterial and bourgeois dream of ascent through the private manipulation of wealth featured in *The Pursuit of Happyness*; a producerist paean in the age of global financialization. Lest we suspect that the interracial cooperation on display in either film offers a palliative to the growing racial wealth gap, we are relieved of that misgiving straight away. From the opening credits of *The Blind Side* onward, Michael's homelessness within the strictures of Memphis's poor and working-class black neighborhoods does not simply contrast with the abundant green spaces and large detached homes of the white middle and upper classes populating its suburbs, but also stands to indict them. The findings of the Kerner Commission's 1968 report—"that white society is deeply implicated in the ghetto"—resonate throughout the film, albeit filtered through the neoconservative retrospective of the 1980s Reagan Revolution. Although the Tuohys, who will become Oher's legal guardians and adoptive family, regard the economic security inherent to their racial and class power as a genuine blessing—"There, but for grace of God, go I"—they at the very least encounter the notion, abstract

---

[3] Not for nothing, Gardner has expressed abiding admiration for the late "King of Oil" Marc Rich, a well-known international white-collar criminal whose dealings helped to finance a range of military conflicts around the world. Rich, while living comfortably in Switzerland to avoid extradition for federal prosecution, was belatedly pardoned by President Bill Clinton after making generous political campaign donations to the Democratic Party (Baghdjian 2013). Gardner named his brokerage firm Gardner Rich & Company in Rich's honor.

Fig. 4.1 Michael Oher (Quinton Aaron) walks through his old Memphis neighborhood in John Lee Hancock's *The Blind Side* (2009). Image reproduced under terms of fair use

and concrete, that something more is at play in the distribution goods and services than divine providence, work ethic, family values, and the free market. Yet, because the encounter is strongly framed by a reduction of the complex theological virtue of charity (*caritas*) to the mere practice of benevolent giving, it occults the true sources of suffering and yields a redoubled commitment to faith-based philanthropic paternalism (Fig. 4.1).

Michael Lewis describes his book on the promotional website as follows: "*The Blind Side*, published in 2006, tells the story of Michael Oher, a poor, illiterate African-American kid living on the streets of Memphis whose life is transformed after he is adopted by white Evangelical Christians." That teaser leaves out even the barest of details about how and why Michael came to live "on the streets" or how and why Leigh Anne and Sean Tuohy came to adopt him in turn. From the back cover of the paperback edition, then, we gather these crucial elements:

> When we first meet Michael Oher he is one of thirteen children by a mother addicted to crack [cocaine]; he does not know his real name, his father, his birthday, or how to read or write. He takes up football, and school, after a rich, white, Evangelical family plucks him from the streets. Then two great forces alter Oher: the family's love and the evolution of professional football

itself into a game in which the quarterback must be protected at any cost. Our protagonist becomes the priceless package of size, speed, and agility necessary to guard the quarterback's greatest vulnerability: his blind side.

With this fuller account, the operative terms of the drama are established. On the one side, the question of family is posed, along with the concomitant matter of heritage; on the other, the question of vocation is posed, along with the related issue of remuneration. But since the structure of kinship and the scene of exchange are precluded by violent state intervention, heritage is disrupted by the jolt of recurrent dispossession, and remuneration is displaced by the prior obligation of reparation—to recover or return what was taken, to restore or renew what was damaged or destroyed.[4] Moreover, Leigh Anne is the true focus of the film, a point underscored by the entirely lopsided casting of Hollywood A-list actress Sandra Bullock in the lead role (and country music icon Tim McGraw as her supportive husband Sean) opposite the novice Aaron. The film is shot almost entirely from Leigh Anne's perspective, including her bookend voice-over narrations, all of which bars Michael from any scenes of sustained reflection, private dialogue, or, with one notable exception, independent action. (The subsequent accolades for Bullock reflect this reading.) And due to this structured attitude, the film and its protagonist are left to create a world out of need, even neediness, in which Michael is understood through an increasing knowledge of origins and those origins are understood as a milieu of general deficit.[5]

---

[4]The themes of dispossession and reparation are, of course, particular to Michael's biography in this case. But they also evoke the entire history of racial slavery that provides the basic conditions and coordinates of Michael's lived experience and of the disavowed inheritance shaping the interracial encounter eventuating in his adoption. On the fundamental assault against the possibility of black family under slavery, and the central role played by the control of black women's sexuality therein, see Sublette and Sublette (2016). On the living legacy of racial slavery in the contemporary operations of child welfare, see Roberts (2009). Sublette and Sublette provide some very germane comments in the coda to their massive study: "we have seen that no matter how bad we thought slavery was, it was even worse. There's no end to it" (668).

[5]To contradict the highly restricted viewpoint of *The Blind Side*, the book and the film, Oher published his own autobiography with former *Sports Illustrated* writer Don Yeager in 2011. *I Beat the Odds* provides much of the crucial missing material about Oher's early life, the years prior to his adoption by the Tuohys. In so doing, he points out that he was not, as it were, raw material molded by his well-intentioned and highly-resourced adoptive white family, but rather someone *already* involved, with a range of limitations, in his own academic development and athletic training, and someone *already* cared for, however intermittently, by friends and relatives and neighbors throughout the black community. Regarding the former, Oher said that one of his main issues with the film was that it "portrayed me as dumb instead of as a kid who had never had consistent academic instruction and ended up thriving once he got it" (Noland 2011). There are other examples of such corrective statements throughout the text. And while Oher's testimony serves to challenge powerfully the relative silencing of his flattened characterization in the book and film, it nevertheless fails to address the structural dynamics analyzed in the present chapter more generally.

The Tuohys fear Michael is living without heritage in its fullest sense, in the absence of inheritance, birthright, legacy or benefaction. Heritage: from the Latin *hereditas*, the root *hērēs* gives us heir or heiress; from the Greek *khḗra* or *chíra*, meaning widow or relict, one that is relinquished, let go or left behind, but also one that survives or remains after the loss of others. Yet Michael's inheritance is not lost; it is taken away, stolen. His mother does not abandon him; state agents actively separate him from her and thrust him into the inoperable foster care system. His father is no mystery; they simply hold no memorable relationship before he learns his father's identity posthumously, as the victim of a spectacular homicide. He is not estranged from his siblings; the law disperses them throughout the municipality. His is a situation of shattered bonds rendering a proscribed maternity, a lethal patrimony, and an unkindness of scattered relations. It is this other, illegible kinship, a racialized *akinship* forced and forged in the crucible of modern slavery, that absorbs the attention of sports commentators and fans throughout the world of professional football and its tributaries.[6] It provokes a fascination with the matter of origins in the most profound sense, especially to the extent that the athletic contest is viewed as a site for the discovery and adjudication of human capacity, of limit and possibility, but also of social recognition and the reiteration of official morality. In every respect, it represents a test of character.

Sports commentary in the NFL is focused consistently on the question of the production of *talent* and of its proper evaluation and management. Spectators at all levels of involvement are enjoined to ask, in terms decidedly against the present vocabulary: What social labor is required for the production of (athletic) labor-power capable of creating (entertainment) value greater than itself (Engels 1891)? To be more precise, how can the labor-power of those otherwise deemed antithetical to value serve as a source of surplus value? In less adorned language, it is to wonder: Where do black athletes come from and how should we feel about their arrival and appearance, to say nothing of their achievement, in theaters historically reserved for the fabrication of white masculinity?

For the modern athlete, whose vocation is unmoored from any notion of the immemorial, "the determination of initial conditions has… become both a necessity and a near-impossibility" (Hussein 2002, 72). One is inundated with factual data about the arbitrary formulation of every rule and

---

[6]The idea of "akinship," which could be read as both akin-ship and a-kinship, is borrowed from Chamberlin (2014), who offers that: "Akinship… gives one name to the proximity between sexuality and violence."

regulation and the contingent date and location of each significant inaugural event, and so unable to hark back to the mist of origins for legitimation of the contemporary endeavor. Determination of proper membership and its benefits is equally troubled and as such some new effort must be made to justify the maintenance of patterned discrimination, exploitation, hierarchy or marginalization. The rise and fall (and return) of scientific racism has rendered its discourse untenable as a naturalist rationalization in the current conjuncture, and in its place, or alongside its remnants, culturalist conceptions of racial difference have settled in with the force of gravity (Goldberg 2011). If the NFL is understood by critics to be an institution for the discipline and punishment of black men, as much as for the (commodity and sexual) fetishization of their bodily forms and physical prowess, it must also be addressed as a sort of public salon for the oblique appraisal of the black family in general, and of black child-rearing in particular. Thence the lurid speculation about black reproduction insinuated into every sports-related assessment, whose primary feature is an unceasing denigration of black motherhood within "a cultural situation that," according to the patriarchal commitments of the dominant vantage, "is father-lacking" (Spillers 2003, 227).

The Blind Side's greatest feint—both the book and the film—is to suggest that only young black men like Michael Oher, who had "some kind of miserable childhood in the worst part of West Memphis" (Lewis 2006b), must seek to establish "beginnings in the absence of origins" (Hussein 2002, 72). In point of fact, what Jacques Derrida once termed "the prosthesis of origin" is as much a lure for white communal protocols as for any black strivings, and perhaps even more so. For the salient difference at play in the encounter between the (rich and white) Tuohys and (poor and black) Oher is a matter of *symbolic activity*, rather than some empirical distribution of lack and plenty. This is not to ignore the gross and wholly unjust disparity between the Tuohys' material abundance and Oher's material deprivation, but to acknowledge that the former's wealth only amplifies the fictions of whiteness that enshrine—across the class divide—a devastating mythology of filial purity and its related fantasies of unsullied genesis and succession. The Tuohys' relationship with Oher begins to reveal to them, though the lesson remains fully beyond their reach, that: "Beginning is inevitably found to be already underway in a fundamental sense" (Hussein 2002, 71). The origin, in other words, is irretrievably lost, complicated, non-originary; it consists of a theology piety.

A beginning, by contrast, "is a first step in the intentional production of meaning and the production of difference from preexisting traditions" (Said

1985, 32). It refers to what one makes—in the double sense of *interprets* and *creates*—of what one has been made. Though we are familiar by now with a battery of sophisticated arguments that this is the general condition, it is a persistent effect of the mark of slavery that the social category of racial blackness bears the burden for this immanent critique of the metaphysics of presence. The slave code at once foreclosed relations among captives from the political and economic orders, disorganized their social aspirations, and declared that such precluded form and standing to be the stuff of civilization. "The arcane of reproduction," whose elision has obtained even within much of the international movement of workers, is crucial to the maintenance of the relations of capitalist patriarchy and its gendered division of labor (Fortunati 1996; Hader and Mohandesi 2015). And yet Marx's hidden abode of production is riven in a more elementary way where the domestic sphere carries only the weight of pretense. Michael's childhood home is not a locus for the reproduction of labor-power, except as an unintentional by-product of a general warehousing. There is throughout the public housing projects and the adjacent neighborhoods not only a state of permanent unemployment, but also, more pointedly, a state of everyday social incarceration, an interdiction of the private sphere that preempts the trappings of storybook childhood. The Tuohys anxiously fill in the blanks of Michael's complicated history with compensatory bedtime reading, accelerated house training, an individualized education program, and, most brazenly, a falsified baby picture culled from online advertisements[7] (Fig. 4.2).

A Different Type of Bull

Michael Lewis' bestselling book is a telling not just of the story of Michael Oher, but also of an important development in the world of professional football. With the emergence of faster, stronger backside pass rushers in the 1980s, most famously in the person of New York Giants' Hall of Fame linebacker Lawrence Taylor, offensive blocking schemes had to adjust to a

---

[7]"There was one final piece of unfinished business in Michael Oher's Briarcrest career. The senior yearbook picture was due, and Michael didn't have one. It was a Briarcrest tradition for every senior to have his baby picture in the senior program. Her lack of a baby picture for Michael drove Leigh Anne to distraction. 'You don't want to be the only senior who doesn't have a baby picture in the annual!' she told him. [...] But the picture didn't solve the problem. It wasn't a baby picture. One spring night Leigh Anne had an idea. She flipped on her computer and went online and found, as she puts it, 'the cutest picture of a little black baby I could find.' She downloaded the stranger's photo and sent it into Briarcrest" (Lewis 2006b).

Fig. 4.2 Leigh Anne Tuohy (Sandra Bullock) reads to Michael and her son Sean (Jae Head). Image reproduced under terms of fair use

new threat. Since most quarterbacks are right-handed, this meant that a novel demand was placed on the left offensive tackle to secure his blindside during pass protection. The gruesome, career-ending injury suffered in 1985 by Washington quarterback Joe Theismann—a double compound fracture of his tibia and fibula—from a Taylor sack live on Monday Night Football remains the iconic moment of this strategic shift. On the night that Theismann was disabled, Washington's All-Pro left tackle, Joe Jacoby, was sidelined with an injury and a patchwork of double-team combinations were attempted to contain Taylor in his stead. Whether Jacoby's presence would have made the difference is impossible to know, but the point had been made nonetheless. Blindside protection meant the left tackle was *essential* on every series. A raise in pay, if not prestige to be sure, accompanied this now essential role. As Lewis writes early on:

> Offensive lineman were the stay-at-home mothers of the NFL: everyone paid lip service to the importance of their contribution yet hardly anyone could tell you exactly what that was. In 1985 the left tackle had no real distinction. He was still expected to believe himself more or less interchangeable with the other lineman. The Washington Redskins' [sic] offensive line was perhaps the most famous in NFL history. It had its own nickname: the Hogs. Fans

dressed as pigs in their honor. And yet they weren't understood, even by their own teammates, in the way running backs or quarterbacks were understood, as individual players with particular skills. "Even people who said they were fans of the Hogs had no idea who we were," said Jacoby. "They couldn't even tell the black ones from the white ones. I had people see me and scream, Hey May!" (Right tackle Mark May was black; Jacoby was not.) (Lewis 2006a, 24)

Jacoby suggests that the height of depersonalization is not to lose one's individuality in racial anonymity, e.g., his being mistaken for Jeff Bostic or Russ Grimm, but to lose one's "proper" racial designation altogether, the crudest and most preliminary manner of social identification. Or perhaps the indignity has to do with a white man being confused for a black man. One imagines that Mark May and George Starke, the two black members of the Hogs, also found such confusion amusing, but they likely would be far more accustomed to being mistaken as someone—or something—else in ways both large and small.

In any case, analogizing offensive lineman to stay-at-home mothers has the rhetorical effect, with respect to *The Blind Side*, of affiliating Michael Oher and Leigh Anne Tuohy as figures of unrecognized and underpaid reproductive labor, crucial to the circuit of capital, but nowhere featured in its central drama of value. Here the labors of the black man and white woman are together meant to minimize risk to the white man's life and limb, his person and property. Leigh Anne will provide a stable home to Michael so that Michael can provide a protective pocket for his (white) quarterback so that he can line the pockets of his white owners. It bears mentioning that Michael will imagine protecting the presumptively white quarterback as if he were protecting his white mother. In this, his on-field proficiency is fueled by a defense of, or defensiveness about, the mother particular to black men in the historic instance.

But Michael is not framed in this film in strict accordance with the prevailing tropes of black athleticism. Frantz Fanon stated at mid-century: "There is one expression that through time has become singularly eroticized: the black athlete" (Fanon 2006, 122). And Ben Carrington, for one, has done much to elaborate this critical insight in his own research. In *Race, Sport and Politics*, Carrington (2010) dedicates considerable space to an analysis of the psychosocial processes by which the black athlete, especially the black male athlete, is "debased and reduced to the status of animal-like savagery" and "*at the same time* imbued with certain hyper-masculine qualities of virility, strength, power and aggression" (87). While the attribution of strength and power certainly pertains to Michael's characterization, the corresponding qualities of virility and aggression, not to mention their stereotypical pairing, are muted. Likewise, while Michael is repeatedly assigned the status of animal-like, he is not thereby understood to be savage, if by that we mean "fierce, violent, and uncontrolled," to cite the *Oxford English Dictionary*.

Surely, Michael is described at the outset in terms reminiscent of commercial livestock or the slave auction block. Leigh Anne explains in her opening monologue: "The ideal left tackle is big, but a lot of people are big. He is wide in the butt and massive in the thighs. He has long arms, giant hands, and feet as quick as a hiccup. This is a rare and expensive combination…" And Michael is soon thereafter compared to a bull, but not, as one might expect, to indicate his hard-charging nature. Rather, he is likened to the eponymous protagonist from Munro Leaf's noted 1936 children's book, *The Story of Ferdinand* (Leaf 1977). Leaf's Ferdinand, an allegorical pacifist opposed to the right-wing Franco dictatorship in Spain, was a bull who preferred to smell the flowers in the field rather than fight matadors in the arena. He eschewed the competition and gamesmanship of the other young bulls, despite the advantage of his greater stature. One day, Ferdinand is stung by a bee while meandering in the pasture and he storms about in pain, barreling through fences and other obstacles. Nearby bullfighting wranglers are duly impressed with his potential and immediately corral him for the spectator sport. Leigh Anne loves the book too, even if its progressive politics are anathema, and she reads it to her own children, Michael included, as she was introduced to it before them. The affinity dawns on her while observing a practice during Michael's first season with the varsity football team. Coach Cotton (!) is exasperated by Michael's passivity on the line. He was being bested play after play by teammates with half his size and strength. The coach blurts out to Leigh Anne: "Most kids from bad situations can't wait to be violent and that comes out on the field. But this kid, he acts like he doesn't wanna hit anyone." Leigh Anne replies epiphanically: "He's Ferdinand the Bull."

Lewis first proffered this bit of wisdom in his 2006 *New York Times Magazine* book excerpt, "The Ballad of Big Mike," where he wrote: "The N.F.L. was loaded with players who had mined a loveless, dysfunctional childhood. The trouble with Michael Oher as a football player was the trouble with Ferdinand as a bull: he didn't exhibit the anger of his breed. He was just a sweet kid who didn't particularly care to hit anybody. Or as [Coach] Freeze puts it: 'He just wasn't aggressive…'." The anger of his breed, then, would be the racially overdetermined response to conditions of racial domination, of impoverishment and homelessness, of physical and emotional abuse, of miseducation and illiteracy, among other things. Michael's suffering, in its similarity to so many of his predecessors in the top ranks of football, was supposed to provide the raw material for his athletic exploitation. The men charged with his training—first Big Tony Henderson (who lobbies for Michael's acceptance to the wealthy, white private high school), then Coach Cotton at the Wingate Christian School, and later Coach Orgeron at Ole Miss—share the pop psychological assumption that a "miserable childhood… was typically excellent emotional preparation for what was required" in football.[8]

But it is the women (and feminized men and boys like Sean and S.J.) who take him in and offer assistance that inspire him most—first Leigh Anne, then his teacher Mrs Boswell and his tutor Miss Sue, and later his adoptive sister Collins. Their care and guidance enable Michael to call up aggression and channel it into his game play as part of the same dubious "pedagogy of confidence" that elicits his kindness and good manners and sparks his imagination (Jackson 2011). This is done in a precise and pernicious way. Leigh Anne overcomes Michael's passivity by asking him to imagine that she is the quarterback and that the oncoming pass rushers were seeking to harm her. She takes this tack based upon her understanding of Michael's eighth-grade transcript, augmented by a *deus ex machina*: although Michael scores dismally in "spatial relations" and "ability to learn" on the career aptitude test, he places "in the 98th percentile in one category: protective instincts." For those wondering when and whether any such test exists, filmmaker David Kenrick offers this in his review for *Psychology Today*: "This test, as near as we can tell from reading the *New York Times* story that is the basis of the script, is something added to the real story, and a quick look online suggests that it's a score you can get if you take your dog to a canine psychologist, but not something your son will get from the high school counselor" (Kenrick 2010). And protect Michael does: he protects Coach Cotton against an undeserved penalty from a biased white referee; he protects S.J. from the

---

[8] Beyond the racist animalization involved in this all-too-common description of black athletic talent, the staff of Memphis Child Protective Services shared the basic assumption of inherent black male rage. As Noland (2011) recounts in his review of Oher's autobiography for the *Los Angeles Times*: "By his own admission, Michael Oher preferred to observe rather than participate in social settings when he was a young man. In fact, his silence was so disconcerting to social workers in Memphis, Tenn., he says, that it was misdiagnosed as repressed rage, and he was locked up in a hospital for observation." Note the pat hydraulics of his medical incarceration. The hospital inverts his silent, passively observing disposition, locking him up for not saying or doing anything in particular. His rage—and the threat it entailed—was presupposed even in its apparent absence. When it is later discovered that he is not especially enraged, he becomes a charming peculiarity—not unlike Ferdinand—to the people of the Wingate Christian School.

Fig. 4.3 Leigh Anne inspires Michael to be more aggressive on the field. Image reproduced under terms of fair use

impact of the passenger side airbag when they get into a minor accident in Michael's new pickup truck; and, above all, he protects Leigh Anne, her image and her good name (Fig. 4.3).

This is not the protection of a junior patriarch, but rather, as Kenrick's comment suggests, the protection of a pet, or, better, a loyal slave. What recommends the last of these terms is a pivotal pair of scenes in the display of Michael's growing facility with physical violence as a result of his football regimen. This couplet also bears on our opening comments regarding the bifurcation of racialism in the moral economy of the film. The first scene occurs during Michael's high school debut in the game between the Wingate Crusaders and the nearby Milford Lions. Though it is a home game for Wingate, the overwhelming presence of the Milford fans, described by Leigh Anne as "so many rednecks," sets a tone of immediate hostility. One Milford man stands out as the leading "redneck" in the bleachers and his son, a defensive pass rusher, will prove equally bigoted on the field below. Leigh Anne must contend with the elder; Michael with the younger. The Milford father refers to Michael derisively as a "big ole' black bear" and a "blue gum," and the son, in kind, taunts him by calling him a "buck" whose "fat black ass I get to kick all night." Leigh Anne shuts up the father, who is boasting about his son, by turning around and shouting: "Hey crotch mouth! Yeah, you! Zip it or I'll come zip it for ya!" Michael deals with his opponent, after absorbing several quarters worth of racist harassment, by drive-blocking him all the way down the field, out of bounds, up and over the fence. Leigh Anne adds the *coup de grâce*, exclaiming to the bigoted father: "See number seventy-four? Well, that's MY son!" Michael's force here is not violence, however, because it is sanctioned by the rules of the game. It would not even have drawn a penalty—for the spurious offense of "excessive blocking"—except that the referee, like most of the crowd, was against Michael's very presence on the field. The chief instigator, the "redneck" father who had raised his son in the same reactionary tradition, is effectively checked, humbled even, by Michael's athletic excellence and good sportsmanship which Leigh Anne interprets in her condescending riposte as his vicarious just deserts.

We should read this confrontation in the stands alongside Leigh Anne's earlier rift with the high-society "ladies that lunch" after one of them, over drinks at a posh restaurant, makes an offhand comment comparing the odd couple of Leigh Anne and Michael to Jessica Lange and the giant ape in John Guillermin's Academy Award-winning 1976 *King Kong*, a remake of the notorious 1933 original. The luncheon is, importantly, linked to the previous scene, in which Leigh Anne's cousin Bobby, drinking a six-pack of beer in a reclining chair, feels compelled to call and ask, "Do y'all know that there's a *colored boy* on your Christmas card?" Perhaps he lives in Milford too. The comment, played aloud on the answering machine, elicits chuckles and bemused looks of disapproval from Leigh Anne, Sean, S.J., and Michael himself, who are sitting around the kitchen together. This laughter forms a sound bridge to the subsequent scene in which we hear Leigh Anne's friend Elaine in voice-over saying about the same card: "Leigh Anne, you looked teeny-tiny next to him." Another friend, Sherry, quips: "I taped your card to the fridge. The next morning [my husband] Frank almost gagged on his orange juice." Leigh Anne's circle of friends persists in badgering: "Is this some kind of white guilt thing?" "What will your daddy say?" After Leigh Anne artfully sidesteps the questions, the inquisition cuts to the heart of the matter. Elaine asks directly after the safety of Leigh Anne's teenage daughter Collins: "Aren't you worried, I mean even just a little? He's a boy, *a large black boy*, sleeping under the same roof." Leigh Anne's response is as self-righteous as it is hypocritical: "Shame on you," she scolds, as she picks up the tab and walks out. Hypocritical because immediately following her lunchtime throw down, Leigh Anne goes straight home to ask Collins, in that vein, "Is Michael being here weird for you?" If so, Leigh Anne promises vaguely, "I can make other arrangements." After Collins reassures her mother that Michael is no (sexual) threat to her or her younger brother S.J., the worst, it seems, is over. The next day at Wingate the preteen white girls on the playground who previously ran away from Michael in fear are now comfortable greeting him and even accepting his offer to push them on the swing set. Collins that same day breaks ranks with her skeptical white classmates—shades of Leigh Anne's lunch circle—and joins Michael for study hall in the school library. Having been rendered sufficiently asexual, the larger Wingate family is prepared to accept Michael into the fold.[9]

But Michael has not sufficiently proved himself for all his best behavior in the white community of his adoptive family. He must accentuate his good intentions by violently differentiating himself from the sexual threat—and broader moral degeneracy—associated with his natal surround. While doubting for the first time the motives of the Tuohys' generous spirit, after he is investigated by the National Collegiate Athletic Association for potential ethics violations in his recruitment to the University of Mississippi, Michael breaks off communication with Leigh Anne and seeks out his birth mother, Denise Oher.[10] He returns to the Hurt Village public housing complex of his earliest years in search of what we do not know—solace, perhaps, or advice. En route, he runs into a local drug dealer, Alton, a former neighbor who implies he is also Denise's supplier. Alton invites Michael inside his apartment, where members of his crew are relaxing, to wait for Denise's return. The exchange becomes heated in short order:

ALTON: It's good to see you, Big Mike. You lookin' fit. I heard you playin' some ball.

MICHAEL: Yeah.

[…]

ALTON: You stayin' on the other side of town, that's what Dee Dee [Denise] said. Said you got a new mama. She fine, too. I seen her when she come to see Dee Dee.

MICHAEL: She came here?

---

[9] In a cultural project committed to sanitizing racism, it is worth noting the sheer volume of epithets used to refer to Michael in the film and book—"colored boy," "black bear," "blue gum," "brute," and "King Kong," to name a few. He is also compared to a cow (after being weighed on cattle scale), a dog (in relation to his "protective instincts"), and so on. But, crucially, none of these slurs are ever subject to challenge.

[10] The NCAA investigator, Jocelyn Granger, is the only other significant black woman character in the film and she is drawn so harshly as to evoke hostility toward the very idea of regulatory oversight she represents. For a critical response from the actual NCAA assistant director for enforcement, Joyce Thompson, see Lawrence (2011).

ALTON: She got any other kids? She got a daughter?
(Michael nods)
You tap that?
(Michael, agitated, rises to leave.)
Where you going? Sit down. I wanna hear about your fine white sister. 'Cause I like me some mommy/daughter…

MICHAEL: Shut up.

ALTON: Shut up? You tellin' me to shut up? I'll cap your fat ass. Cap your ass, drive east, and pay a visit to your cracker Mama and her…

Before Alton can reach for his gun, Michael explodes in a fit of anger and attacks Alton, throwing him across the room while fending off Alton's sidekicks. The apartment is nearly demolished in the process. The script direction describes it as "eighteen years of subdued rage coming out in seconds." Bear in mind that this is *after* Michael has been legally adopted by the Tuohy family; *after* he has become a high school All-American with scholarship offers from dozens of top college football programs; *after* he has committed to attend Ole Miss; *after* he has closed the gap in his formal education to become academically college-ready. It is only now, when a poor black man from the projects, a perverse shadow of Michael's now-deceased father, a black man with a criminal history and violent tendencies who enables Denise's drug use and, it is implied, sexually exploits her as well, a black man who would derail Michael's dreams of higher learning and professional sports, who maligns his adoptive sister, and who threatens to murder him for his audacity; only *now*, when he threatens interracial sexual violence against Leigh Anne, that Michael draws the line and unleashes his wrath. And it is this singular campaign of violence that constitutes Michael's only autonomous action in the entire film.[11]

This scene catalyzes Michael's final reconciliation with the Tuohys. Leigh Anne admits in the aftermath that her heavy-handed guidance unscrupulously steered Michael toward Ole Miss and she accepts, at this late hour, whatever decision he now makes about his future, even if he opts to work

---

[11] The attentive viewer will notice that Alton refers to Michael specifically as "fat ass" in the same manner as the junior "redneck" from Milford during the game. Though Michael is insulted in many ways by many people in *The Blind Side*, this particular put-down binds the two racialists—one white, one black—into a common domain and each is dealt with by force. In both cases Michael is, to repeat, defending Leigh Anne, imaginatively during the game and preemptively during the apartment brawl. But even with his demonstrated loyalty and asexual presentation, Leigh Anne still threatens castration if he impregnates a woman outside of marriage.

at a fast food restaurant (like those that made her family rich) or to attend her alma mater's arch-rival, the University of Tennessee. It also signals Michael's definitive departure from Hurt Village and his relinquishment of any remaining ties to his birth mother, all of which serves to redeem Leigh Anne's questionable efforts to date. Leigh Anne tracks Michael to the complex, where Alton sits outside nursing his wounds. Alton informs her that Michael has already left, but that there is now a price on his head for his rampage: "So you tell him, sleep with one eye open. You hear me, bitch?" Leigh Anne leans in and says menacingly: "No, you hear me, bitch. You threaten my son, you threaten me. You so much as cross downtown, you'll be sorry. I'm in a prayer group with the D.A. [District Attorney], I'm a member of the NRA [National Rifle Association], and I am always packing." Her promise to solicit the state violence of fast-track prosecution and long-term imprisonment and/or to mete out state-sanctioned, financially-backed interpersonal gun violence in Michael's defense is tantamount to a vow to protect his blindside against Lawrence Taylor's off-field double. For her recourse to a disavowed organized violence, marshaling it and managing it at once, she is bestowed the coveted title. Upon returning to her car, Michael calls Leigh Anne on the phone and, spilling over with symbolism, asks, "Mama?" (Fig. 4.4).

Fig. 4.4 Leigh Anne visits Michael's mother, Denise Oher (Adriane Lenox), to discuss the new arrangement. Image reproduced under terms of fair use

Something more is at stake, again, than the asymmetry of wealth, power, and resources between Denise and Leigh Anne. We are not simply bearing witness to a son gravitating, practically and emotionally, toward the mother more capable of providing for him. This much is a common enough feature in the political economy of adoption, especially those patterns of interracial adoption indexed to class inequality. The transfer of maternal title, despite Leigh Anne's matter-of-fact statement that Denise will "always be Michael's mama," involves, at its base, a normative rearrangement of the vectors of generational obligation. Denise explains to Leigh Anne during their one brief visit: "Every foster home they sent [Michael] to, he'd slip out the window at night and come looking for me. No matter where I was that boy would come find me, *take care of me*" (emphasis added). Michael's mother is, then, not only unable to protect him from dangers in his home and neighborhood or the regular incursions of the state, not only unable to ward against the structural conditions of ghettoization; she is also in need of protection herself. The black mother, in this scenario, is not merely incapable or incapacitated in her role; she is, more accurately, *made vulnerable* in a comprehensive way. That is to say, the childhood insecurity Michael and his siblings experienced was not a failure, moral or otherwise, of their mother (or even of their fathers for that matter), but rather a feature of her own position, one encapsulated by the exchange between Leigh Anne and Michael's Child Protective Services caseworker, Ronald, early in the adoption process.

> **LEIGH ANNE:** We'd need her [Denise's] permission [for the adoption] though, right?
>
> **RONALD:** No. Michael is a ward of the state. Just apply and get a Judge to sign off on it.
>
> **LEIGH ANNE:** So you would give him away without even telling his mother?
> (Ronald shrugs.)

Under these circumstances, Michael's frequent returns (or escapes) from foster care, even if driven by an impossible childhood wish to help his mother, were also, of necessity, inchoate attempts to create the conditions of his own recovery, reminding us that black children's welfare is indelibly linked to the status of black women and the value assigned to black motherhood (Roberts 2009). But because global Hollywood is unlikely to allow *The Blind Side* to contemplate *that* earthshaking ethical dilemma and remain solvent, the audience must resign itself, with a certain relief, to save Michael and, with regrets, to abandon Denise and her kin to their destiny. Leigh Anne, after all, is our guide. Her closing voice-over monologue is as follows:

> **LEIGH ANNE**: I read a story the other day about a boy from the projects. No daddy, in and out of foster care. He'd been killed in a gang fight at Hurt Village. In the last paragraph they talked about his superb athletic skill and how different his life might have been if he hadn't fallen behind and dropped out of school. He was twenty-one years old the day he died. It was his birthday. That could have been anyone. It could have been my son, Michael. But it wasn't. And I suppose I have God to thank for that. God and Lawrence Taylor.

By "anyone," of course, Leigh Anne means anyone from the projects, on the other side of the city, on the far side of the color line. It turns out that the murder victim was Michael's old friend David, who had been playing football at a local junior college before Alton convinced him to drop out and work for his local drug operation. David, as he told Michael in an earlier scene, was tired of going to class: "Always somebody tellin' me what to do." *That* is the very lesson that Michael learns in the Tuohy home and at Wingate Christian School: how best to relate to somebody telling you what to do. While working on a book report with Miss Sue, at a critical time in the boosting of his grade point average for the upcoming college admissions requirements, Sean suggests a topic to Michael. Rather than write about Dickens' *Great Expectations* and its orphaned protagonist's incipient criticism of class society, as Miss Sue had urged, Sean encourages Michael to take on Tennyson's "Charge of the Light Brigade" and contemplate the mission and mindset of dutiful soldiers, whom Sean conventionally analogizes to football players, following orders even with knowledge of their leader's ruinous error. Michael interprets:

> **MICHAEL**: Courage is a hard thing to figure. You can have courage based on a dumb idea or a mistake, but you're not supposed to question adults, or your coach, or your teacher because they make the rules. Maybe they know best but maybe they don't. It all depends on who you are, where you come from. [...] That's why courage is tricky. Should you always do what others tell you to do? Sometimes you might not even know why you're doing something. I mean, any fool can have courage. But honor, that's the real reason you either do something or you don't. It's who you are and maybe who you want to be.

If you die trying for something important then you have both honor and courage and that's pretty good. I think that's what the writer was saying. That you should try for courage and hope for honor. And maybe even pray that the people telling you what to do have some too.

Redemption Rebooted

Honor in the (quasi-)military contest: heady stuff for a young black man from the projects to mull over on his way to the University of Mississippi, described by James Meredith, the first black student in attendance, as "the Ivy League of the Southern way of the life." To say that the Hospitality State's flagship institution, and the Southern society it was meant to epitomize, has a problematic understanding of what constitutes honor, on or off the field of battle, would be the understatement of the present essay. Meredith, on the fiftieth anniversary of his historic matriculation, stated plainly: "The reason Ole Miss was established was to refine and define and perpetuate the theory of white supremacy" (Elliott 2012). Michael Oher made the Dean's Honor Role and earned a bachelor's degree in criminal justice there in the years leading up to this landmark 2012 celebration. Oher's athletic feats during his tenure also distinguished him as among the most accomplished players to ever wear the Rebels uniform. But the true-to-life story of Oher's uncommon success as a black student-athlete—bridging the promise of equal access to higher education with the prestige of sporting achievement—inhabits a sordid legacy only hinted at in the various literary, journalistic, and cinematic depictions of his journey.

Nineteen sixty-two represents the high-water mark for Ole Miss football, arguably the best season it has enjoyed to date. That year, under longtime coach John Vaught, the Rebels went 10-0, securing the only undefeated record in school history. They won the Southeastern Conference Championship, claimed a piece of the disputed national title, and finished with a #3 national ranking overall. Vaught and the Rebels, who had already established themselves as top contenders in the immediately preceding seasons, were especially keen to excel this time out so that their weekly marches to victory might progressively counteract the scathing international press coverage then marring the concentric reputations of the university, the state, and the region. For 1962 was also the year of James Meredith's arrival to campus as the living embodiment of the imperative for desegregation established with *Brown* v. *Board of Education* in 1954. Meredith, a retired US Air Force veteran from the small town of Kosciusko, applied for admission to the University of Mississippi with assistance from Medgar Evers, head of the state chapter of the National Association for the Advancement of Colored People (NAACP) and the NAACP Legal Defense Fund.[12] After twice being denied admission according to the administration's longstanding Jim Crow policy, Meredith successfully sued Ole Miss in a case decided by the US Court of Appeals for the Sixth District and affirmed by the Supreme Court. Governor Ross Barnett, a Dixiecrat, defied the Supreme Court's injunction and declared during a statewide radio and television broadcast:

> We must either submit to the unlawful dictates of the Federal Government or stand up like men and tell them "NEVER!" The day of reckoning has been delayed as long as possible. It is now upon us. This is the day—and this is the hour… I have made my position in this matter crystal clear. I have said in every county in Mississippi that no school in our state will be integrated while I am your Governor. I repeat to you tonight—NO SCHOOL WILL BE INTEGRATED IN MISSISSIPPI WHILE I AM YOUR GOVERNOR! (Katagiri 2007, 104–105)

For Barnett and the vast majority of white Mississippians, to capitulate to "social integration" was to "drink from the cup of racial genocide." Historian Frank Lambert describes Barnett's speech as a bold articulation of popular sentiment:

> Barnett knew his audience. For Mississippians, race was not just an important political issue, it was the paramount issue. One reporter from outside the state found in his daily rounds that whites associated race with everything, no matter how mundane. As he traveled through the state in 1962, [Rhodes Scholar and future Pulitzer Prize-winner] Robert Massie [then writing for *Newsweek*] visited white Mississippians of all socioeconomic backgrounds and of various cultural sensitivities and found that the one thing that they shared was a preoccupation with race. (Lambert 2010, 100)

This was not the first time a Southern Governor had taken center stage in the strategy of "massive resistance" to federal desegregation orders in the postwar era (Webb 2005). One thinks immediately, for instance, of Governor Orval Faubus's stance at Central High School in Little Rock,

---

[12] Evers would be assassinated in his driveway by the white supremacist Byron De La Beckwith in 1964 (Williams 2011) and, two years later, Meredith would be shot by an unknown white gunman while marching in support of black voter registration in Mississippi (Meredith 2012). For critical reflections on the political fate of the *Brown* decision, see Bell (2004), Klarman (2007), and Patterson (2001).

Arkansas in 1958 or Alabama Governor John Patterson's refusal to intervene on white mob violence in his state against the 1961 Freedom Riders. Nor was it the first time that the White House would exercise executive power to countermand. But what followed surpassed any previous show of force in the name of federal civil rights law enforcement since Reconstruction. Heeding Governor Barnett's call, hundreds and eventually thousands of mostly young white men, including many students, descended on the courtyard in front of the Lyceum Building at the center of campus just prior to Meredith's first day of classes. President John F. Kennedy had already sent 500 US Marshals to accompany Meredith in his first weeks, but when the mob that had assembled began to riot, attacking the Marshals and laying waste to university property, Kennedy knew he had a much larger problem on his hands. The Marshals were quickly overwhelmed in the melee, while dozens of local and state police stood down on orders from state officials. The President, following reluctantly the precedent set by Dwight Eisenhower five years earlier in Arkansas, then deployed troops from the 108th Armored Cavalry Regiment of the Mississippi National Guard and the 70th Army Engineer Combat Battalion stationed at Fort Campbell, Kentucky, who had been mobilized in anticipation of the heightened conflict.

When the rioting was finally quelled on the second day, over 300 people had been injured, including fully one-third of the Marshals and dozens of military personnel. Two men had been murdered in execution-style shootings, including Agence France-Presse journalist Paul Guihard. Tens of thousands of dollars of damage had been inflicted by rocks, firebombs, and bullets from the mob. The police presence at the scene never returned fire. On the following day, October 1, 1962, James Meredith began what would be his senior year at Ole Miss, having already accrued the bulk of his credits at the historically black Jackson State University while awaiting the outcome of his case. He lived under 24-hour police protection until graduating the next summer with degrees in history and political science. He would go on to earn a law degree at Columbia. All told, it required a force of arms nearing 30,000 to secure his entrance, all of which did nothing to subdue the daily barrage of taunts, threats and slurs.[13]

James Meredith has referred to the Ole Miss Riot of 1962 as the final and belated cessation of hostilities between the Union and the Confederacy. Historian William Doyle, who co-authored Meredith's memoir and penned

---

[13]For a more comprehensive history of the 1962 Ole Miss Riot, see Doyle (2001), Robertson (2012), and Thompson (2009). For additional detail regarding the life of James Meredith at Ole Miss and beyond, see Eagles (2009) and Gallagher (2012).

an award-winning study of the events, concurs and echoed the thought in his comments for Fritz Mitchell's recent contribution to ESPN's *30-for-30, The Ghosts of Ole Miss* (Billman 2012).

> **DOYLE**: Mississippi is really just a symbol, it's a microcosm for America. It's the emotional heart and soul of America on the issue of race. To conduct a military strike on this piece of land, which was symbolically the heart of the old South, was completely audacious and very dangerous. I think of it as the last battle of the Civil War.

Mitchell is a noted documentary filmmaker and television producer, recipient of three Peabody Awards and seven Emmy Awards in an impressive career stretching back to the early 1980s. He is also a dyed-in-the-wool white Southerner and a Mississippian, despite his liberal leanings. He made *Ghosts* as an attempt to reconcile himself to history, personally and politically, on the semi-centennial of the riot. Mitchell notes that the Ivy League of the Southern Way of Life has not renounced its vocation, inscribed as it is into the built environment, the customs and culture of the institution, and the deep structures of the state that authorizes it.[14] The Rebels take their namesake from the University Grays, a Confederate regiment of Ole Miss students who fought at the Battle of Gettysburg in 1863. All of them were killed or seriously wounded. There is also a monument on campus in memory of the Confederate General Albert Sidney Johnston, whose death at the Battle of Shiloh Jefferson Davis claimed to be "the turning point of our fate" in the Civil War. Johnston is, following Davis and Robert E. Lee, perhaps the most esteemed Confederate war hero in the pantheon.

But, Mitchell argues, things have begun to change for the better.[15] The university undertook in 2010 to change its official mascot from the embarrassingly partisan Colonel Reb to the seemingly anodyne Rebel, The Black

---

[14] There is a vast literature on the twentieth-century conservative movement in the United States, especially in its postwar renaissance. For recent work on this history in Mississippi, see Crespino (2007).

[15] Compare Mitchell's closing narration to Meredith's sardonic commentary about the anniversary celebration. Mitchell muses:

> Yes, some of 1962 remains. But much of it has been replaced by a new world born from its ashes. The kids playing football in the pregame glow might not know the inscription on the nearby statue. Yes, Mississippi was, but Mississippi is. They might not know, but they can see it everywhere they look. James Meredith can see it too. Fifty years after it took the United States Army to get him on the campus, he is now invited by the Chancellor, honored on the same day as the 1962 Rebels. He never got to watch that team play, but at long last he is watching it walk on the field. Yes, Mississippi was, but Mississippi is.

Bear. Fifty years after Meredith's armed escort, the Ole Miss student body is now 16% black (the state of Mississippi is nearly 40% black), and a black woman, Kimberly Dandridge, was elected as Student Body President while also participating as an active member of a predominantly white sorority. Dandridge is, in many ways, a kindred spirit with Meredith under altered circumstance. Nominally liberal, betraying a colorblind meritocratic vision, Dandridge identified the most important decision of her life as the one that faced her when a fellow student denounced her with a racist slur during her campus political campaign. Dandridge tells us that she chose not to respond with anger as a way of refusing to let one person define Ole Miss, and thereby her college experience. Dandridge and Oher were classmates for a year, a point that weaves the history of segregation back into the very fabric of the post-civil rights moment. For Oher, his education at Briarcrest Christian School (the referent for Wingate in *The Blind Side* film) was not only enabled by the largess of the Tuohy family or even the larger support team duly noted in Lewis's text and Oher's own subsequent reflections.[16]

More profoundly, we would not have in the United States a vast system of private K-12 education, now enrolling some 10 percent of students nationally, or, now, a galloping campaign for school vouchers and public charters were it not for the acute and ongoing white backlash against school desegregation (Bonastia 2015; Ravitch 2013; cf. Stulberg 2015). When filibustering, intimidation, and wholesale school closures could no longer circumvent judicial decree and legislative action, white communities throughout the country, not least in Mississippi, set out to establish hundreds of "segregation academies" to preserve the racial exclusivity of their children's education (Carr 2012).[17] What's more, it is the disavowed

---

Meredith, in turn, remarks: "You know, I got a degree from Ole Miss in political science, history and French. I ain't never heard of a Frenchman celebrating Waterloo… They not only kept me out… they kept all of my blood before me out forever, and I'm supposed to celebrate that" (Elliott 2012)?

[16] A comparative reading of Lewis's text and Hancock's film, and of these sources against Oher's subsequent publication, reveals the considerable artistic license exercised in the biography and its screen adaptation. It was important, on that score, for Oher to clarify that he did not learn to play football, much less acquire the necessary on-field aggression, at Briarcrest, but rather much earlier in life (Oher 2012). Moreover, Lewis's account shows, contrary to the pat rescue scene in the film, that Michael only eventually settled at the Tuohy residence, at Sean's suggestion and not Leigh Anne's, after staying with various families, black and white, during his first year at the private Christian academy.

[17] According to the conservative Mississippi Association of Independent Schools, private schools in the state mushroomed from less than 20 member institutions in the 1960s to over 120 at present.

persistence and permutation of racial domination—hyper-ghettoization, mass imprisonment, educational re-segregation, and the dismantling of public services never intended for the general welfare of black communities—that galvanizes stories like *The Blind Side* or *The Ghosts of Ole Miss* in the first place. Rather than debating the relative merits of their respective treatments of the sociological material, however, we could better spend our time and energy talking about how to abolish their conditions of possibility. But in order to do so, we would have to contemplate something more disconcerting than civil war, and it is doubtful that fans would, as yet, fill a stadium for that.[18]

References

Baghdjian, Alice. 2013. Marc Rich, 'King of Oil' pardoned by Clinton, dies at 78. *Reuters*, June 26. Accessed May 28, 2017. http://www.reuters.com/article/us-marcrich-idUSBRE95P0CO20130626.
Baptist, Edward. 2014. *The Half Has Never Been Told: Slavery and the Making of American Capitalism*. New York: Basic Books.
Barrett, Lindon. 2013. *Racial Blackness and the Discontinuity of Western Modernity*, ed. Justin Joyce, Dwight McBride, and John Carlos Rowe. Urbana: University of Illinois Press.
Beckert, Sven. 2014. *Empire of Cotton: A Global History*. New York: Knopf Doubleday.
Bell, Derrick. 2004. *Silent Covenants: Brown v. Board of Education and the Unfulfilled Hopes for Racial Reform*. New York: Oxford University Press.
Bery, Soven. 2013. NFL: Is the Most Popular Sports League in the USA Really Too Big to Fail? *The Bleacher Report*, July 17. Accessed May 28, 2017. http://bleacherreport.com/articles/1707663-nfl-is-the-most-popular-sports-league-in-the-usa-really-too-big-to-fail.
Billman, Andrew. 2012. *The Ghosts of Ole Miss*. TV. Directed by Fritz Mitchell. Los Angeles: ESPN Films.
Bonastia, Christopher. 2015. "The Racist History of the Charter School Movement." *AlterNet*, January 6. Accessed May 28, 2017. https://www.alternet.org/education/racist-history-charter-school-movement.

---

[18]The literature on "the new African-American Sport Studies" (Lomax 2002) generally falls short of the radical analysis necessary to do justice to its various topics, opting instead to argue for diversification of the upper echelons of the industry, *ceteris paribus*, alongside capitalist development proposals for wealthy black professional athletes. See Hawkins (2013), Lewis (2010), Rhoden (2007), and Smith (2009) for recent examples. For a longer view on the field, see Leonard (1998) and Hartmann (2003).

Buttersworth, Matthew. 2017. *Sport and Militarism: Contemporary Global Perspectives*. New York: Routledge.

Carr, Sarah. 2012. In Southern Towns, 'Segregation Academies' Are Still Going Strong. *The Atlantic*, December 13. Accessed May 28, 2017. http://www.theatlantic.com/national/archive/2012/12/in-southern-towns-segregation-academies-are-still-going-strong/266207/.

Carrington, Ben. 2010. *Race, Sport and Politics: The Sporting Black Diaspora*. Thousand Oaks, CA: SAGE.

Chamberlin, Christopher. 2014. Akinship. MA thesis, Culture & Theory PhD Program, University of California, Irvine.

Crespino, Joseph. 2007. *In Search of Another Country: Mississippi and the Conservative Counterrevolution*. Princeton, NJ: Princeton University Press.

Doyle, William. 2001. *An American Insurrection: The Battle of Oxford, Mississippi, 1962*. New York: Doubleday Publishing.

Eagles, Charles. 2009. *The Price of Defiance: James Meredith and the Integration of Ole Miss*. Durham: University of North Carolina Press.

Elliott, Debbie. 2012. Integrating Ole Miss: A Transformative, Deadly Riot. *National Public Radio*, October 1. Accessed May 28, 2017. http://www.npr.org/2012/10/01/161573289/integrating-ole-miss-a-transformative-deadly-riot.

Engels, Frederick. 1891. Introduction to Karl Marx's *Wage Labour and Capital*. *Marxists Internet Archive*. Accessed May 28, 2017. https://www.marxists.org/archive/marx/works/1847/wage-labour/intro.htm.

Fanon, Frantz. 2006. *Black Skin, White Masks*, trans. Richard Philcox. New York: Grove Press.

Fortunati, Leopoldina. 1996. *The Arcane of Reproduction: Housework, Prostitution, Labor and Capital*. New York: Autonomedia.

Gallagher, Henry. 2012. *James Meredith and the University of Mississippi: A Soldier's Story*. Jackson: University Press of Mississippi.

Goldberg, David Theo. 2011. *The Threat of Race: Reflections on Racial Neoliberalism*. New York: Wiley-Blackwell.

Hader, Asad, and Mohandesi. 2015. Making a Living. *Viewpoint Magazine*, October 28. Accessed May 28, 2017. https://www.viewpointmag.com/2015/10/28/making-a-living/.

Hartmann, Douglass. 2003. *Race, Culture, and the Revolt of the Black Athlete: The 1968 Olympic Protests and Their Aftermath*. Chicago: University of Chicago Press.

Hawkins, Billy. 2013. *The New Plantation: Black Athletes, College Sports, and Predominantly White NCAA Institutions*. New York: Palgrave Macmillan.

Holleman, Hannah, Inger L. Stole, John Bellamy Foster, and Robert W. McChesney. 2009. The Sales Effort and Monopoly Capital. *Monthly Review* 60: 1–23. Accessed May 28, 2017. doi:10.14452/MR-060-11-2009-04_1.

Hughey, Matthew. 2014. *The White Savior Film: Critics, Comments and Consumption*. Philadelphia: Temple University Press.

Hussein, Abdirahman. 2002. *Edward Said: Criticism and Society*. New York: Verso.

Jackson, Yvette. 2011. *The Pedagogy of Confidence: Inspiring High Intellectual Performance in Urban Schools*. New York: Teachers College Press.
Johnson, Broderick. 2009. *The Blind Side*. DVD. Directed by John Lee Hancock. Burbank, CA: Warner Bros.
Johnson, Walter. 2013. *River of Dark Dreams: Slavery and Empire in the Cotton Kingdom*. Cambridge, MA: Harvard University Press.
Katagiri, Yasuhiro. 2007. *The Mississippi State Sovereignty Commission: Civil Rights and States' Rights*. Jackson: University Press of Mississippi.
Kenrick, David. 2010. When Life Imitates a Made-For-TV Movie: The Bland Side of Heroism. *Psychology Today*, March 4. Accessed May 28, 2017. https://www.psychologytoday.com/blog/the-caveman-goes-hollywood/201003/when-life-imitates-made-tv-movie.
Klarman, Michael. 2007. *Brown v. Board of Education and the Civil Rights Movement*. New York: Oxford University Press.
Lambert, Frank. 2010. *The Battle for Ole Miss: Civil Rights vs. States' Rights*. New York: Oxford University Press.
Lawrence, Marta. 2011. Seeing Through 'The Blind Side'. *NCAA.com*, May 10. Accessed May 28, 2017. http://www.ncaa.com/news/ncaa/2011-05-10/seeing-through-%E2%80%98-blind-side%E2%80%99.
Leaf, Munro. 1977. *The Story of Ferdinand*. New York: Puffin Books.
Leonard, David. 1998. What Happened to the Revolt of the Black Athlete? *ColorLines*, June 10. Accessed May 28, 2017. http://www.colorlines.com/articles/what-happened-revolt-black-athlete.
Lewis, Michael. 2006a. *The Blind Side: Evolution of the Game*. New York: W. W. Norton & Company.
Lewis, Michael. 2006b. The Ballad of Big Mike. *New York Times Magazine*, September 24.
Lewis, Thabiti. 2010. *Ballers of the New School: Race and Sports in America*. Chicago: Third World Press.
Lomax, Michael. 2002. Revisiting *The Revolt of the Black Athlete*: Harry Edwards and the Making of the New African-American Sport Studies. *Journal of Sport History* 29: 469–479.
McDonald, Soraya Nadia. 2015. 'Concussion,' the NFL, and the Limits of Empathy. *The Washington Post*, December 28.
Meredith, James. 2012. *A Mission from God: A Memoir and Challenge for America*. New York: Atria Books.
Noland, Eric. 2011. "Book Review: 'I Beat The Odds' by Michael Oher with Don Yeager." *Los Angeles Times*, February 7. Acccessed May 28, 2017. http://articles.latimes.com/2011/feb/07/entertainment/la-et-book-20110207.
Oher, Michael. 2012. *I Beat the Odds: From Homelessness, to The Blind Side, and Beyond*. New York: Gotham Books.
Patterson, James. 2001. *Brown v. Board of Education: A Civil Rights Milestone and Its Troubled Legacy*. New York: Oxford University Press.

Ravitch, Diane. 2013. *Reign of Error: The Hoax of the Privatization Movement and the Danger to America's Public Schools.* New York: Vintage.

Rhoden, William. 2007. *Forty Million Dollar Slaves: The Rise, Fall, and Redemption of the Black Athlete.* New York: Broadway Books.

Robertson, Campbell. 2012. 50 Years After Integration: Ole Miss Grapples with History. *New York Times*, September 30.

Roberts, Dorothy. 2009. *Shattered Bonds: The Color of Child Welfare.* New York: Basic Books.

Robinson, Cedric. 2000. *Black Marxism: The Making of the Black Radical Tradition.* Chapel Hill: University of North Carolina Press.

Rovell, Daniel. 2014. NFL Most Popular for 30th Year in Row. *ESPN.com*, January 26. Accessed May 28, 2017. http://espn.go.com/nfl/story/_/id/10354114/harris-poll-nfl-most-popular-mlb-2nd.

Said, Edward. 1985. *Beginnings: Intention and Method.* New York: Columbia University Press.

Schermerhorn, Calvin. 2015. *The Business of Slavery and the Rise of American Capitalism, 1815–1860.* New Haven, CT: Yale University Press.

Smith, Earl. 2009. *Race, Sport and the American Dream*, 2nd ed. Durham, NC: Carolina Academic Press.

Sparrow, James. 2011. *Warfare State: World War II Americans and the Age of Big Government.* New York: Oxford University Press.

Spillers, Hortense. 2003. *Black, White, and in Color: Essays on American Literature and Culture.* Chicago: Chicago University Press.

Stulberg, Lisa. 2015. "African American School Choice and the Current Race Politics of Charter Schooling: Lessons from History." *Race and Social Problems* 7: 31–42.

Sublette, Constance, and Ned Sublette. 2016. *The American Slave Coast: A History of the Slave-Breeding Industry.* Chicago: Chicago Review Press.

Thompson, Wright. 2009. Ghosts of Mississippi. *Outside the Lines*, August 1. Accessed May 28, 2017. http://sports.espn.go.com/espn/eticket/story?page=mississippi62.

Wacquant, Loïc. 2002. From Slavery to Mass Incarceration: Rethinking the 'Race Question' in the US. *New Left Review* 13: 41–60.

Webb, Clive. 2005. *Massive Resistance: Southern Opposition to the Second Reconstruction.* New York: Oxford University Press.

White, Earl. 2009. *Race, Sport and the American Dream*, 2nd ed. Durham, NC: Carolina Academic Press.

Williams, Jean. 2007. Will Smith in Pursuit of Excellence. *Black Collegian*, October 25.

Williams, Michael Vinson. 2011. *Medgar Evers: Mississippi Martyr.* Fayetteville, AR: University of Arkansas Press.

Zirin, Dave. 2008. *A People's History of Sports in the United States: 250 Years of Politics, Protest, People, and Play.* New York: The New Press.

5

Comedy and Romance: On *Diff'rent Strokes* and *Webster*

Introduction

The cinema of policing examined in the preceding chapters has shown itself to be preoccupied with the question of black men's origins, if only to devise a means of disciplining their development through moral education and athletic training or punishing their seemingly inevitable failure to conform to normative expectations. Put differently, this cinema is concerned with producing and policing the exceptions to the rule in defense of the constituted imperatives of law enforcement. Along the way we have moved toward increasingly literal forms of the adoption of black boys and men. Alonzo Harris in *Training Day* is figuratively adopted by the Three Wise Men who oversee his operations in the gray zones of legality. The black athletes who co-star in *Pride*, *Friday Night Lights*, and *Coach Carter* are mentored by black and white father-like coaches who variously provide for their wellbeing or leave them to their own devices. And in *The Blind Side* the interracial adoption motif is again complicated by the centrality of a white mother as protector and guide through the black male's rites of passage. This chapter examines such dynamics at earlier points in the life course of black boys, a prehistory of sorts for the coaching stage. It discusses, to that end, the post-civil rights era television situation comedy as an oblique commentary on the racial politics of kinship in the afterlife of slavery, taking *Diff'rent Strokes* and *Webster* as case studies. It traces the black man-child characters that featured in primetime programming throughout the 1980s to earlier figures in US popular culture: the black rascals of the *Our Gang* film series of the

1920s and 1930s and, before that, Topsy of Harriet Beecher Stowe's 1852 novel *Uncle Tom's Cabin*. The intervening years of the mid-twentieth century witnessed sustained attempts by a new generation of black professionals and community advocates to politicize, yet again, the matter of black family preservation against ongoing attempts by state and civil society to shatter the bonds between black parents and children. We will see that this ongoing struggle is inscribed in the discourse of the television sitcom as a tributary to the broader cinema of policing under review and it returns symptomatically in both its performance and its reception.[1]

Buckwheat's Return

In 1966, the late Kristin Hunter-Lattany, award-winning author of the novel *God Bless the Child*, published her second major work of fiction, *The Landlord*. The novel was adapted for the screen several years later by Bill Gunn and on the initiative of Norman Jewison the film production was directed by Oscar Award-winner Hal Foster for United Artists and released in 1970 to mixed reviews. (Its 2007 re-release, interestingly enough, drew unanimous critical acclaim.)[2] *The Landlord* is a political satire about the belated coming-of-age of one Elgar Enders (Beau Bridges), a liberal and affluent young white man—a recent critic describes him as an "indolent American princeling" (Hoberman 2007)—who buys a rundown tenement building in a poor, predominantly black Brooklyn neighborhood in order to displace the local residents, renovate the property, and move into his spacious new accommodations—all to assert a putative independence from the stifling blueblood family dynasty whose accumulated wealth made the folly possible in the first place.

Along the way, Elgar doubts the morality—though not necessarily the ethics—of his original plan as he develops obscure feelings of concern for

---

[1] The black man-child trope persists up to the moment. Consider subsequent black sitcoms like, most notably, William Bickley and Michael Warren's *Family Matters* (1989–1998), starring the nerdy Steve Urkel (Jaleel White); and, more recently, Kenya Barris's *Black-ish* (2014–), where the negligible difference in maturity between the protagonist Andre Johnson (Anthony Anderson) and his sons, teenaged Junior (Marcus Scribner) and eight-year-old Jack (Miles Brown), are a constant theme. One could consult as well the many episodes of Ellen Degeneres and Steve Harvey's children's variety show, *Little Big Shots* (2016–), where, among the guests, young black boys are regularly featured in comic exchanges with Harvey to emphasize their premature badness, boldness, and boastfulness.

[2] See, for instance, the online film review clearinghouse, Rotten Tomatoes, where it was rated "100% Fresh." Leading critics writing for the *Chicago Sun-Times*, *Salon*, *Variety* and the *Village Voice* all offered positive reviews.

those he would evict and, in a sense, adopts the wary tenants as his *ersatz* family, friends, and community; or, at least, as his very passionate preoccupation. This change of heart is prompted in no small part by his budding intimate relationship with Lanie (Marki Bey), a young, light-skinned woman living in the building (she is described in the story as having a white father), and a brief and strained affair with Francine Johnson (Diana Sands), a somewhat older brown-skinned woman and wife of a militant Black Power activist, Copee Johnson (Louis Gossett Jr., who garnered a nomination for the Academy Award for Best Supporting Actor). The affair results in an unplanned pregnancy and, after giving birth to a son, Francine announces in the hospital recovery room that she will relinquish her parental rights, but with a twist. She tells Elgar that she wants their newborn son put up for adoption as a *white* child. When Elgar, taken aback, asks why, Francine replies with biting candor: "Cause I want him to grow up casual, like his daddy" (Jewison 1970).

It turns out that Elgar, now chastened by the profound limits of his self-styled transformation, retains custody of his son and elects to raise him together with Lanie, with whom he has patched things up and will now cohabit somewhere a good distance away from the tenement where they met. With a birth mother like Francine and an adoptive mother like Lanie, it is hard to know if the unnamed son will achieve the desired results seamlessly, light complexion and inherited assets notwithstanding. But the point not to be missed here has to do with the close and problematic association between racial whiteness and the versatile invocation of "the best interest of the child" or, rather, the inverse relation between ascriptions of, or proximity to, racial blackness and the presumed absence or, often enough, the enforced denial of family ties.[3] In this sense, Foster's rendition of Hunter-Lattany's literary intervention manages to touch a central nerve of the post-civil rights dispensation, wherein the restructuring of the welfare state and the retrenchment of conservative racial politics meet the resurgence of mass-mediated popular culture in the service of a severe agenda.

Hunter-Lattany, who would go on to pen another half-dozen novels and short story collections alongside several books for young readers, also worked successfully as a journalist for the *Pittsburgh Courier*, a lecturer on

---

[3]Roberts (2002) speaks directly to this association: "White families…benefit from the presumption of parental fitness and valuable family ties. […] [Holding] up white families as the superior standard against which all other families fail is entrenched in American culture" (67). Throughout the text, however, she speaks to the ongoing denigration of black parental fitness in general and black maternal fitness in particular.

the faculty of the University of Pennsylvania Department of English, an advertising copyeditor and a television screenwriter. She knew something about the ways and means of American popular culture, in other words, and she bore witness to its troubling ideological underpinnings across a range of media for the long haul. Writing some two decades after her debut novel, well on the other side of the revolutionary zeitgeist of the 1960s and now inhabiting an "openly reactionary" political context she described sardonically as "Reaganstruction" (a title justified, in part, by "the images it has produced of Blacks"), Hunter-Lattany observed that "today's producers and screenwriters have no governors on their racist fantasies, no authority to answer to, and no one around to set them straight" (Hunter-Lattany 1984, 84).[4] What the esteemed writer-critic is referencing in the most immediate sense is the dissolution of the Black Power movement of the 1960s and 1970s and the manifold repression—absorption—cooptation of the broader, midcentury resurgence of the longstanding black freedom struggle. What she attempts to expose to a harsh light is the fundament of a cultural formation seemingly frozen in time and without spatial parameter: the black stereotype.

> Black stereotypes were put on the shelf in the 1960s and 1970s—this century's era of Rebellion and Reconstruction—because Blacks were scaring the hell out of the society and "Anything to pacify those people!" was the response. Now that the threat of Black rebellion seems to be past, now that the pacification programs have withered, and now that "affirmative action" has become a tired phrase rendered meaningless by its being stretched to accommodate a broad spectrum called "women and minorities," the Black stereotypes are being hurled at us again with a vengeance, as if TV and film producers were getting even for having to shelve their pet fantasies for so long. And they come at us unrelentingly, without the relief of any realistically human Black portrayals. (Hunter-Lattany 1984, 79–80)

"Put on the shelf," which is also to say held in reserve for future use against the rebellion seeking to dislodge, dismantle or defuse them in pursuit of a radical reconstruction of society. The return of the stereotype in popular culture appears, then, as retribution, or punishment in return for wrongdoing, and it appears without relief or respite, as a state or condition of counterinsurgency. We might wonder about the demand for verisimilitude and the "positive Black images" to which it might give rise, but the description of

---

[4] Thanks to Professor Jennifer Reich for bringing this article to my attention.

the predicament is astute. Indeed, one could have chosen almost at random from the portfolio of cultural imagery unleashed in the historic instance, but the present outrage was catalyzed by the return of a figure of the diminutive black man-child, tracing a line of descent from Billie Thomas' first portrayal of Buckwheat in the 1934 short film *Mama's Little Pirate* as President Franklin Roosevelt implemented the First New Deal all the way to Eddie Murphy's satiric reincarnation of the little rascal on *Saturday Night Live* in the first year of the Reagan Administration's imposition of supply-side economics.

Hunter-Lattany discovers a whole set of contemporary film and television characters within this dubious genealogy, but her paradigm example is Arnold Jackson (Gary Coleman) of the hit situation comedy *Diff'rent Strokes*, which ran for eight seasons and 189 episodes between 1978 and 1986. The analysis, from the title onward, is suffused with a righteous indignation that lends clarity of vision and provides a safeguard against the tendency to forgo necessary judgment in the name of endless complexity. The author is interested in locating the black stereotype and identifying it properly in order to kill it forthwith. Like all of those "Black viewers who [remember] the original Buckwheat and [understand] the dangerous implications of his reincarnation on national television," she watches with "smoking psychological pistols aimed at the screen" and urges all of those of like mind to "ready our guns" for all of those stereotypes that remain alive and well in the popular imagination (79, 84). As a voice of the spirit of rebellion that survives in the minds of black viewers, she claims with pride a vicarious responsibility for killing Buckwheat's latter-day reincarnation (Fig. 5.1).

In reality, it was Eddie Murphy himself who ordered the hit on Buckwheat, an attempt on his part to undo what had immediately become his earliest public persona. It marked an attempt on his part, that is, to interrupt the culture's predisposition to see him as the very stereotype his performance on the popular sketch comedy show was meant to satirize (Miller and Shales 2014). What, then, are we to make of this unacknowledged alignment, this shared discontent, between Murphy and his erstwhile critics? What do they collectively understand about the necessary recourse to (figurative or symbolic) violence in order to counteract the "dangerous implications of [Buckwheat's] reincarnation on national television?" Why does it require such lethal violence to tell the difference between the black stereotype and the black actor who performs it? And why does the attempt at satire seem to fail so completely? What does this say about the force, the ungoverned fantasies, by which the conflation is achieved in the first place?

Fig. 5.1 Eddie Murphy plays "Buckwheat" on Lorne Michaels's *Saturday Night Live* circa 1982. Image reproduced under terms of fair use

Topsy's Legacy

For all that Buckwheat may seem to suggest, pace Hunter-Lattany, about the misrepresentation of black masculinity in US popular culture, it is important to note that the character was initially drawn as a girl and was played by a young actress named Carlena Beard, sister of Matthew "Stymie" Beard of the original *Our Gang* cast. In fact, even after the character was recast and played thereon by Billie Thomas, the actor most widely associated with the role, Buckwheat remained a female onscreen for another two years. To say that Thomas played the role in drag, however, would presuppose a prior gender differentiation that the unremarked nature of his performance would belie. The interchangeability of Beard and Thomas points instead toward a persistent denial, or perceived derangement, of gendered difference for the black child; and this confusion installs the black child as the backdrop before which the gendered figures of white boys and girls can be highlighted.

Like the other black rascals (e.g., Booker T. Bacon, Farina, Mango, Pineapple), Buckwheat can be played either by a young actress or by a young actor and the character can morph from female to male (and back again?) without requiring any significant change in role. The distribution of feminine and masculine features, as it were, does not follow the conventions established by the dominant vantage. The whole system of marks is short-circuited, or hot-wired, in such a way that the black child becomes, in a sense, available for anything—seduction, betrayal, peril, disfigurement, death—a condition of social formlessness that renders the genderless child at once insubstantial (and so beyond any ethical consideration whatsoever) and pure substance (and so immune to any suffering whatsoever). The black child in this rendering is not only the constitutive outside of the social domain that indexes a relation to the coordinates of human sexuality, but also the archaic point of abiogenesis preceding the advent of reproduction itself.

On this note, Buckwheat invokes Harriet Beecher Stowe's earlier literary figure, Topsy, the young enslaved girl purchased by "the kind-hearted plantation owner Augustine St. Clare" (Nyong'o 2002, 376) in her magnum opus *Uncle Tom's Cabin*, the bestselling novel of the nineteenth century and principal text of the international abolitionist movement. We are introduced to Topsy in Chapter XX of that famous work, wherein St. Clare presents Topsy as a challenge to the Christian faith and missionary zeal of his cousin, Miss Ophelia, whose charge it is to "bring [Topsy] up in the way she should go."[5] Unkempt and uncouth, Topsy embodies in Stowe's universe the physical, mental, and spiritual degradation born of slavery: "life among the lowly." More importantly, Topsy is parentless, a normative state of natal alienation and genealogical isolation indicating that enslaved children are, as it were, paradigmatically orphans.

In point of fact, orphan is too strong a word here because, again, it presupposes a parental bond that has been lost after the fact rather than one that is shattered in advance. As Topsy proffers her own origin story: "Never was born… never had no father nor mother, nor nothin'." Topsy, before she is converted and civilized and "adopted" by the family that has bought her, comes from no one and nowhere; she has no sense of time, historical or biographical, and no sense of place, no hearth or home. She is perfectly deracinated or, better, she is without an original origin; her origin is non-originary (Marrati 2005).[6] When Miss Ophelia queries Topsy about her knowledge

---

[5]All citations for Harriett Beecher Stowe's text are from the Project Gutenberg online copy of *Uncle Tom's Cabin, Or Life Among the Lowly* (1852, 2006, 2011).

[6]There are, needless to say, generative possibilities inherent in the political terror of deracination.

of God and the source of divine creation, she replies to the point: "I spect I grow'd. Don't think nobody never made me." It will be Miss Ophelia's principal learning objective to instill in Topsy the fundaments of her abiding faith in Christian salvation. The precondition for Topsy's conversion from ideal slave to nascent Christian lies in her willingness to develop, in the first instance, a capacity to receive love, white love—what is, on this account, tantamount to a capacity for relationality as such—against which can be registered the "outrages of feelings and affections" that constitute, for Stowe, the core evil of slavery as institution.

To this end, Topsy is moved along the righteous path less by the diligent pedagogy of her pious and condescending mistress (for whom a "feeling of repugnance remains in the heart") than by the pristine example of her "sibling" Eva, St. Clare's angelic daughter, who promises Topsy, in one of the pivotal scenes of the story, that "you can go to Heaven at last, and be an angel forever, just as much as if you were white," if only Topsy will accept Eva's enjoinder to "try to be good." Yet, beneath Topsy's seemingly characteristic incorrigibility, it is revealed, finally, that she suffers from a profound fatalism. "Couldn't never be nothin' but a nigger, if I was ever so good," she declares. "There can't nobody love niggers and niggers can't do nothin'!" Eva's outpouring, then, gives the lie to this racist axiom: "Oh Topsy, poor child, *I* love you!" It is here, where Eva, the moral centerpiece of the text, has her first and most instructive effect, that the abolitionist sermon gains its coherence. Topsy's conversion is determinant for Miss Ophelia's and St. Clare's respective changes of heart; Eva's memory becomes crucial to Uncle Tom's renewed commitment to his own Christian faith, opposing as he does unto death the slaveholder Simon Legree and becoming thereby a martyr to the cause of Quimbo's and Sambo's (the slaves who were ordered to kill Tom) subsequent conversions, and so on.

Topsy's chief role in the novel is thus to provide an object lesson in the power of white Christian love to overcome wretchedness among *both* the perpetrators *and* the victims of great moral evils, a love epitomized by the innocence of youthful white femininity. This innocence is not autochthonous, however. It is produced in the moment of juxtaposition between black and white female children in profile, Topsy ("with her usual air of careless drollery and unconcern") and Eva ("her whole face fervent with feeling"). Eva can appear "like the picture of some bright angel stooping to reclaim a sinner" only because Topsy is repeatedly described as "odd and goblin-like" in turn. Topsy plays darkness to Eva's light, crudeness to Eva's refinement, despair to Eva's hope, but, most importantly, incredulity to Eva's belief, reestablishing against the cynicism of the culture of slavery that the abolition

5 Comedy and Romance: On *Diff'rent Strokes* and *Webster*   129

of "heathenism," wherever it be found, is the proper occupation of white Christian women and men.[7]

Cultural critic Tavia Nyong'o observes that dramatic adaptations of *Uncle Tom's Cabin* became "the indispensable play of the late nineteenth-century American theater and para-theater" and remarks the particular popularity of the Topsy character therein (Nyong'o 2002, 376). Most relevant for present purposes is the fact that, while such stage versions "sometimes capitalized on Topsy's transformation from wild child to demure Christian" to advance the text's redemptive vision, they more commonly "misread Stowe's novel and took St. Clare at his word when he claimed [initially] to have bought Topsy as entertainment [rather than to spare her further abuse at the hands of her previous owners], and left her laughably reprobate" (376). He continues:

> As an entertainer, Topsy quickly became one of the most popular characters in the play, as necessary as Uncle Tom. Actors playing Topsy sometimes received top billing in mid-nineteenth-century productions, and Topsy's song was a hot seller in sheet music. Rival productions of *Uncle Tom's Cabin* were soon advertising two Topsies—double the fun and fidelity to Stowe's novel be damned. Topsy's conquest of the landscape of United States popular culture makes her an inaugural figure in the genealogy of performing black children. (376)

It is in this light that Buckwheat can be seen to hyperbolize (perhaps to the point of satire) for a modern filmgoing audience the already exaggerated attributes of the "pickaninny" stereotype that Stowe's sentimental novel both drew upon and canonized in the antebellum period. But if Topsy "appears at a historical moment where a white supremacist and slaveholding nation was actively debating 'the character and destiny' of black folk" (Nyong'o 2002, 376) and the character is mobilized to argue alternately, sometimes simul-

---

[7]Stowe's novel argues that Christianity is anathema not only to slavery and its "outrages of feelings and affections" but also to racism and "the feeling of personal prejudice" it entails, even among abolitionists. Indeed, the convergence of slavery and racism is represented in the character of Simon Legree, a northern racist turned slaveholder, the quintessential godless man. In Chapter XXXIX, she writes of Legree: "No one is so thoroughly superstitious as the godless man. The Christian is composed by the belief of a wise, all-ruling Father, whose presence fills the void unknown with light and order; but to the man who has dethroned God, the spirit-land is, indeed, in the words of the Hebrew poet, 'a land of darkness and the shadow of death,' without any order, where the light is as darkness. Life and death to him are haunted grounds, filled with goblin forms of vague and shadowy dread." The "goblin forms" that Legree sees in Tom and the other slaves on his plantation surely recall the "goblin-like" countenance that Miss Ophelia observes on Topsy's face up until the point of her late conversion, just prior to Eva's untimely death. The question remains, obviously, about how the author, as she is wont to do, ensures her own distance toward the very racist discourse her text invariably reproduces.

taneously, for ultimate assimilation or extinction, then "what is interesting about the black rascals [Buckwheat above all] is less their fit within then current racial policies of segregation" and more "the lack of fit between the racial formation of the time, ideologically considered, and the general economy of innocent pleasures to which *Our Gang* caters" (380).

That is to say, insofar as our critique focuses exclusively upon Buckwheat et al. as the reproduction of stereotypes, it misses the ways in which the popular film and television series seeks "a production of the appropriate ambience for the insinuation of racially unmarked innocence, an innocence predicated upon a forgetfulness of the past that is one of the greatest privileges of whiteness" (381). Buckwheat emerges not so much as a repetition of Topsy, who is firmly embedded in the partisan politics of the day, as an artifact forged in the aftermath of her transformation, or perhaps as an effect of the transformation in the post-bellum white public sphere now supposed to be—or wishing it were—capable of loving black children as its own, "just as much as if [they] were white." Of course, in order to insinuate racially unmarked innocence per se, the marks of racial difference must be reiterated and it is the function of the stereotype to manage the ambivalence generated by the operative contradiction.

We can track in this instance the procedure of a subtle political dynamic identified by historian Robin Bernstein in her book *Racial Innocence* (2011). There she examines, from the antebellum period to the civil rights era in the United States, "the pivotal use of childhood innocence in racial politics" (Bernstein 2011, 65). Her researches in American literature, drama and material culture across the massive upheavals of civil war, industrialization, urbanization, and the rise of mass media find that

> When a racial argument is effectively countered or even delegitimized in adult culture, the argument often flows stealthily into children's culture or performances involving children's bodies. So located, the argument appears racially innocent. This appearance of innocence provides a cover under which otherwise discredited racial ideology survives and continues, covertly, to influence culture. (51)

The emergence of the figure of the pickaninny in popular culture in the mid-nineteenth century preserves for the pro-slavery ideology and beyond what Bernstein calls "the libel of black insensateness" (51) in the face of abolitionism's growing moral force and political power. Insensateness is perhaps the signal attribute of the "pickaninny" stereotype. This is not to say that she is indestructible or even invulnerable, for she is constantly endangered, disfigured and killed; but rather that she does not genuinely feel the pain of the injuries she receives. In a word, she does not suffer. She may experience fear or fright or threat, she may cry out, but none of this actually registers (34–36).[8] This is why and how she inhabits her condition with such strange ease. She may be wretched, as the story runs, but she knows nothing about it. It is all lost on the black juvenile and this imputed incapacity to feel is the very source of amusement, and vindication, for white audiences.

In the *Our Gang* series, the black rascals, unlike their white counterparts, are "subjected to consistently imaginative punishments that frequently culminate in an implied off-screen death" (Nyong'o 2002, 381). To be sure, the emerging generic conventions of the slapstick comedy film render all violence humorous, but its clear racial distribution prompts us to ask: Does the racially unmarked innocence sought onscreen serve, in the final instance, to reassert the whiteness of "the category of the child and, ultimately, the human" (Bernstein 2011, 36) by expelling the black juvenile from its domain over and over again? Does this depressing feature of Buckwheat's first public life in the post-Reconstruction era become an inescapable inheritance for Murphy's satirical man-child post-civil rights? And does it become a contiguous and overwhelming influence on Coleman's Arnold Jackson as well? How might the denial of black childhood—as it migrates from the stage to the silver screen to the television sitcom—supplement the unraveling mythology of the childlike black adult? How might the insensate black juvenile onstage or onscreen counteract arguments circulating in the political sphere about the realities of black suffering, first by the abolitionist movement and later by the twentieth-century black freedom struggle (Fig. 5.2)?[9]

Like the "peculiarly genderless" (Nyong'o 2002, 37) Topsy and the parentless non-child juveniles (and, by implication, the childless "adult" slaves) for which she stands, it would seem that the black also betrays no index of generational movement. Whether young or old, male or female, the black appears in racist culture as a figure whose traits afford no reliable measure of human differentiation. "They all look alike" is more than a notion. It describes in a phrase an entire cultural apparatus whose psychic life not only shapes the visual field, but also structures the social, the political and

---

[8]Bernstein (2011) concludes: "Pain divided tender white children from insensate pickaninnies. At stake in this split was fitness for citizenship and inclusion in the category of the child and, ultimately, the human" (36).

[9]"The unfeeling, un-childlike pickaninny is the mirror image of both the always-already pained African American adult and the 'childlike Negro'" (Bernstein 2011, 35).

Fig. 5.2 Billie Thomas plays "Buckwheat" in Gordon Douglass's *Glove Taps* (1937), part of Hal Roach's *Our Gang* series (1922–1944). Image reproduced under terms of fair use

the economic spheres. And lest we be misled by the eventual emergence in popular culture of black juvenile figures (from Buckwheat to Arnold and beyond) deemed "cute" by the dominant vantage, we are cautioned to recall that even "when a pickaninny was well-dressed and adorable… this icon of insensateness did not call for protection. Whereas the white child manifested innocence, the pickaninny deflected it: the pickaninny made not itself, but its violent context, appear innocent" (Bernstein 2011, 65).

Reforming the White Family

We have already had occasion to label the violent context of the 1980s "Reaganstruction." It bears repeating, however, that this context also provides the conditions of emergence and relations of production for our central point of interest, *Diff'rent Strokes* (1978–1986): the vehicle that thrust Gary Coleman into overnight celebrity and made Arnold Jackson a household name, installed the young protagonist's signature phrase ("What you talkin' bout, Willis?") as an item of common parlance, and laid the

5 Comedy and Romance: On *Diff'rent Strokes* and *Webster*

groundwork for both a successful spinoff, *The Facts of Life* (1979–1988), and its primetime heir, *Webster* (1983–1987), starring Emmanuel Lewis in the eponymous lead role. *Diff'rent Strokes* owes a good deal of its popularity to the towering influence of producers Norman Lear and Bud Yorkin, whose Tandem Productions dominated 1970s television with a series of top-rated and award-winning sitcoms: first and foremost, *All in the Family* (1971–1979), the most watched television show in the country for a record-breaking five consecutive years, but also the notable spinoffs *Maude* (1972–1978) and *The Jeffersons* (1975–1985), alongside another pair of respectable productions featuring black main characters, *Sanford and Son* (1972–1977) and *Good Times* (1974–1979). Yorkin went on to produce the modestly successful black-cast sitcom *What's Happening!!* (1976–1979), under auspices of the short-lived TOY Productions company he co-founded with Bernie Ornstein and Saul Turteltaub.

Lear, in particular, exercised a progressive political influence on the culture of 1970s primetime, pursuing an array of programming that shrewdly integrated social issues into evening television for a diverse viewing audience attempting to make sense of the ongoing social, political, and economic conflicts associated with what the late historian (and distinguished food writer) Josh Ozersky understatedly terms "an era of change" (Ozersky 2003). *All in the Family* staged the countervailing forces of radicalism and reaction unleashed throughout the United States, setting the rants of an unreconstructed white working-class bigot, the infamous Archie Bunker (his name signifying the very personification of Silent Majority *retrenchment*), against a constellation of pithy rejoinders and well-formulated critical commentary from his moderate wife, his hippy daughter and son-in-law, and his diligent, upwardly mobile black neighbors—George and Louise Jefferson and their bright and handsome son, Lionel. *All in the Family*, garnering at its height fully one-fifth of the national population as its audience, kept in productive and pleasurable tension the profound ethical questions and pressing everyday challenges posed by the new social movements for civil rights and Black Power, feminism and women's liberation, sexual revolution, and peace. In the midst of the Nixon Administration's politics of backlash, the sitcom warded against the demonization and caricature afoot in the shifting political climate and held open a space for the normalization of, among other things, alternative family forms, gender equality, and racial integration. Popular culture for Lear, then, was a site for political education and adjudication as much as it was for entertainment and escape.

The Jeffersons, as the Bunker's neighbors came to be known after relocating from the modest row houses of Queens to the posh high-rises of Manhattan's upper east side, elaborated the integrationist theme adumbrated by *All in the Family*, introducing viewers to the first professional middle-class black family in American television history. And the principals, despite the patriarch's trademark antics, were unapologetic about their residence in "a deluxe apartment in the sky." *The Jeffersons* remains one of the longest-running sitcoms in general—outlasting *Friends* (1994–2004), for instance—and the single longest-running black sitcom in particular, surpassing by three seasons the more celebrated *The Cosby Show* (1984–1992). Lear's work not only attempted to symbolically desegregate privilege within the existing arrangements. It also sought to sustain, within generic and institutional constraints, the public discourse of social justice and economic equality articulated most forcefully by the black freedom struggle and, in more attenuated form, the social democratic vision of the Great Society, enabling downward redistributions of wealth, power, and resources. *Sanford and Son*, set in the Watts section of South Central Los Angeles, and *Good Times*, set in the Cabrini-Green housing projects of Chicago's South Side—both locales of major civil disturbances during the "long hot summers" of the late 1960s—dramatized the lives of poor and working-class black families in urban ghettoes, adding a degree of texture to the grim conditions of "American Apartheid" officially acknowledged by the 1968 Kerner Report and perhaps lending a degree of urgency to that federal commission's propositions as well.

This is not to say that the sitcom, even in the hands of a Hollywood liberal like Lear, could become a cultural accompaniment to the sort of revolutionary change that defined the political horizon. Quite the contrary, the genre and the medium have tended in the historic instance to depoliticize, which is to say privatize and individualize, the social problems of the moment. Sociologist Darrell Hamamoto, writing in the twilight of the Reagan—Bush era, discusses this ideological maneuver in his aptly-titled *Nervous Laughter*:

> The symbolic resolution of dilemmas inherent in interpersonal relations has long been the signal strength of the television situation comedy. [...] If macroeconomic events were beyond all comprehension and personal control, then at least a certain measure of solace, security, and autonomy might be found at the level of interpersonal relations revolving around domestic life. In the situation comedy, sociopolitical contradictions become transcoded into personal problems. (Hamamoto 1991, 126–127)[10]

---

[10]For further reading on the history of the situation comedy in American television, see Dalton and Lindner (2005), Moore et al. (2006), Morreale (2003), and Taylor (1989). For treatments of the African American presence in television in particular, see Acham (2004), Fearn-Banks (2006), and Squires (2009).

There is a double movement at work here. First, sociopolitical contradictions, or macroeconomic events, are transcoded into personal problems and sequestered to the sphere of domestic life. Second, after "the dilemmas inherent in interpersonal relations" are loaded with such immense freight, they are brought to a symbolic resolution affording "a certain measure of solace, security, and autonomy." Yet, if interpersonal relations, all things remaining equal, are already complicated by *inherent* dilemmas, and so must always make due with symbolic resolutions where real contradictions remain irreducible, then the second-order ideological labor that this symbolic resolution must perform when interpersonal relations stand in for "events beyond all comprehension and personal control" becomes tenacious indeed. This for the ideal viewer during good times, better known in this case as the postwar liberal consensus of the brief American Century from Harry Truman to Lyndon Johnson. But just as President Dwight Eisenhower, the pivotal figure between the end of the New Deal and the rise of the New Federalism, appointed Richard Nixon as his Vice President, coupling his moderately reformist domestic policies with the anti-communist politics of containment, the liberal consensus contained within itself the seeds of its undoing.

As the full effects of global economic restructuring (e.g., stagnating wages, rising unemployment, decreased social spending) were beginning to be widely felt across the USA and the radical implications of a genuine commitment to the egalitarian ideals of the social movements worked their way into the common sense, media executives, with their fingers held up to the political wind and their noses pressed to the ledger, mandated a return to the guidelines of normalcy that dominated network television programming from its inception in the 1940s through the 1960s. The permission for political experimentation inspired by the era of change was effectively revoked. We might think of this as the cultural accompaniment of the counterrevolutionary political restoration that would usher in the neoliberal orthodoxy informing the dominant discourse of the late twentieth and early twenty-first centuries, including the ascendant doctrine of colorblindness. By the time President Carter took action to address the 1978 public health scandal regarding the Love Canal toxic waste superfund in Niagara Falls, NY, "the salience of 'socially relevant' themes in the television situation comedy as seen in the 1970s gave way to the micropolitics of intimacy" (Hamamoto 1991, 126).[11]

---

[11]For a discussion of this return to normalcy and its relation to internal developments in the corporate structure of the television industry, see Ozersky (2003), especially Chap. 6.

Whither the Black Family

Whereas the relevancy boom of Norman Lear's 1970s attempted to catalyze in its audience an intelligent consideration of the social milieu along with a certain measure of solace, relief, and personal autonomy, the new ratings-driven programming led by NBC's newly appointed president Fred Silverman sought to crush any such consideration and sever any such linkages between education and entertainment as the decade expired. Before coming to NBC, Silverman produced the hit miniseries *Roots* for ABC, earning the latter network the honor of airing the most-watched television event in history (over 70% of the viewing audience tuned into watch the final episode) and destabilizing the longstanding position of CBS as industry leader. What is telling about the success of *Roots*, however, is less its artistic merit or political saliency in its rendering of the story of an African American family "from slavery to freedom" and more its capacity to circulate as commodity, demonstrating to elite decision-makers that empty innovation, rather than stale repetition, was the frontier of expansion: not original, timely or relevant, but simply new, shiny, and different. Nolan Davis, writing for the *New West*, asked at the time, "Is Kunta Kinte the New Fonzie?" (quoted in Ozersky 2003, 177)?

Diff'rent Strokes and *Webster* entered the fray of this post-civil rights era "ratings mania," in which programming selected in order to capture maximum market share was monitored on a daily basis and risks were minimized ruthlessly. What made *Diff'rent Strokes* a safe bet? To begin, it followed the integrationist theme established by *The Jeffersons* several years earlier (Acham 2004, 171). In fact, Gary Coleman made his network television debut in a guest appearance as George Jefferson's streetwise eight-year-old nephew, linking the forthcoming sitcom directly to the ethos and environs of its predecessor. But something was lost in the gap between the launch of *The Jeffersons* in 1975—flanked as it was by *Sanford and Son* and *Good Times*—and the first season of *Diff'rent Strokes* in 1978—when these leading black working-class sitcoms, and the antagonism they inscribed, disappeared. *Diff'rent Strokes* is not just another integrationist sitcom. Rather, like its contemporaries *Benson* (1979–1986) and *Gimme a Break!* (1981–1987), and its next of kin, *Webster*, it features lone black characters isolated in white settings with scant connection to any larger black community, history, culture, or politics. Communications scholar Catherine Squires glosses the distinction in her comprehensive study, *African Americans and the Media*, as follows:

5 Comedy and Romance: On *Diff'rent Strokes* and *Webster*   137

> The networks continued to play it safe in the later '70s and early '80s, with Black TV characters. One prominent trend featured White adoptive parents and mentors who took on the task of socializing Black kids and teens. […] Like the "exceptional" Black characters of the 1960s, these Black children were situated in all-White worlds. Unlike the isolated, middle-class Black predecessors like Julia, though, these characters did not live amongst Whites to prove Blacks were "just like" them, but to provide comic (and some might say racial) relief. Through their sassy, comic uses of Black slang and "street smarts," characters like Gary Coleman's Arnold livened up the "square" White environments, and safely integrated them. But like Julia, these children were divorced from contact with Black communities, suggesting that their Black origins had little to offer them. (Squires 2009, 224)

The suggestion that "Black origins [have] little to offer" children was hardly novel at this time, but it was nonetheless glowing red from the heat of public debate. The National Association of Black Social Workers (NABSW), in light of extensive analysis and direct observation by its professional membership of myriad "barriers to preserving families of African ancestry" in the pursuit of child welfare, issued a comprehensive policy statement at their Fourth Annual Conference in 1972 (NABSW 2003). Known primarily—and almost always reductively—in both the scholarly literature and the mass media for its trenchant (and, to date, unwavering) criticism of interracial adoption and its advocacy of race-matching in child placement, the NABSW actually grounds its controversial position, including the proposal to treat interracial placement as an option of last resort, within an overarching formulation of antiblack racism as ideology, institutional practice and structural condition.

One could, for what it's worth, interrogate the theorization of cultural identity that underwrites much of the NABSW's argument that black children receiving interracial out-of-home placements by child welfare agencies for foster care or adoption "are disengaged from their cultural background" and are therefore "denied the opportunity for optimal development and functioning" (NABSW 2003). One could cite, on that score, existing scholarship that demonstrates how, for instance, no demonstrable difference exists between black and white foster families, and black children adopted interracially fare as well as black children adopted interracially; or how, to take another example, the earlier the age of adoption the higher the chances for successful adjustment are, a prime rationale advanced for permitting, or even promoting, interracial adoption in lieu of extended periods in foster care awaiting eligible black adoptive families; or how even the NABSW's preference for kinship care with extended family members (who are most likely to be black) over out-of-home placement in foster care or adoption (where both of the latter options are more likely to be interracial) nonetheless presents problems of oversight for those relatives not trained and monitored as registered foster families (Moran 2001). I say one could do this, for what it's worth, because the above points are merely arguments in favor of interracial placements without consideration of the bedrock motivation of NABSW's general position: protecting black families from group-based harm.[12]

For those that might presume that family preservation is a categorical public policy goal, the NABSW makes clear that black families, or families of African ancestry, are particularly targeted for destruction. How is this so? Clearly, it is unrelated to any racial disparities in rates of abuse or neglect. As the NABSW states: "contrary to popular opinion, parents of African ancestry are no more likely to abuse or neglect their children but they are more likely to be investigated, have children removed from their home, and receive fewer services that are often found to be substandard." Instead, it has to do with a host of institutional factors that are as readily identifiable as they are deeply entrenched. It is a well-known fact that the child welfare system in the United States has, to put it mildly, serious design flaws. Among these is the tendency to ignore abuse and neglect among the middle and upper classes and to punish abuse and neglect with undue severity among the poor.

Those with resources are not only better able to defend themselves against the intrusions of child welfare agencies, legally if need be; they are also shielded from scrutiny by a geography of privacy and a presumption of fitness even when evidence of trouble presents itself. This is especially true for instances of neglect, representing the lion's share of child welfare cases. Child welfare as a profession systematically conflates child neglect with the material effects of poverty. It fails to recognize the distinction between parental *care*, or lack thereof, and parental *resources*, or lack thereof. When cases of abuse or neglect are found to exist among families of means, those families are much more likely to receive in-home support services leading to rehabilitation and preservation. In cases where out-of-home foster care placement is deemed necessary, the emphasis is laid upon reunification rather than adoption. Since black families are disproportionately poor, it stands to reason that they are more likely to be subjected to intervention and disruption.

---

[12]See Part Three of Roberts (2002) for a theory of African American group-based harm in relation to the child welfare system.

To this extent, the structural effects of the racial wealth gap shape the unequal operations and outcomes of child welfare.[13]

However, the "color of child welfare" is overdetermined by systemic racial discrimination by policymakers, agency administrators, and caseworkers. Legal scholar Dorothy Roberts, a leading commentator on the issue, is unequivocal: "America's child welfare system is a racist institution" (Roberts 2002, 99). That is, even when controlling for a host of typical indicators of child endangerment—from parental substance abuse to physical or sexual violence—black families are far more likely than their white counterparts to experience state intervention and that intervention is far more likely to be punitive, resulting in permanent separation of parents and children and of siblings from one another. The disqualification of black family rights is rooted in what Roberts calls "the system's fundamental flaw": "The child welfare system is designed not as a way for government to assist parents to take care of their children but as a means to punish parents for their failures by threatening to take their children away" (74). The child *welfare* system is more accurately described by the official title it carries in many states throughout the country: child *protective* services. For this reason, the system is activated "only after children have already experienced harm and puts all the blame on parents for their children's problems" (74). Importantly, this shift in orientation toward protection is strictly correlative with the shift in the racial demographics in child welfare from overwhelmingly white to disproportionately black.[14]

The group-based harm of the system's child "protection" orientation is bound up with a set of popular assumptions about black family dysfunction and parental unfitness that draw upon and reinforce longstanding stereotypes about "deviant Black mothers and absent Black fathers," painting a picture of an anomalous "matriarchal" structure that distorts child development and undermines community development. At bottom, these "myths about Black mothers," dating back to pro-slavery ideology and, later, the

---

[13]Roberts reports that "the economic fortunes of white and Black children are just the opposite: the percentage of Black children who *ever* lived in poverty while growing up is about the same as the percentage of white children who *never* did" (Roberts 2002, 46). See Part One of Roberts (2002) for more on the intersections of race and class in child welfare.

[14]The sharp statistical disproportion between white and black families that Roberts cites in her research has eased slightly in the last 15 years or so, but the structural dynamics remain firmly intact. Black families remain far more likely than their white counterparts to face forced separation, black children remain vastly overrepresented among children in child protective services and foster care, and they remain the least like to find adoptive homes, especially black male children. See, generally, Child Welfare Information Gateway (2017).

attack on Reconstruction and the defense of segregation, "confirm the need for the state to intervene in their homes to safeguard their children and to ensure that their children do not follow their dangerous example" (Roberts 2002, 61). The careless mother, the matriarch, the welfare queen all represent the frightful destiny of Topsy grown up, still suffering from "outrages of feeling and affection" despite gaining family rights post-emancipation. As such, the modern child welfare system inherits, in inverted form, the moral dilemma of *Uncle Tom's Cabin*: how to save black children? Like the liberal sentimental abolitionism of the nineteenth century, the neoliberal child welfare system of the twentieth century must maintain the very segregation, and domination, of black children that its mission is, ostensibly, meant to overcome.

It is in this context that the seemingly contradictory fear of miscegenation and the fear of black separatism in the white imagination can be understood as two sides of the same coin. Whereas miscegenation represents a supposedly biological threat to mythic white racial purity, black separatism is regarded as a sociological threat of greater familial and communal dysfunction, leading inexorably to increased crime and general social disorder. The contorted mechanisms of black children's state-sponsored discipline and punishment, particularly with respect to "un-parented" black boys, overlays the otherwise unspoken belief that black reproduction *as such* is a problem. William Bennett, conservative moralist and former Secretary of Education for the Reagan Administration, said as much during an episode of his Morning in America radio program in 2005, an outlet with over one million active listeners. While addressing a caller who opined that legal abortion hurt the US economy by reducing the number of productive workers paying into the Social Security system, Bennett offered his own hypothetical to chasten such wild speculation.

> **BENNETT**: All right, well, I mean, I just don't know. I would not argue for the pro-life position based on this, because you don't know. I mean, it cuts both—you know, one of the arguments in this book *Freakonomics* that they make is that the declining crime rate, you know, they deal with this hypothesis, that one of the reasons crime is down is that abortion is up. Well…
>
> **CALLER**: Well, I don't think that statistic is accurate.
>
> **BENNETT**: Well, I don't think it is either, I don't think it is either, because first of all, there is just too much that you don't know. But I do know that it's true that if you wanted to reduce crime, you could—if that were your sole purpose, you could abort every black baby in this country, and your crime

rate would go down. That would be an impossible, ridiculous, and morally reprehensible thing to do, but your crime rate would go down. So these far-out, these far-reaching, extensive extrapolations are, I think, tricky. (Seifter 2005)[15]

Tricky indeed: Bennett and his defenders went to considerable lengths to rationalize his assertion by denegation (e.g., "We should never commit this atrocity, but if we did..."). And the agonizing public debate that ensued served mainly to entrench the condemnation of blackness, even among Bennett's anti-racist critics (e.g., "OK, black male crime rates may, in fact, be higher, but the reasons are not racially inherent...").[16] The problematic assumptive logic and conceptual framework of Senator Daniel Patrick Moynihan's infamous 1965 report, *The Negro Family: The Case for National Action*, was reiterated broadly across the board.[17]

Roberts, then, helps to clarify why the problem of interracial adoption that emerged in full force in the discourse of Black Power in the 1970s is important but not essential to the historical analysis of state violence against the black family, and the refraction of this violence in the products of popular culture. The crucial element here is, to borrow the phrasing of literary critic Hortense Spillers, the continuing negation of black women's "mother right" as a "feature of human community" (Spillers 2003, 227). This negation is the hard core of the more general fact that "the laws and practices of enslavement did not recognize, as a rule, the vertical arrangements of their family" (Spillers 2003, 249), a general fact that also characterizes the

---

[15] Some might rightly hear a resonance between Bennett's comments and those offered more recently by Congressman Steve King (R-Iowa). King shared on social media that he concurred with the public positions of far-right Dutch politician Geert Wilders, then leader of the racist, xenophobic Party of Freedom (*Partij voor de Vrijheid*). Wilders was convicted in 2016 by a Dutch court of inciting racial and religious discrimination against North Africans in the Netherlands. King, who had already made past public statements extolling the superiority of the civilization of the white Christian West, wrote in March 2017: "Wilders understands that culture and demographics are our destiny. We can't restore our civilization with somebody else's babies." When asked to clarify in an interview with CNN later that week, King doubled down by saying, "Of course I meant exactly what I said," and then concluded: "If you go down the road a few generations or maybe centuries with the intermarriage, I'd like to see an America that's just so homogenous that we look a lot the same, from that perspective" (Gupta 2017). From the present discussion, we see that King's fears of a demographic threat posed by immigration from Asia, Latin America and the Middle East is rooted in a deeper, more long-standing tradition of antiblack sexual regulation, segregation and population control endemic to the racialization of modern slavery from at least the fifteenth century onward.

[16] For an overview of the debate, including the mischaracterization of Steve Levitt's *Freakonomics*, see Saletan (2005). The phrase "condemnation of blackness" is from Muhammad (2010), who tracks the development of the social, economic and political conflation of blackness and crime in the post-Reconstruction-era USA.

[17] For reflection on the Moynihan Report on the 50th anniversary of its publication, see Geary (2015).

political culture and policy environment of "the afterlife of slavery"—post-emancipation, post-civil rights (Hartman 2007). Adopting this critical insight, family matters for the African American personality assume a different hue and cry. As such, "one aspect of the liberational urge for freed persons is not so much the right to achieve the nuclear family as it is the wish to rescue African-Americans from flight… essentially, to bring the *present* into view rather than the past" (Spillers 2003, 249).

Perhaps, then, this is why William Merritt, the former president of the NABSW, describes interracial out-of-home placements as a "particular form of genocide" (quoted in Rothman 2004, 195). If to some it may seem "absurd and hurtful to use the language of genocide when you look at the acts of individual loving white parents of black children" (Rothman 2004, 196), then they only need to look upstream to those processes that systematically displace black children and push them into the adoption stream in the first place. This is why, according to sociologist Barbara Rothman, "it is not absurd to think in terms of genocide when you look at social policy" (Rothman 2004, 196).[18] Accordingly, the seemingly banal micropolitics of intimacy depicted in the television sitcom, if re-inscribed, or if viewed for what is already inscribed there as subtext or throwaway line or opening gambit, can follow a thread back to those occluded macroeconomic events and sociopolitical contradictions that otherwise remain beyond comprehension.

Arnold Emerges

To be sure, *Diff'rent Strokes* was a "safe" show, as Squires notes above. But nominal safety begs the question: safe for whom and from what? If NBC was indemnifying itself against financial risk, it did so by addressing the paramount political issue of black freedom, at least this one "aspect of the liberational urge for freed persons," through a process of inoculation. Mr. Drummond (Conrad Bain), a wealthy white widower living

---

[18]Rothman explains further: "Adoption is the result of some very bad things going on upstream, policies that push women into having babies that they then cannot raise. Racism is of course the other feeder stream: More women of color find themselves placed just there, placed willingly or very much against their will. Some make adoption plans and place their babies in waiting arms; some have their children wrenched away by a deeply neglectful state, which then finds neglect. A lot of what adoption is about is poverty; a lack of access to contraception and abortions; a lack of access to the resources to raise children. In addition, a lot of what poverty is about in America is racism. Moreover, as much as the black community stands there with open arms, absorbing as many of those babies and children as it can, the same poverty that pushes all those babies and children into the adoption stream ensures that there won't be enough black homes to take them all" (Rothman 2004, 197–198).

in a Park Avenue high-rise, has agreed to look after his recently deceased black housekeeper's two sons, Arnold (Gary Coleman) and Willis Jackson (Todd Bridges). Mr. D, as he is affectionately known, describes the late Mrs. Jackson in terms redolent of the mammy stereotype: "a sweet wonderful woman…like a member of the family" with a "great sense of humor." And his description of her sons as "orphans…from Harlem…two innocent, sweet, helpless little boys" would not be altogether unfamiliar to Stowe's Augustine St Clare.

In Season 1, Episode 2, "Social Worker," the Drummond family is visited by a social worker, *Ms.* (she emphasizes, "not Mrs") Aimsley, for a routine evaluation of post-placement adjustment. After being coached by Mr. Drummond to give positive reviews of their home life to date, the boys put on a dog and pony show to placate the stern government agent. Referring to themselves as "Happy Willis" and "Delirious Arnold," the former describes Mr. D as "a real cool dude" and the latter reveals as an obvious aside that "confidentially, the man is loaded… L-O-D-I-D." Ms. Aimsley notes the material comforts of their new surrounds (we learn later in the episode that Mr. D is so rich, in fact, that he has never even heard of a garage sale). However, she is compelled nonetheless to ask: "Boys, have you ever lived in a non-black neighborhood before?" Willis deflects this first query: "Just once when our landlord in Harlem painted our building white." Ms. Aimsley continues: "Arnold, do you miss seeing other black children your age?" And Arnold parries: "No ma'am! If I miss seeing a black kid *my* age, all I gotta do is look in the mirror" (Fig. 5.3).

Throughout the consultation, the boys put on airs *as* rich white children (i.e., adapted), and not the children *of* a rich white man (i.e., adopted), as evidence of Mr. D's fitness. They smile broadly, they walk arm-in-arm, they affect proper enunciation and grammar, and they use a Pollyannaish tone and idiom reminiscent of Mr. D's prep schooled daughter, Kimberly (Dana Plato). Ms. Aimsley, of course, sees through the amusing act, punctuated as it is by Arnold's black vernacular punch lines, but she admits to Mr. D after the fact that 'the boys seem to be getting along just fine and, frankly, I'm surprised.' 'Why should you be?' asks Mr. D.

MS. AIMSLEY: Well, it's been my observation that white children are usually happier in white families and black children with black families.

MR. D: Oh, really?

MS. AIMSLEY: Mm-hmm, but then it just might be that money *can* buy happiness. It must be nice to be L-O-D-I-D.

Fig. 5.3 Arnold Jackson (Gary Coleman) and his brother Willis (Todd Bridges) raise their concerns with Mr. Drummond (Conrad Bain) in Jeff Harris and Bernie Kukoff's *Diff'rent Strokes* circa 1979. Image reproduced under terms of fair use

Ms. Aimsley is suggesting, of course, that Arnold and Willis have fallen in love with their own upward mobility, rather than forming any genuine emotional bond with their new guardian. Mr. D replies to the point: "It's true, I do have money. But I really do care a lot for those boys." And that is that.

Following this visit, however, Mr. D is so astonished by the evident facts of racial segregation in the United States that have been brought politely to bear against his studied inattention to the world beneath his thirtieth-floor balcony[19] that he repeats to his white housekeeper, the unflappable Mrs. Garrett, what was offered by the caseworker as a—to boot, computer-generated—truism of the profession: "black children belong with black families." Arnold inadvertently overhears this distressing fragment of the conversation and takes it, out of context, as a racist rejection of their nascent filiation. Arnold relays the message to his older brother and Willis registers the mood of disappointment: "And all the time I thought that was one dude who was colorblind." Beyond the immediate hurt, though, Arnold is perplexed:

ARNOLD: Why would he pretend to like us, Willis?

WILLIS: I guess cause we're the latest fad in honkyland.

ARNOLD: What does that mean?

WILLIS: It means we better get outta here before he puts us in a jockey suit and plants us in the front lawn.

While the reference to the racist connotations of the black lawn jockey replica is meant to insinuate the young boys into the historical derogation of adult black masculinity, they are both, and Arnold in particular, too young to fit the mold. Moreover, "the latest fad in honkyland" has placed them, not on the exterior, but on the interior of the domestic sphere of this "man of means," perhaps not unlike the ceramic "pickaninny" figurines evoked by Topsy and Buckwheat in earlier moments. As Mr. D has already recounted for them in the opening episode the ostentatiously long list of his possessions—the elite education, the high art collection, the square footage of Manhattan real estate, the antique furniture, the hot tub, the color TV and stereo, the priceless city view—Willis is rightly concerned that he and Arnold have become part of Mr. Drummond's collection of things.

---

[19] Although this isn't entirely true. Mr. D, in the same episode, quips that he's had a good day because he walked all the way home from the office through Central Park without being mugged. He also jokes, in the first episode, when bragging to Arnold and Willis about the obscene wealth they will now enjoy as his new charges, that on a clear day one can see from his balcony all the way across the Hudson River to New Jersey—likely the multiracial, multiethnic working-class neighborhoods of Jersey City—"not that anyone would want to."

Willis' clarification is lost on Arnold, of course, since Arnold is, if not unaware of, then at least underwhelmed by, the force of antiblack racism. (The general dynamic between the brothers is one in which Willis tries to impress upon Arnold the cold, hard truths of the world—as he understands it in light of his thirteen years—and Arnold tries to encourage Willis to lighten up.)[20] Arnold and Willis notify the social worker forthwith to indicate their dissatisfaction at Mr. Drummond's residence and announce their preference for re-placement with a black adoptive family. When Ms. Aimsley puts Mr. D on notice about the impeding change, he attempts in vain to talk to the boys about their apparent change of heart. He finds them in their room watching TV, laughing, intent on ignoring him.

> **MR. D**: What's so funny guys?
>
> **WILLIS**: The whites were attacking the Indians and the Indians are winning.
>
> **ARNOLD**: Aw man, talk about a fast haircut!

This oppositional reading of a scene from the Western film genre sets the stage for what the boys believe is their defensive and reactive rejection of Mr. D in the face of his racist pronouncement, and their rejection is rendered through a curious racial transposition, like Indians repelling the aggression of white colonial expansion through armed self-defense. When Willis reiterates Arnold's reiteration of Mr. D's reiteration of Ms. Aimsley's reiteration of the professional common sense—"blacks belong with black and whites belong with white"—their newfound preference for a black family is offered without explanation and, for all intents and purposes, requires no rational justification. "It's just that things ain't working out," says Willis. Dejected and confused, but credulous, Mr. D does not press the issue and in his very brief concession speech he simply states: "I see. Well, I only want to do what's best for you,' cause I love you." With that, Mr. D accepts the failure of his final promise to Arnold and Willis' mother and his former housekeeper. Recall that Mrs. Garrett replaced Mrs. Jackson in her capacity

---

[20]On Arnold's role as comic relief, see Heffernan (2006). There the author writes that *Diff'rent Strokes* "is the representative document of the surreal race politics of 30 years ago, which made gods of limousine liberals and allowed minstrelsy to inform black roles for children. If the 60s had radical chic, the 70s and 80s had radical cuteness. The face of this ideology in primetime was Arnold Jackson... At the time Arnold struck audiences as an endlessly endearing trickster figure, whose Harlem-bred sensitivity to being hustled had been reduced to a sweetie-pie affectation: 'What you talkin' about, Willis?' Arnold was supposed to be shrewd and nobody's fool, but also misguided; after learning his lessons, he was easily tamed and cuddled."

and so, as her proxy, the white woman who now occupies the position inflects the latter's wishes without account. Mrs. Garrett consoles Mr. D accordingly:

> You're very kind and loving, and you make a wonderful father. Besides, look what they got here. I'm telling you, these kids are living in the lap of luxury. [...] Believe me Mr Drummond, that black couple is gonna have to be something else before those boys will give up all of this and… leave you.

As it turns out, "that black couple," Geoffrey and Olivia Thompson, *is* something else. The heads of a successful manufacturing business that provides barrels to overseas oil refineries, Mr. Drummond's luxury apartment—seven-figures, two-stories, four-bedrooms *and* a housekeeper—simply reminds the Thompsons of the "little flat in London" they use "just for weekends." Now that the gross material advantages Mr. D represents with respect to their tenement in Harlem seem quaint in comparison to the Thompsons' fortune, the boys must address the racial dimensions of their prospective adoption *ceteris paribus*. And, under the circumstances, they do choose to vacate the premises. Yet before Arnold's *faux pas* can run its course—and Arnold is designated the "big dummy" here—the "rather opinionated" social worker, in a moment of self-satisfaction, repeats the race-matching mantra, reveals the source of misunderstanding, and catharsis begins. Importantly, it is Olivia Thompson, appearing as Arnold and Willis' prospective black adoptive mother, that rearticulates the last wishes of their recently departed black birth mother. And, according to this strange calculus of race, class and gender, only *she*, a black woman of means, can give the (posthumous) blessing: "Black or white, it's *love* that counts."

The triangulation is thus complete. Mrs. Garrett is the working-class *white* counterpart to Mrs. Jackson the working-class *black* woman; Mrs. Thompson is the *owning-class* black counterpart to Mrs. Jackson the *working-class* black woman. Mr. Drummond would seem to be the fourth term, the *white owning-class* male counterpart to Mrs. Jackson the *working-class black* woman, but within the semiotic square that positions these women along axes of race and class, the missing and unspoken term is, in fact, the late Mrs. Drummond. What makes it possible for Mr. Drummond to establish the double substitution of his custodial claim is this series of relays or mediations wherein the terms of racial domination and class struggle are progressively isolated and negated. What remains, however, is the gender trouble and sexual panic of a wealthy, middle-aged, presumptively heterosexual white widower who must, on his word, take up the task of raising two young black boys—in place of the white son he always wanted and alongside his teenaged white daughter.[21] In this way, the question of interracial intimacy that had been, as noted, only recently broached in the history of America television by the late 1970s, debuts in the proper sense as a matter of male bonding, intergenerational and patriarchal, in the relative absence, or management, of white women and the total absence of black women (Fig. 5.4).

Here the desire that black children might have for filiation with black caretakers or relatives, and perhaps even the larger idea and ethos of black community as such, has no positive value; it exists, on this telling, only as a reaction formation against the rejection of intimacy by white society.[22] More importantly, though, the subject of the drama has been changed from considerations of "the best interests of the (black) child" to "the best intentions of the (white) parent." This much should give pause to the careful viewer. But, ultimately, it is the displacement of "the vertical arrangements of [black] family" in general and of black "mother right" in particular that makes possible the entire dialectic between white father and black sons, the enduring dream of interracial fraternal bond. When Ms. Aimsley reports at the end of the episode that she will tell the computer to "go suck a lemon," she is not refuting a racist presumption, even one taken up in a misguided white liberal's attempt to provide for black child welfare. Rather, she is endorsing, and thereby giving state sanction to, the rejection of the very concern raised by the NABSW, in the name of Black Power, for the

---

[21] Given the history of American film and television, one would think that *Diff'rent Strokes* would generate controversy for placing under the same roof a pubescent black boy (Willis) and a pubescent white girl (Kimberly), both ages thirteen. In a sense, the too obvious objection to that doubly taboo interracial, incestuous sexuality was repressed, only to return in a fascination with the perversion attributed to the cast off-screen. All three of the former child stars—Gary Coleman, Todd Bridges, and Dana Plato—struggled with substance abuse and various legal problems that led to financial ruin. Plato additionally gained some notoriety when she posed nude for *Playboy* magazine and later starred in several soft-core pornographic films. A similar aura of perversion would attach itself to Emmanuel Lewis, star of *Webster*, with the emergence of his close and public friendship with Michael Jackson, especially as the latter faced allegations of sexual crimes against children.

[22] This dynamic has been noted regarding questions of identity for black characters broadly in contemporary American television. See, for instance, Ibelema (1990), who summarizes as follows: "There is a definite pattern in all the episodes on African or racial identity. First, concern with African identity results from a personal crisis. The African American character does not project his African cultural identity in normal times. Overt awareness and projection are triggered by an event or in moments of self-doubt. Secondly, the character begins to engage in uncharacteristic behavior, rejects most social norms, and acts in exaggeratedly strange ways. In other words, overt awareness and expression of African identity is portrayed as a form of personal revolution and social rebellion. Thirdly, the character is confronted with 'evidence' that convinces him that assertion of African identity is not necessary. Fourthly and finally, the character reverts to his old ways, and the identity crisis is over" (Ibelema 1990, 122–123).

5 Comedy and Romance: On *Diff'rent Strokes* and *Webster* 149

Fig. 5.4 Gary Coleman poses for press pictures as "Arnold" on Diff'rent Strokes circa 1980. Image reproduced under terms of fair use

preservation of black families. It is not unreasonable to conclude, then, that *Diff'rent Strokes* is, first and foremost, *about* the death of the black mother. Whatever other ancillary themes and topics the show may take up (e.g., the growing pains of adolescence, the moral training of children, the contemporary reconfiguration of the nuclear family), the critical point is that this foundational violence is sedimented into its symbolic universe for the duration; first, by restricting the matter to the distal question of interracial adoption and, second, by preempting that question altogether with the canard of colorblindness. In fact, the alternative white family formation—single parent and blended—becomes the site for the re-institutionalization of black natal alienation, a gentrified revision of the bourgeois family that insulates interracial intimacy from the potential turbulence of its historic association with miscegenation.[23]

Arnold Redux

Noting the success of NBC's production over five seasons, ABC launched its own spinoff in 1983. *Webster* presents the story of George Papadopolis (Alex Karras, former standout defensive lineman for the Detroit Lions), a sports newscaster and former professional football player, and his wife Katherine Papadopolis (Susan Clark), a socialite, philanthropist, and consumer rights advocate. Theirs is an interethnic and cross-class marriage: George, a working-class child of Greek immigrants and Katherine, a member of the WASP upper crust. These factors of minor internal difference will sensitize the newlywed couple to the fortune that awaits them and provide degrees of mediation for the major difference they will broach in their adoption of Webster, the son of George's former football teammate, after his parents are killed in a car accident. And the troubles involved are announced directly.

In Episode 1, "Another Ballgame," Webster arrives at the Papadopolis residence "special delivery" by way of a courier service, rather than through the intermediaries of an adoption agency. After George receives Webster from the courier, Katherine asks apprehensively, "George, did we just buy a child?" Webster's commodity status is highlighted in this opening scene by a number of formal elements, including George's objectifying grip—arms outright with hands beneath his armpits, at the level one would position a ventriloquist's dummy—and Webster's costume-like "little man" suit and tie, stiff posture, and rolling eyes, silently searching the apartment. It dawns on the couple in short course what they are being asked to assume, and Katherine objects strongly to the consequent restructuring of the domestic sphere. The ensuing exchange is telling:

---

[23]Wiegman (2002) makes a related argument is made with respect to Richard Benjamin's *Made in America* (1993). She writes about how "the absence of interracial sexuality… is critically important to the presence of white multiracial desire" in narratives of liberal whiteness for the post-segregationist era" (Wiegman 2002, 861).

5 Comedy and Romance: On *Diff'rent Strokes* and *Webster*

GEORGE: Well, he's kinda cute.

KATHERINE: That's not the point.

GEORGE: Then I can't keep him?

KATHERINE: He's not a puppy, he's a child. [...] We'll do everything we can for him. We'll find him a nice home.

GEORGE: What is he a puppy?

KATHERINE: That's not fair, George.

Webster, who has wandered into the bedroom where the adults are talking, overhears the deliberations. He feels himself an imposition in his new home and leaves the following note on his way out the door: "You have a nice house here. A boy would be happy." George tracks down Webster at the football stadium nearby and attempts to explain why he and his wife cannot or, rather, *should* not adopt him. Webster, in turn, appeals to George's latent desire for children despite his and Katherine's decision to remain childless by choice in pursuit of their respective careers. Webster pleads: "I don't eat much. I know how to make my own bed. I'm tidy." George demurs: "You can stay with us as long as it takes for us to find you a good home." Webster parries: "What am I, a puppy?" George, taking the point, asks, finally: "Don't you want a family?" Webster, undaunted, retorts: "Don't you?" So, whereas George impresses upon Webster the value of living a life with people who are eager, rather than reluctant, to care for you, Webster impresses upon George the improbable prospect of a life with a child who, like a puppy, actively solicits your care rather than one that, at best, makes a virtue out of necessity.

George is won over by Webster's persistence, a persistence that is curious not only for the age of seven, even in TV land, but also given the fact that Webster is, at the time we meet him, in the most immediate shock and mourning over the sudden loss of his parents, his home, and the whole of his natal surround. Together now, George and Webster attempt to prevail on Katherine, who makes defensive recourse to the pluralist idea of different strokes. She explains to Webster: "Take the zoo, for instance. Some women go to the zoo. They love to go to the zoo. They go to the zoo all the time. I am not one of those women. I don't like the zoo." Webster's task, and his stake, is to convince Katherine why a trip to the zoo, where presumably she will encounter Webster as if for the first time, can provide a source of enrichment rather than displeasure. No longer a stray animal, he is now a caged one, "radical cuteness" intact. The appeal to family by surrogate succeeds by and by, so much so that this very odd white couple begins to rethink their life plan, which is to say principally that the liberal feminist ideals Katherine lives by become attenuated. Over the course of the first several episodes we witness the reconversion of the decidedly non-domestic career woman trying diligently to learn the traditional gender roles she previously rejected, making a bid, for Webster's sake, to start "homesteading in Middle America," as she puts it. Within this sweep, white masculinity can remake and reassert itself through a political rapprochement with the social effects of the movements for racial justice and gender equality, betraying a kinder, gentler white man for the new age (Fig. 5.5).

The true reckoning, however, is delayed but not evaded, returning with misleading openness in Episode 8, "Travis." It is not immediately clear how the title is related to the themes of the episode, except that we know Webster's father is Travis Long (Harrison Page), George's former teammate. Travis asked George to serve as Webster's legal guardian in the event of his and his wife's untimely death and that request comes under intense and belated scrutiny here. In the opening scene of the episode, Katherine chats after exercising with her friend Ellen, a black woman who Katherine knows well from her college days. Despite their otherwise cordial rapport, Ellen is bothered, on principle, by Katherine's interracial adoption and says so without further explanation: "I don't think a white couple should be raising a black child." When Katherine takes this news to George for discussion, her practical-minded husband counsels: "It's an opinion… Does an opposing opinion automatically make you wrong? […] What makes her the expert?" But Katherine has a serious contention: "Well [Ellen is] a housewife, mother of three, she's black, she has a Ph.D. in sociology specializing in the placement of minority children, and she's written this book, *Trauma and Culture Shock of the Adolescent Victims of the Liberal White Left*. […] She is an expert in her field." Furthermore, Katherine concurs, "Webster has a right know about his culture, about his background, about his heritage, about where he comes from," assuming Ellen's objection is grounded, after all, in a concern for Webster's awareness of "culture," "background," and "heritage."

It remains perfectly ambiguous what precisely is the source of Ellen's expertise—her being black, a wife, a mother, a sociologist, a published author or a specialist in the placement of minority children—though one would think the last would be decisive. In any event, the summary judgment of a black professional—whose "rather opinionated" research might be cited by Ms. Aimsley's computer—stands in for the pointed and complex debate inaugurated, or reignited, by the NABSW more than a decade earlier. And, much as in the case of *Diff'rent Strokes*, the issue is reframed beyond

Fig. 5.5 Webster Long (Emmanuel Lewis) hugs George Papadapolis (Alex Karras) in Stu Silver's *Webster* circa 1983. Image reproduced under terms of fair use

recognition, as the very notion of black expertise on race matters, and the legitimacy of the political demands it recalls, is not so much refuted as it is circumvented. George, now impatient, says: "Do you think that kid in there has got a problem because we're white?" "I don't know," Katherine replies.

"But I sure would like to find out." And so they do. Predictably, Webster does not have a problem with the fact that George and Katherine are white, but this is not revealed without routing the determination of the child's approval, already a displacement of the adjudication of his best *interest*, into an economy of sacrifice.

> **KATHERINE**: Are you ever embarrassed that George and I are your guardians?
>
> **WEBSTER**: I'm confused. Do I do that to you?
>
> **GEORGE and KATHERINE**: No.
>
> **WEBSTER**: Then I guess you don't do that to me.
>
> **KATHERINE, to GEORGE**: Maybe he doesn't understand what we're trying to say. He is only seven.

Indeed, Webster interprets his guardians' concerns wrong side up. "They're very nice, Teddy," he muses to his stuffed animal companion. "They wouldn't ever want to hurt my feelings. But I don't think they were telling the truth. I think I do embarrass them." Webster is sure that his guardians would not *want* to hurt his feelings, but they have, in raising this awkward question in so awkward a way, inadvertently done just that. In asking him about embarrassment, that is, they cause him embarrassment, a "confusion or disturbance of mind." Webster seeks consolation in a young white playmate, Melanie, but her ingénue's advice only compounds the misunderstanding. Consulting the dictionary entry for "embarrassment," Webster and Melanie, through a process of elimination, land on a definition indicating "difficulty arising from the want of money to pay debts" and conclude thereby that Webster presents a financial burden to George and Katherine. Having defined, and more importantly, *quantified* the problem in this way, Webster sets out to remedy the situation by selling off his toys to neighborhood kids, raising $1.87 for the cause.

As Webster plies his wares, Katherine is shown following Ellen's advice to bone up on the scholarly research on white families raising black children, suggesting a parallel in her and Webster's respective, albeit well-meaning errors. Each of them mistakenly believes that they are a problem to the other. George remains the skeptic, dismissing outright or, rather, disavowing the very question of race-conscious parenting as nothing more than an unnecessary source of discomfiture for parents and children alike. Katherine notices the impromptu clearance sale and interrupts Webster's commerce.

5 Comedy and Romance: On *Diff'rent Strokes* and *Webster*

Fig. 5.6 Webster talks with Katherine Calder-Young Papadapolis (Susan Clark) circa 1983. Image reproduced under terms of fair use

After learning of Webster's plan, Katherine explains: "Our problem is much more serious than money. I don't know if we're the right parents for you. I like you very much, but the truth is that you're black and we're white and I'm not sure if being together as a family is for the best." Webster reiterates his earlier stance and, again, misinterprets: "I don't mind that we're different colors. Oh, I see, *you* mind." Fed up with the sort of handwringing that characterizes the "liberal white left," George insists to Katherine: "I'm sure this arrangement is gonna work. Darling, we're not black, I can't help that, but we're the right family for Webster." "How do you know?" Katherine implores. "How can you be so sure? Make me sure" (Fig. 5.6).

George, meeting the demand, gathers his newly blended interracial family on the couch to "settle the whole thing" in a scene deeply reminiscent of Spencer Tracy's climactic soliloquy in Stanley Kramer's 1967 film, *Guess Who's Coming To Dinner?* In this instance, however, the director makes use of a flashback sequence to add an important authorial twist to the white patriarch's pronouncement. It is seven years prior, on Webster's birthday, and George has just walked off the field in the middle of a professional football game with his friend and teammate, Travis. Now at the hospital, they are buzzing with excitement about Webster's arrival when Travis asks George to be Webster's godfather. George is honored by the request, but concerned about its implications.

GEORGE: Travis, you think it's okay for a white guy to bring up a black child?

TRAVIS: I don't know about that, man. But if you're the white guy, and it's my kid in question… just why you being so difficult, you want the gig or not?

GEORGE: Well, I was only thinking about people. You know how people are.

TRAVIS: People are going to think whatever they want to think. Nothing is going to change, George, not completely. If people look at what we do as some kind of social statement then that's their problem. But I'm not giving you my kid to make a social statement. I'm giving you my kid because I love you, George Papadopolis. You got the same values, same standards, same soul. You're the closest thing to me that I can think of.

Aside from the evident way that George distances himself from responsibility for and inhabitation of the structures of antiblackness by rendering racism a problem of other people (white people? black people?), it is crucial that black people establish that considerations of race and racism do not enter their thinking when pursuing their children's best interests. "Social statements" on the welfare of black children are not made by black parents with meaningful personal ties to white people; they merely nominate the best person for "the gig" on the basis of "values," "standards," and "soul," rather than some putatively segregationist logic of race-matching. It is worth noting, on this point, that both Mrs. Jackson in *Diff'rent Strokes* and Travis Long in *Webster* are from working-class communities (Travis' recent ascent to the NFL notwithstanding), and the barriers to their stated desire for the posthumous interracial adoption of their own children are middle-class black professionals like Ellen or adherents like Ms. Aimsley or even, temporarily, Katherine herself, all educated fools. White men, whether bluebloods like Philip Drummond or *nouveau riche* white ethnics like George Papadopolis, have little trouble with the prospect of interracial adoption because they experience no compunction in their interactions with black people in general. White women with professional aspirations, under the influence of liberal feminism, are susceptible to doubt about white parental fitness, for white and black children alike. White men have heard it from the horse's mouth, as it were, and their word is their bond. Better yet, they are bonded to the ghostly word of departed black mothers and fathers, to honor their singular final wishes as a testator's veto against the interference of political pressure, government mandate, or public opinion (Fig. 5.7).

Fig. 5.7 Webster sits with his uncle Phillip Long (Ben Vareen) circa 1985. Image reproduced under terms of fair use

GEORGE: So this is why I trust this, why I'm so sure. And if you don't trust me, trust Travis Long. […] Travis didn't say anything about easy. It wouldn't be easy if Web was white. I think we have a pretty good head start. Here's a little kid that loved us enough to sell all his toys for a buck-eighty-seven. And a woman who cared enough to risk losing that little boy, if it would be the best thing for Web. And a man, your pop, who was closer to me than his own brother. I don't see easy, but I do see family, don't you?

In the symbolic universe of Reaganstruction, the vindication of white interracial adoption, and the negation of the political demand for black family preservation that underwrites race-matching policy, is grounded in the earnest and profound intimacy that blacks ostensibly feel toward whites and the moral acceptance and eventual reciprocation of that intimacy by their white obligatees. White parents of black children cannot be interested; they must consider the best interests of the child, however perfunctorily, and be willing to relinquish custody in order to be rediscovered in that interest and as its ultimate guarantee. If black parents choose to give their children to white surrogates because they are kindred spirits, then we cannot fail to appreciate the acuity of Fanon's observation that "what is called the black soul is a construction by white folk" (Fanon 2006, xviii).

References

Acham, Christine. 2004. *Revolution Televised: Prime Time and the Struggle for Black Power*. Minneapolis: University of Minnesota Press.

Bernstein, Robin. 2011. *Racial Innocence: Performing American Childhood from Slavery to Civil Rights*. New York: New York University Press.

Child Welfare Information Gateway. 2017. Foster Care Statistics 2015. *Children's Bureau*, Numbers and Trends, March. Accessed May 28, 2017. https://www.childwelfare.gov/pubs/factsheets/foster/.

Dalton, Mary, and Laura Linder (eds.). 2005. *The Sitcom Reader: American Viewed and Skewed*. Albany, NY: SUNY Press.

Fanon, Frantz. 2006. *Black Skin, White Masks*, trans. Richard Philcox. New York: Grove Press.

Fearn-Banks, Kathleen. 2006. *The A to Z of African-American Television*. Lanham, MD: Scarecrow Press.

Geary, Daniel. 2015. *Beyond Civil Rights: The Moynihan Report and Its Legacy*. Philadelphia: University of Pennsylvania Press.

Gupta, Prachi. 2017. GOP Rep. Steve King Would Like to See an America That's 'So Homogenous That We Look a Lot the Same'. *The Slot*, March 13. Accessed May 28, 2017. http://theslot.jezebel.com/gop-rep-steve-king-would-like-to-see-an-america-thats-1793212880.

Hamamoto, Darrell. 1991. *Nervous Laughter: Television Situation Comedy and Liberal Democratic Ideology*. New York: Praeger Publishers.

Hartman, Saidiya. 2007. *Lose Your Mother: A Journey Along the Atlantic Slave Route*. New York: Farrar, Straus and Giroux.

Heffernan, Virginia. 2006. Revealing the Wages of Young Sitcom Fame. *New York Times*, September 4. Accessed May 28, 2017. http://www.nytimes.com/2006/09/04/arts/television/04stro.html.

Hoberman, James. 2007. The Slums of Park Slope. *Village Voice*, September 11. Accessed May 28, 2017. https://www.villagevoice.com/2007/09/11/the-slums-of-park-slope/.

Hunter-Lattany, Kristin. 1984. Why Buckwheat Was Shot. *MELUS* 11: 79–85.

Ibelema, Minabere. 1990. Identity Crisis: The African Connection in African American Sitcom Characters. In *Sexual Politics & Popular Culture*, edited by Diane Raymond, 121–130. Bowling Green, OH: Bowling Green State University Popular Press.

Jewison, Norman. 1970. *The Landlord*. DVD. Directed by Hal Foster. Santa Monica, CA: MGM/United Artists.

Marrati, Paula. 2005. *Genesis and Trace: Derrida Reading Husserl and Heidegger*. Palo Alto, CA: Stanford University Press.

Miller, James Andrew, and Tom Shales. 2014. *Live From New York: The Complete, Uncensored History of Saturday Night Live as Told by Its Stars, Writers, and Guests*. New York: Little, Brown and Company.

Moore, Barbara, Marvin Bensman, and Jim Van Dyke. 2006. *Prime-Time Television: A Concise History*. Westport, CT: Praeger Publishers.

Moran, Rachel. 2001. *Interracial Intimacy: The Regulation of Race and Romance*. Chicago: University of Chicago Press.

Morreale, Joanne (ed.). 2003. *Critiquing the Sitcom: A Reader*. Syracuse, NY: Syracuse University Press.

Muhummad, Khalil Gibran. 2010. *The Condemnation of Blackness: Race, Crime, and the Making of Modern Urban America*. Cambridge, MA: Harvard University Press.

National Association of Black Social Workers. 2003. Preserving Families of African Ancestry. Accessed May 28, 2017. http://nabsw.org/?page=PositionPapers.

Nyong'o, Tavia. 2002. Racial Kitsch and Black Performance. *Yale Journal of Criticism* 15: 371–391.

Ozersky, Josh. 2003. *Archie Bunker's America: TV in an Era of Change, 1968–1978*. Carbondale, IL: Southern Illinois University Press.

Roberts, Dorothy. 2002. *Shattered Bonds: The Color of Child Welfare*. New York: Basic Books.

Rothman, Barbara Katz. 2004. Transracial Adoption: Refocusing Upstream. In *The Politics of Multiracialism: Challenging Racial Thinking*, ed. Heather Dalmage, 193–202. Albany, NY: SUNY Press.

Saletan, William. 2005. Natural Unborn Killers: The Bigotry of Bill Bennett's Low Expectations. *Slate*, October 4. Accessed May 28, 2017. http://www.slate.com/articles/health_and_science/human_nature/2005/10/natural_unborn_killers.html.

Seifter, Andrew. 2005. "Media Matters Exposes Bennett." *Media Matters For America*, September 28. Accessed May 28, 2017. https://www.mediamatters.org/video/2005/09/28/media-matters-exposes-bennett-you-could-aborte/133904.

Spillers, Hortense. 2003. *Black, White, and In Color: Essays on American Literature and Culture*. Chicago: University of Chicago Press.

Squires, Catherine. 2009. *African Americans and the Media*. Malden, MA: Polity.

Stowe, Harriett Beecher. 1852. *Uncle Tom's Cabin, Or Life Among the Lowly*. Salt Lake City, UT: Project Gutenberg Literary Archive Foundation. Accessed May 28, 2017. http://www.gutenberg.org/files/203/203-h/203-h.htm.

Taylor, Ella. 1989. *Prime Time Families: Television Culture in Postwar America*. Berkeley, CA: University of California Press.

Wiegman, Robyn. 2002. Intimate Publics: Race, Property, and Personhood. *American Literature* 74: 859–885.

6

Shadow and Myth: On *Stranger Inside* and *Moonlight*

Introduction

If we have learned a few things about contemporary figures of black masculinity in the previous chapters, it is not only that blackness and masculinity are articulated by way of a cultural discourse and social practice of policing, material and symbolic; but also that the sexed embodiment of this figure is in no ways guaranteed. We have seen, instead, that the appearance of blackness in an antiblack world produces a crisis of category; the lines between and among the most salient binary oppositions become unstable, subject to inversion or oscillation or indistinction, including: cop/criminal, citizen/slave, white/black, male/female, human/animal, adult/child, thought/feeling, and so on. Alonzo Harris performed the whiteness of law enforcement with a recognizable black style, succeeding before failing to fulfill the earlier determination of his predecessor Agent J (Will Smith) in Barry Sonneberg's 1997 blockbuster *Men in Black*. When talking to his white partner and training officer, Agent K (Tommie Lee Jones), about the difference that obtains between them, J declares confidently: "I make this look good." Not for nothing, *Men in Black* is an action-*comedy*. When the tables are turned and the black officer trains the white one in an action-*drama*, the cool pose struck by Smith's character (a *faux-cool* used mainly to stand out against his signature slapstick comedy, from the *Fresh Prince* persona onward) becomes the stalwart composure of Ethan Hawke's Jake Hoyt, rather than the slick maneuvering of Denzel Washington's Alonzo Harris. The jester in the former genre is entertaining, but the would-be trickster figure in the latter winds up dead after crossing the line once too many times.

Pride shows us that the racist culture spanning from maritime slavery to municipal segregation condemns blacks for not swimming well but then animalizes and quarantines them when they do. And moving up the learning curve from the one condition to the other—from sinking like rocks to swimming like alligators—we see how patriarchal striving among black men aligns them with the same antiblack state and civil society they hope to subvert. Boobie Miles in *Friday Night Lights* becomes indistinguishable from the Permian Panthers' rivals at Dallas-Carter, confusing the line between teammate and opponent, as does Ty Crane for the Richmond Oilers in *Coach Carter*. Michael Oher in *The Blind Side* is repeatedly chided for exhibiting incongruously feminine traits of passivity, sensitivity, and gentleness, bonding primarily with women and children in his quest for masculine courage and honor. Arnold and Webster confound, in turn, the demarcations of age and generation, just as their fictional forebears, Buckwheat and Topsy, trouble differences of sex and gender and even those between the plant and animal kingdoms (recall Topsy was not born to known parents, but "just growed"). In every case, the deconstruction of difference and degree that blackness provokes opens up a space to think again about the formulation of criterion as such.

Extimacy, or the Intimate Exterior

Cheryl Dunye has taken up this challenge better than most. Her filmmaking has consistently questioned the criteria by which we separate fact from fiction, history from speculation, memory from desire, friend from foe, coercion from consent, and freedom from captivity—all at the nexus of race, class, gender, and sexuality. Dunye's award-winning 2001 made-for-television film, *Stranger Inside*, is the director's second feature-length project. It follows upon the critical acclaim of her 1996 debut, *The Watermelon Woman*, and prefigures the commercial success of her subsequent 2004 Miramax Films production, *My Baby's Daddy* (which, despite the Hollywood constraints and unreconstructed male leads, managed to make statements consonant with black feminist and queer critical sensibilities). The earlier work, the first feature-length film directed by a black lesbian in the United States, is a docudrama following the efforts of "Cheryl," a young Philadelphia-based black lesbian filmmaker and video store clerk played by Dunye, as she reconstructs the life and work of one Fae Richards, a black lesbian screen actress and stage performer cast in a series of so-called "mammy" roles in Hollywood studio films of the 1920s and 1930s. Richards is the eponymous "Watermelon Woman," so nicknamed by Cheryl after she discovers Richards listed in the credits of the undated black-and-white film, *Plantation Memories*.

Cheryl is drawn into the vortex of this historical endeavor—requiring great expenditures of time, energy and resources—because she is captivated by the found image of a black woman that she invests with deep psychosexual and sociopolitical significance. She remarks to the point: "Something in the way she looks and moves is serious, interesting." The film thus unfolds, largely, as a multidimensional pursuit and production of this "something" that Cheryl discovers surreptitiously within the image. After ninety minutes of Cheryl's subsequently painstaking research—availing herself of interviews, archives, and personal collections—*The Watermelon Woman* punctures and punctuates the climactic presentation of the awaited film and video montage that finally installs Fae Richards into a revised and expanded US film history with this famously revealing disclaimer: "Sometimes you have to create your own history. *The Watermelon Woman* is fiction."

Reviewers report a range of responses to this revelation, but most note a feeling of surprise, followed by an ensuing sense of loss, and then an ultimate yearning: "I wanted Fae to be real." The tracing of the enigmatic itinerary of *that* desire and the development of a capacity to inhabit it is the dramatic achievement of the film. And that achievement is enabled by a fiction that is licensed by an exigency. Yet, there is a rich ambiguity in the statement. Is this a descriptive indication that "you have to create your own history" in order to do something or another (best read as an instrumental statement), or is it a categorical imperative that "you have to create your own history" (best read an ethical injunction)? How conditional or absolute is the warrant, or mandate? We might wonder whether the ambiguity collapses or oscillates interminably in this particular case because the "subject" of the film—subject as focus, as protagonist, as author—is, from the dominant vantage, no subject at all: among other things, it involves a black lesbian filmmaker shooting a film featuring a black lesbian actress in the role of a black lesbian filmmaker making a film about a black lesbian actress (and along the way several vexed and shifting configurations of interracial same-sexuality and gender variance).

Yes, *The Watermelon Woman* is fiction, but what sort of fiction is it? It is certainly one that, as one review put it, "effectively [blurs] the line between fiction, nonfiction, and biography" (Vesey 2011). But is there not more at stake than a mixing of genres? Or, rather, does the formal complication that blurs the line between genres not raise the question of the law or rule of genre itself? The punch line, or punctuation mark, at the film's conclusion redacts the very terms that would seem to animate its project and mobilize its various audiences: truth and accuracy, visibility and voice, recovery and representation, history and memory. The film has thereby all the elements of a seduction, but one that underlines its ruses so boldly that they become nearly imperceptible, until they hit you, in the flash of an inter-title, in the interregnum between the opening and closing shutter of a camera obscura, in the logical time before dying, where the time for understanding after the instant of seeing never, finally, allows for the moment of concluding.

Mark Winokur describes *The Watermelon Woman* as "a primary text whose fantasy archaeology preempts any critique and history of itself" (Winokur 2001, 232). One cannot argue with the film on the grounds of its verisimilitude. But neither can its motive force be doubted. What Cheryl discovers in the image of Fae Richards is something that she has invented, a projection onto the image she constructs of "something" that she will find there as if it were a solicitation; it is a redoubled desire. This is a fantasy archaeology, which is to say an imagination of a past that never was (and perhaps could not have been otherwise), but also an archaeology of fantasy, which is to say an imagination of a future that is yet to be (and perhaps can never arrive); it is both a memorial and an announcement. One could read Dunye's cinematic historiography, beginning with *The Watermelon Woman*, and the short films preceding it, in light of the methodological problematic formulated several years later by Matt Richardson, that is, "not only to recover submerged *voices* but also to lay bare the *conditions* that create and subjugate black, female, woman-loving sexualities and transgressions of gender norms" (Richardson 2003, 64, emphasis added). To read not only what is not there, so to speak, but also what is already there, present in the form of distortion, interference, inhibition, symptom, anxiety. Conditions that create *and* subjugate, subjugate *and* create: there is no way to determine a precise and linear temporality for this structural relation, no way to extricate the voices and sexualities and transgressions from the conditions and norms that create and subjugate them, and vice versa. It's all the matter and material of the investigation, the excavation, the activity of laying bare, disclosing, discovering, of finding what is desired and desiring what is found. Put differently, the binary opposition of power and resistance is displaced here, those terms can no longer be thought as binary opposites, and, moreover, the nature of binaries in general must be rethought altogether. "I would say—when all is said and done, it is less a matter of remembering than of

6 Shadow and Myth: On *Stranger Inside* and *Moonlight*

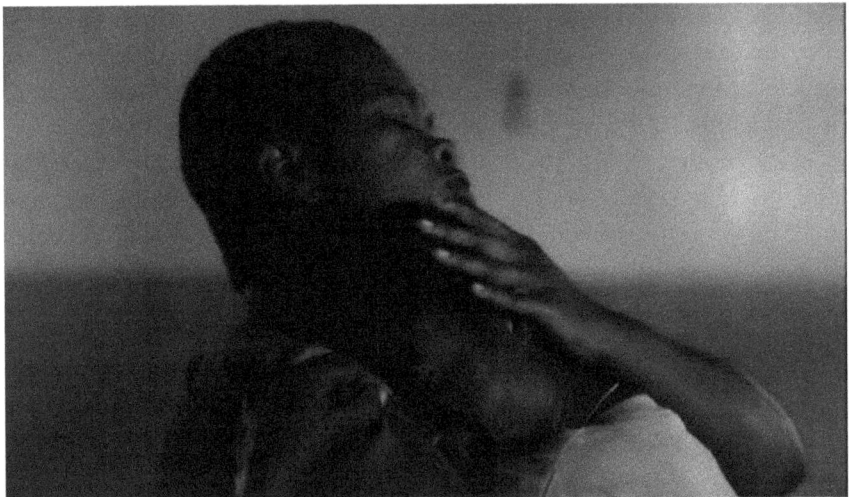

Fig. 6.1 Brownie (Davenia McFadden) comforts Treasure Lee (Yolonda Ross) in Cheryl Dunye's *Stranger Inside* (2001). Image reproduced under terms of fair use

rewriting history," Jacques Lacan offered early in his famous seminar on the technique of Freudian psychoanalysis. "What is essential is reconstruction" (Lacan 1991, 56) (Fig. 6.1).[1]

What would it mean, then, to think of supposed opposites as those that take on their meaning, not at the point of greatest distance or divergence (wherever that may be), but at the point of greatest proximity or convergence? How do we think of difference—especially at the extremes—as an intimate matter? This is a bridge between *The Watermelon Woman*, with its appropriation of the conventions of romantic comedy, and *Stranger Inside*, with its appropriation of the conventions of melodrama, these characteristic genres of women's films in the historic instance. Both films rehearse a deconstruction of "the documentary impulse" and thereby participate in "a counter-tradition" of black cultural productions "that masquerade as true in order to prompt interrogations of prevailing notions of historical fact," if not the notion of history itself, history, in any case, as the past or a story emerging from a simple origin, or a story of origins as such (Smith 1992, 56).

---

[1] The fuller passage reads: "[The] restitution of the subject's wholeness appears in the guise of a restoration of the past. But the stress is always placed more on the side of reconstruction than on that of reliving, in the sense we have grown used to calling *affective*. The precise reliving—that the subject remembers something as truly belonging to him, as having truly been lived through, with which he communicates and which he adopts—we have the most explicit indication in Freud's writings that that is not what is essential. What is essential is reconstruction" (Lacan 1991, 56).

Stranger Inside, like *The Watermelon Woman*, begins and ends on the matter and material of a captivating image, an image or imago that at once compels and confounds the search for origins, a search that has to do, for our protagonist as for everyone else, however disavowed, with the issue of the black mother. It has to do with the impossible and unavoidable matter of black maternity, and of the kinship that is foreclosed thereby. We cannot make sense of this search, its possibility or impossibility, without recourse to a conception of natal alienation that would plot this story of mothers and daughters otherwise. And we have to think about that alienation—imposed by law and culture, economy and society, but above all by *force*—in such a way that allows the natal occasion as such to become susceptible to deracination in the most universal way. *Stranger Inside* projects a "fantasy archaeology" too; it is about the fantasmatic nature of archaeology itself, and the archeological nature of fantasy, the ways in which sedimentary layers of identification and desire, rage and aggression, mourning and loss are inscribed symbolically, circulated, transmitted, inherited: fantasy archaeology and plantation memories. Maria St. John notes in an interview with the filmmaker that "an array of female masculinities are inhabited within the prison walls and are portrayed not as stigma but as signs of strength and pride" (St. John and Dunye 2004, 327). This performance of masculinity at the margins, where the power with which it is typically associated is undercut and reconfigured by female embodiment, poverty, incarceration and, above all, racial blackness, supports the overarching question of *relation* in the most fundamental sense (Fig. 6.2).

Treasure Lee (Yolonda Ross), our protagonist, suffers from reminiscences of childhood torment: "You ain't got no mother" is the recurrent taunt that indexes a preemptive separation or severance—a cleaving—around which she organizes her psychic life. "I'm going home," she declares, further and further into the very state of confinement from which one is supposed to flee. But here, strangely, the abyssal inside of domestic aspiration—from juvenile facility to women's prison to isolation unit to the women's voices heard and hallucinated through the walls, the sink, the toilet—converges with the extremity of psychosexual and sociopolitical exclusion. Treasure has nothing to give or take from the social dynamics of group therapy because she is unlike other women. Prison was her destination, not a terrible detour. She does not desire the supposed freedom and normalcy of life outside. And even when she dreams of leaving prison with her mother and living together somewhere else, she wants only to return to the hood, to the confinement of the ghetto, as it were, without another horizon. She wants her mother, so much so that she is not only willing to risk death—physical and civil—but

Fig. 6.2 The prisoners line up for roll call. Image reproduced under terms of fair use

also, more to the point, to risk *belief*, a belief in her image: the archaic imago of a lost black mother. Again, Treasure declares in the opening scene: "I'm going home." A former occupant of her current prison bunk etches a similar statement in unadorned graffiti on the wall just above her head: "I wanna go home." What is the difference or relation these two claims, between the doing and the desiring? And how is that difference or relation brought into relief, and obscured entirely, by the fact that Treasure has been wanting the *mistaken* image of the woman, Brownie (Davenia McFadden), who murderously usurped her mother's place, a woman whose place she will, in turn, occupy in the wake of matricidal violence? Scar (Almayvonne Dixon) quips facetiously: "What do you think, we all look alike?"

Treasure will not accept her maternal grandmother's declaration that her mother is dead, what is also a maternal declaration that a daughter has died. Treasure follows instead the fateful word of her play sister and fellow gang member, Shadow (LaTonya 'T' Hagans), that her mother was alive and "doing life" at the Women's Correctional Facility. The quest that takes Treasure through the descending planes of incarceration, during which she is reunited with her mother's tenderness through discipline and punishment, requires the sacrifice of all her kin, in a restoration of the dyadic bond. That dyad provides a semblance of order and of what will become, at last, destiny. But that consuming relation, in which the world falls away entirely and reduces to the signification of a global threat, entails an even more profound potential for violence from the inside of a rivalry that lends it any orientation whatsoever. If the mother must be let go before a relation can be established in the proper sense, then what if such letting go is interdicted by a taking that never admits the theft? "To lose your mother was to be denied your kin, country, and identity. To lose your mother was to forget your past… I was an orphan. […] This sense of not belonging and of being an extraneous element is at the heart of slavery. Love has nothing to do with it; love has everything to do with it" (Hartman 2007, 85).[2] This dispossession also gives rise to a new set of possibilities for Hartman, and so too for Dunye. A new set, like that invoked by the final image of the film: Shadow, the messenger and documentarian, the photographer photographing the shadow of her own image, laid flat on the prison yard, elongated, hand bearing the sign and offering of peace, anonymous and singular, standing perfectly still, only to disappear once more, out into the blackness, into the shade (Fig. 6.3).

Stranger Inside is a complex meditation on the psycho-politics of black kinship, and of black maternity specifically, as the disinherited matrix of gendering and ungendering as well as the orientation and disorientation of sexuality. Black female masculinity, under conditions of extremity, is the formation here that questions the relation between the psychic life of a state-sanctioned interdiction of black kinship and the willingness to suffer and/or inflict forms of physical, mental and emotional violence to undo—or preserve or pervert—its effects. The racialized dislocation of embodiment, gender expression, and sexual practice—where it is unclear in advance, and at various points along the way, who identifies with whom, who is related to whom, who is attracted to or involved with whom—serves also to upset the normative striving for a coherent social identity aligned with the dominant conceptions of filial love and loving affiliation. In this regard, Dunye's work stands in powerful contrast to the contemporary Hollywood representations of black masculinity discussed in previous chapters. And, as another important contribution to the history of black feminist and queer filmmaking, *Stranger Inside* constructs a prismatic lens to review the critical itinerary travelled in our investigation to this point.

---

[2]Hartman writes further: "Love encourages forgetting, which is intended to wash away the slave's past. Love makes a place for the stranger; it domesticates persons from 'outside of the house' and not 'of the blood'; it assuages the slave's loss of family; it remakes slaveholders as mothers and fathers. Owning persons and claiming kin are one and the same; so love cannot be separated from dispossession or property in persons. Affection perhaps softens the sting of dishonor but does not erase it… Love extends the cover of belonging and shrouds the slave's origins, which lie in acts of violence and exchange, but it doesn't remedy the isolation of being severed from your kin and denied ancestors" (Hartman 2007, 87).

Fig. 6.3 Treasure talks with Shadow (LaTonya 'T' Hagans) on the yard. Image reproduced under terms of fair use

Counter-Cinema

We have arrived, circuitously, at this final onscreen meditation, wherein black kinship operates in and through interdiction, not in spite of it; and the coordinates of gender and sexuality, no less than the distinctions of class, are devised and revised in an atmosphere of violent dispossession: from cop to prisoner, from coach to player, from parent to child, from birth to adoption, from father to mother, from black man to white woman, from housing projects to high-rise penthouse, from post-civil rights retrenchment to antebellum abolitionism and back again. We are now in a position to see, through the half dozen examples given above, that while "Black males are American cinema's perennial outsiders and antiheroes, as well as its most stereotypically depicted ones" (Tate 2016), that cinema is, for the same reason, a site for equally perennial modes of critical reading. So, while the crises and contradictions that condense in highly patterned ways upon the forms and figures of black masculinity are perhaps brought into starkest relief *between* the seemingly stock characters of standard Hollywood fare and their more complex, multidimensional counterparts in the universe of (black) independent filmmaking, they are, in fact, immanent to *every* representation, from the margin to the mainstream.

It is tempting to hold out hope for a promising counter-cinema where, among other things, a critical appraisal of black masculinity can be more fully developed; and, in that vein, it is hard not to be excited by the intervention of a film like *Stranger Inside* or, indeed, a whole range of recent productions from documentaries like Daniel Peddle's *The Aggressives* (2005) and Kortney Ryan Ziegler's *Still Black: A Portrait of Black Transmen* (2008) and Stephen Dest's *I Am Shakespeare: The Henry Green Story* (2017) to narrative features like Tina Mabry's *Mississippi Damned* (2009) and Dee Rees's *Pariah* (2011) and Barry Jenkins's *Moonlight* (2016). Yet, any counter-cinema worth its name, however compelling and intelligent, still demands of that viewers step back and think again. Kara Keeling (2009) has demonstrated the richness of such engagement with regard to Peddle's critically acclaimed work, tracing an aesthetics and politics of *disappearance* produced at the heart of the film that challenges at once the erasure of invisibility and the pitfalls of visibility for the eponymous subjects of the film. The concomitant audience shift would eschew both the passive habit of *looking at* the cast as spectacle and, insofar as their stories take leave of the image track and narrative frame, the active reflex of *looking for* the missing in the manner of a search party or, worse, a police operation. Rather, Keeling suggests, we might be prompted to adopt a perceptual mode of *looking after*, that is, looking in the spirit of caretaking and about what is no longer in view. This might be summarized as an abiding concern for the afterimages of life and death.

I Am Shakespeare traverses territory familiar to viewers of the cinema of policing, namely how black men can and do move across the borders of racial segregation, navigating spaces of exclusive social and cultural capital while managing the difficulties of their offstage home life. Henry Green is a fledgling actor from the predominantly black and working-class Newhallville section of New Haven, CT, just a few miles away from the Yale University campus. He excelled in the Cooperative Arts and Humanities High School theater program there and in the summer after his graduation landed a role as Tybalt in a well-received production of *Romeo and Juliet* for the nearby Elm Shakespeare Company. Shortly thereafter, he was shot and severely wounded in an armed robbery by another young black man from his neighborhood. Green, we learn, was also previously involved with a street gang and credited his acting abilities, in part, for his rapid ascent to a position of leadership and respect. His professional accomplishments, meanwhile, had little traction or legibility outside of the theater world. But, contrary to its customary framing, Green's is not just a tale of two cities and his circulation between its alternate realities. It is also, more importantly, a commentary on the difficulty of understanding the internal relations of Newhallville itself and the interiority of each and every one of its residents. The central soliloquy regards the lesson Green learns, not coincidentally, from the young man who shot him:

I saw a lost child in this kid's eyes. A human being that was confused and hurt and angry. I saw a mirror in his eyes. It was that second that changed me. I'm exactly like that person. There's people who can't get the full picture of me; they want me to be one or the other, renegade or Henry Green, and they can't imagine a world where I'm both. Every person is both. There is no black or white person. You cannot label people; we're too complex. My *shooter* is too complex for me to just label him 'shooter.' Tell me you'd still be as interested in me if you only knew my renegade. It'd be easy to call me a monster, but understanding people is not about being easy. It's not easy to do that. I am Shakespeare, and so are you.

Green does not just empathize with his shooter; he identifies with him. He declares to his audience that he too is one of the "renegade" young black males so feared by the people of Greater New Haven. As he battles the ghost pain of his gunshot wound and works slowly through the effects of post-traumatic stress, he holds on to the mirroring exchange of glances with another black man, one intent on robbing and killing him, and defends the latter against labeling and stigmatizing, against reduction and simplification. He also insists that his shooter, like himself, is knowable, or rather understandable, insofar as one is willing to live with the requisite difficulty. The most profound assertion is no doubt the universalizing of his singularity—the identity of renegade *and* Henry Green, gangster *and* thespian, criminal *and* artist—his insistence that *everyone* is *both*. He allows for no distancing from his own culpability in events leading up to the near-fatal shooting; he calls himself, to that end, "a stained individual." But, likewise, he refuses the judgmental morality of the viewer, who is no less implicated in his account, just as the shooter is more than a shooter and the shooting itself was, in fact, more than a shooting.[3]

This ethical refusal of the morality of good and evil and the concomitant inversion and suspension of the distinctions between black and white, high and low, civilian and outlaw culminates in the leading metaphor and its extension: "I am Shakespeare, and so are you." Green, in claiming to be The Bard of Avon, does not misrecognize himself or aggrandize his talents or

---

[3]One of the most powerful articulations of this ethics, against the morality of good and evil, is found in Bataille (1991). He writes: "We cannot be *human* until we have perceived in ourselves the possibility for abjection in addition to the possibility for suffering. We are not only possible victims of the executioners, the executioners are our fellow creatures. We must ask ourselves: is there anything in our nature that renders such horror impossible? And we would be correct in answering: no, nothing. A thousand obstacles in us rise against it… Yet it is not impossible. Our possibility is thus not simply pain, it extends to the rage of the torturer" (Bataille 1991, 18).

overstate his aspirations. He references instead something like the spirit of Shakespeare, and of all great art, to confront audiences with a critical reflection of their own disavowed conditions of existence, to challenge all of us to see a mirror in his renegade eyes too. In his testimony about the night he was shot, Green recalls that he chose not to run for his life when he realized he was being pursued: "I wanted to face that harm, I wanted to face that danger alone… I opened my arms and said, 'Whatever you are ready to do, let's get it done.'" Why run from something he can't escape, what is, perhaps, his fate? And in facing his attacker and rival, he sees his double, a semblance of himself against which he is also doing battle, his inner and outer worlds collapsing into one another, becoming indiscernible, and all the better to rethink their interrelations.

Something similar is at work in all of the films mentioned in this chapter, from Dunye to Jenkins. If Treasure, in *Stranger Inside*, loses her mother twice over to a double, or doubled, homicide only to regain a new and different sense of kinship-in-captivity on the other side of such compounded loss; then Chiron (pronounced Shy-*Rone*), the protagonist of *Moonlight*, seeks the proper means to separate from his mother, through a no less complex doubling, forging his way between the father's law and the brothers' recognition. Though Chiron, like Treasure, does a stint in prison, off-screen, his story is focused on the life and death that orbits in many ways around the prison, in the everyday, open-air incarceration of the ghetto. *Moonlight* is arguably the most successful black cast film in US history to date, critically and commercially. Winner of a Golden Globe for Best Motion Picture—Drama and Academy Awards for Best Picture, Best Adapted Screenplay and Best Supporting Actor, it was lauded by film critics across the board for its artistic and technical achievements as much as for its powerful social commentary and broad political significance. It landed at number one on more than a dozen of the major annual top ten lists for 2016, including the *New York Times*, the *Washington Post*, the *Los Angeles Times*, and the *Chicago Tribune*, and it grossed over $55 million at the box office on a modest $1.5 million budget (Fig. 6.4).[4]

The critical establishment's praise was immediate and lavish. Peter Bradshaw and Benjamin Lee at the UK *Guardian* described *Moonlight*, respectively, as "a visually ravishing portrait of masculinity" and as "proudly

---

[4]Nico Lang (2017) reminds us that *Moonlight* is also the first LGBTQ film to win an Oscar for Best Picture, citing the persistent homophobia of the Academy of Motion Picture Arts and Sciences. Ang Lee's *Brokeback Mountain* (2005), which most critics thought a shoe-in for the barrier-breaking award, was snubbed in favor of Paul Haggis's trite social message film, *Crash* (2004).

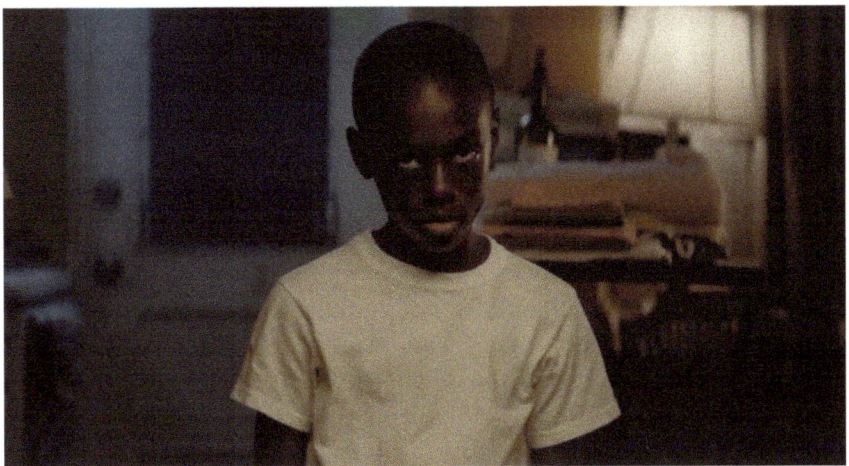

Fig. 6.4 Little (Alex Hibbert) stands in the kitchen in Barry Jenkins's *Moonlight* (2016). Image reproduced under terms of fair use

black and refreshingly queer," and their colleague Deborah Orr offered that it "is probably one of the most emotionally revealing films about a man ever to have been made" (Bradshaw 2017, Lee 2016a, Orr 2017). Mark Kermode, for the same venue, called it "an astonishingly accomplished work—rich, sensuous and tactile, by turns heartbreaking and uplifting" (Kermode 2017). A.O. Scott at the *New York Times* found *Moonlight* to be "both a disarmingly, at times almost unbearably personal film and an urgent social document, a hard look at American reality and a poem written in light, music and vivid human faces" (Scott 2016). The *Washington Post*'s Ann Hornaday was even more fulsome, calling it "a perfect film, one that exemplifies not only the formal and aesthetic capabilities of a medium at its most visually rich, but a capacity for empathy and compassion that reminds audiences of one of the chief reasons why we go to movies: to be moved, opened up and maybe permanently changed" (Hornaday 2016). In all such accounts, we find mention of the film's penchant for cultivating vulnerability where it is supposedly needed most, among poor black boys and men, in ways that allow them to escape, if momentarily, the 'façade' or 'armor' or 'straightjacket' of masculinity in its more hyperbolic and heterosexist expressions, "our hackneyed masculine conventions" (Tate 2016). "The Sensuous *Moonlight* Dares to Let Black Men Love," wrote Melissa Anderson for the *Village Voice*, in homage to Marlon Rigg's 1989 classic *Tongues Untied* (Riggs, as narrator, declares famously in the final section: "Black men loving black men is *the* revolutionary act") (Anderson 2016). Naomie Harris, who plays Chiron's mother, Paula, went so far as to say in one interview that "being human *means* being vulnerable" (Lee 2016, emphasis added). Such are the stakes.

Black male critics, gay and straight, had especially strong praise for the film (with the notable exception of a particularly acerbic Armond White (2016), writing for the conservative *National Review*, who unsurprisingly dismissed it as a politically-correct "plea for pity"). Ashon Crawley at *The Root* was inspired to extended reminiscence upon viewing *Moonlight*, summing up his impression thusly: "Everything in the film, this masterpiece, was a reach for connection" (Crawley 2017). Greg Tate, also for the *Village Voice*, exclaimed: "The poignant brilliance of *Moonlight* derives from the many-splendored ways it enshrines… Black male erotic repression and unconsummated desire in the face of bullying and familial breakdown" (Tate 2016). And Hinton Als, in a Pulitzer Prize-winning piece for the *New Yorker*, found *Moonlight* to be a "brilliant, achingly alive new work about black queerness" (Als 2016). Although he provided the best guided tour of the film among a cohort of reviews displaying some of the top critics' best writing, much of Als's celebration of *Moonlight* revolved around its historic impact on black gay viewers like himself, many of whom never dreamed they would see a film like this, that is, one concerned principally with black male same sexuality *and* commanding high production values, wide distribution, and international renown.

Finally, there was the oft-cited autobiographical convergence, across differences of sexuality, between the noted playwright Tarell Alvin McCraney, author of the previously unproduced original script, *In the Moonlight Black Boys Look Blue*, and co-writer/director Barry Jenkins, both of whom hail from Liberty City, the Miami neighborhood that provides the film's fictional setting and actual shooting location. *Moonlight* was adapted from McCraney's thesis project at the Yale School of Drama, where he returned in 2017, Oscar in hand, to direct the playwriting program. Much of the material, written by McCraney in his early twenties, was autobiographical, and it was eventually combined in the adaptation with elements of Jenkins's own life and shaped, moreover, by the incredibly dexterous interpretations of the various black male actors who star in the major roles. Greg Tate's playful synopsis of the film is as good as any: "The simplest tag you can put on *Moonlight* is that it's a queer coming-of-age story set in a Negroidal Southern galaxy far, far away from the places it's received world-cinema accolades from" (Tate 2016). Chiron is played successively by three actors bearing three titles in a three-act dramatic structure: (i) Little (Alex Hibbert), the child; (ii) Chiron (Ashton Sanders), the teenager; and (iii) Black (Trevante Rhodes), the adult.

The first two acts of the film find him "[living] in public housing with his single mother, Paula (Naomie Harris), who goes on drug binges, less to alleviate her sadness than to express her wrath—against the world and, especially, against her son, who she thinks keeps her from the world" (Als 2016). Little is neglected and berated at home by a mother who is increasingly remote and unremarkably homophobic, and he is chased and terrorized when he ventures outside by neighborhood boys whose rites of passage include his mortal threat. Early in the narrative arc, Little is taken in by Juan (Mahershala Ali), a drug-dealing father figure who finds him taking refuge one afternoon in a derelict apartment building, and his partner Teresa (Janelle Monáe). "Chiron lives for the moments when he can get away from his mother's countless recriminations and needs, and swim in the unfamiliar waters of love with Juan and Teresa," according to Als. "One indelible scene shows Juan holding Chiron in his arms in a rippling blue ocean, teaching him to float—which is another way of teaching him the letting go that comes with trust, with love" (Als 2016). Juan is, then, doing more in this scene than practically teaching Little the rudiments of swimming; Juan is, alongside Teresa, symbolically baptizing him in the emotional universe of everyday adult caretaking. He is, as well, modeling a paternal masculinity that Little will emulate, in part, later in life; one wherein the street smarts and physical prowess of the drug game can be alloyed with a caring and mutual intimate relationship and genuine concern for the welfare of children, whether one's own or others; one wherein compromises and contradictions can be admitted and suffered openly in the course of one's life (Fig. 6.5).

The obvious association with John the Baptist here seems more overwrought than apposite, yoking Little with the unduly heavy burden of signifying resemblance to Jesus. Though there is something admittedly rich about the idea of rewriting the figure of Jesus as a gay black boy from the ghetto—and the subsequent reframing of the film as a dramatic test of faith for everyone around Chiron ("as you did it to one of the least of these my brothers...")—we risk losing the very focalization of his life in the process. There is a perhaps more justified reading of Juan and Teresa in the tradition of the sixteenth-century Roman Catholic saints Juan de la Cruz (John of the Cross) and Teresa de Jesús (Teresa of Ávila), whose commitment to the Counter-Reformation in Habsburg Spain involved the promotion of a return to the austere monastic practices of the early Desert Fathers and Mothers. Both were born to families with living memory of conversion from Judaism under the Inquisition and, while they emphasized the mystical practice of contemplative prayer in pursuit of Christian holiness, they were

Fig. 6.5 Juan (Mahershala Ali) teaches Little (Alex Hibbert) how to swim in the ocean. Image reproduced under terms of fair use

driven by the belief, unlike many of their Protestant rivals, that both faith and good works were necessary to salvation. As a result, Teresa and John earned the enmity of the Church hierarchy and many of the male members of the order Teresa founded, the Discalced Carmelites, as well (Mujica 2009).

In any case, such religious themes seem to operate ubiquitously in the background, much in the way that Mozart's 1780 *Laudate Dominum* plays as ambient, extra-diegetic accompaniment to the young boys' schoolyard roughhousing. Little, already taunted by peers during a game of sandlot football called "kill the carrier" (or *apropos* "smear the queer"), escapes momentarily from the crushing pressure of fraternity bearing down on him, literally and figuratively. Young Kevin (Jaden Piner), Little's only friend and future object of desire, jogs after him and cajoles him to demonstrate some pre-pubescent toughness as a means of general defense. In a compact moment of foreshadowing—Kevin (Jharrel Jerome) will be responsible in the second act for a teenaged Chiron's first and only sexual encounter as well as the violent assault that catalyzes the latter's transformation to the adult Black—we hear, in Latin, the famous lyrics of Psalm 117: "O praise the Lord, all ye nations: praise him, all ye people. / For his merciful kindness is great toward us: and the truth of the Lord endureth forever. Praise ye the Lord." *Laudate Dominum*, "one of the most beautiful of its sort in all of church music," is the famous aria from the *Vesperae solennes de confessore*, K. 339 (Solemn vespers of the confessor) (Summer 2007, 29). Confessor is, of course, another name for a male saint in the Catholic canon and Vespers are the evening prayers performed as part of the Liturgy of the Hours, marking the division of the day as the sun sets and the moon rises, sunlight giving way to moonlight. Layering the religious composition over the children's daytime activities in this way signals their coming evening rendezvous at the baptismal water's edge and sanctifies it. Drawing their latent homoerotic play from a scene of sublimated hostility presages the fateful reversal—homophobic violence drawing from prior sexual acts—once both become manifest in adolescence. The film score's main theme, *Moonlight Suite*, sounds like a slower, more pensive, anagrammatic transposition of Mozart's last choral work for the Salzburg Cathedral, where the great composer, himself a devout Roman Catholic, received his own baptism.[5] The specifically Catholic subtext of the film is only underscored by Juan's immigration from Cuba (placing him among one of several black Catholic populations in Miami, including Dominicans, Haitians, Puerto Ricans, and Afro-Latinos from Central and South America), none of which is to say the film is pious in the least. It is neither pious nor impious. It is non-theistic and non-thetic, venturing through and beyond the logic of positions and propositions as such (Derrida 1987; Wigley 1995).

Not unlike *Pariah*'s main character, Alike (Adepero Oduye), Little's principal, or at least logically and chronologically prior, antagonism is with his troubled and unforgiving mother (herself besieged by a range of social forces and psychic conflicts that the older protagonist later comes to appreciate more fully). The frictions arising between him and the other boys in the neighborhood, especially the acute battle with Terrel (Patrick Decile) that unfolds in high school, seem to represent a generalization of the cruelty he first experiences at home. Little, we learn, hates his mother, as Juan hated his mother before him. The wrinkle introduced by Juan's affirmation of this intergenerational hatred is his realization, after her death, that he was also bonded with her and loved her *within* that hatred, that he misses that strange brew of feelings as an aspect of her absent presence, and that nothing more can be said about it at the moment, chiefly because there has been no opportunity or occasion for further exploration. Little's hatred of his mother, like Juan's, may very well be an inverted expression of her introjected hatred of him. And his experience of communal persecution in the outside world may feel like a perpetuation of the internal sense of

---

[5]For a discussion of the composition process behind the original score, see Shapiro (2017). Nicholas Britell's work was also nominated for an Academy Award.

maternal omnipotence and omnipresence that can come to characterize early childhood under particular conditions of crisis.

Little is able to crack the wall of that encircling aggression, posing a *question* in the heart-wrenching final scene of the first act about why he is hated so viscerally by so many, because Juan and Teresa's calm and stable interaction with the child presents a point of contrast to Paula's volatility. Once that other frame of reference comes to the fore, however, it allows Little to associate that fundamental maternal volatility, rightly or wrongly, with chronic drug use and he cannot explain how that use results in such a fragmented personality and painful relationship, except to think it is directly causal. That arithmetical equation prompts a break in the relation upon which the break is dependent in the first place: Paula uses drugs and Juan sells the drugs she uses, therefore Juan contributes directly to the cause of Paula's permanent disarray and Little's prolonged ordeal. Little exits stage left after the 'clarifying' exchange and Juan dies, somehow, in the interregnum. Little continues to receive Teresa's moral and material support through the end of the second act, keeping a room at her apartment for those times he is unable or unwilling to stay at his mother's place. On the day before Chiron exacts spectacular revenge on Terrel for inciting Kevin to violence (and attempting thereby to destroy Chiron and Kevin's already tenuous rapport), Paula shakes down her son for petty drug money while desperately chastising him for his relationship to Teresa ("I'm your mama! That bitch over there ain't no kin to ya. I'm your blood! Remember?"). Terrel, meanwhile, antagonizes Chiron in a thoroughly sexual manner—accusing him of a quasi-incestuous relationship with Teresa in the wake of Juan's death, insulting him with innuendos about his mother's reputation, and, finally, by threatening directly to rape him if he dares to resist his abasement—betraying a fascination with Chiron that prompts him, repeatedly, to solicit his undivided attention. In this one respect, Terrel is like *all* of the supporting characters in the cast and much of the viewing audience too, driven to distraction with curiosity, or anxiety, about what is on his mind (Fig. 6.6).

Critics, as noted, hailed *Moonlight* as romance and *bildungsroman*, novel for the subject introduced to those timeworn genres. Stephen Hall (2017), posting at the *Black Perspectives* blog, was struck by the film's ability to convey "the power of love to conquer time and space," suggesting that over the course of the film Chiron and Kevin are able to maintain a connection despite the many years and miles—and the painful betrayal—that separate them. Similarly, *New Yorker* columnist Richard Brody's suggestion that *Moonlight* avoids the usual clichés and incorporates the standard criticisms into its very

Fig. 6.6 Naomie Harris as Chiron's mother Paula. Image reproduced under terms of fair use

development turns on the language of character, consciousness and identity, all touchstones of the coming-of-age narrative. He avers:

> [The] subject of *Moonlight* isn't blackness or gayness; it's one man whose many qualities include being black and being gay—and whose own keen awareness of his place in the world, and of its implications, is the high-pressure, high-heat forge of his densely solid, relentlessly opaque, yet terrifyingly vulnerable and fragile character. Blasting aside conventions, archetypes, and stereotypes, Jenkins conjures the birth of an individual's consciousness, the forging of a complex and multifaceted identity; he restores complexity to the very idea of identity, of the multiplicity as well as the singularity of being oneself—and he conveys his own primordial sense of wonder that art itself can conjure it. (Brody 2016)

Wonder is a major theme of the film, but not quite in the way the above passage would suggest. The protagonist wonders, precisely, about matters of character, consciousness and identity, and no less about matters of desire, intimacy, and pleasure, rather than arriving at, or even approaching, any final product in that regard. Nor does he come to adopt some 'life is a journey, not a destination' type of outlook. This wondering sensibility jars against the knowing attitude of those around him who seem to be saying, in one way or another, that a resolution, or at least some resolve, is on the horizon. Negatively, Chiron's tormentors, from his mother to his classmates, have decided *they* know who and what he is, long before he has any real sense of himself. Positively, Juan and Teresa assure him that *he* will know who and what he is in due time and, in the pivotal baptismal scene, Juan declares: "At some point you gotta decide for yourself who you're going to be. Can't let nobody make that decision for you." There is much in this material, and even more in the contextual media coverage of the film, to suggest that *Moonlight* features a process of empowering self-discovery and self-realization. But, to my mind, that reading of the film, or the limitation of the film to that aspect, pressgangs its fine details into the service of a coarser expectation—for character, consciousness, and identity; for desire, intimacy and pleasure—despite its very welcome and more evident demolition of conventions, archetypes, and stereotypes.

Chiron is better understood as a figure of wonder than of identification or desire. His experiences of contact—interpersonal, physical, sexual—and his relations of connection—with his mother, with Juan and Teresa, with Kevin—all seem to unfold without intimacy, rather than in its pursuit or preservation. While his early and persistent encounter with the aggression and hostility of his natal surround might reasonably result in a powerful estrangement, Chiron seems more likely struck by the strangeness of his, and all, social life, from the otherness of the body and the internal foreignness of desire to the inevitable failure to adequately grasp the entire system of operations that has composed the Liberty City of his earliest memories. Chiron moves about in states of *contemplation* that repeatedly peel away from the inevitable demands of material and symbolic wayfinding, whether the dead reckoning of his walking around the neighborhood as a child or the map reading of his dejected commute on the Metrorail as a teenager or, later, the global positioning of his spontaneous road trip from Atlanta to Miami as an adult.[6] His relative silence, which likely indicates both an inhibition and a protective reticence linked to severe and prolonged mistreatment, is most nearly what defines his personae across the radical metamorphosis in physical appearance, from the soft and diminutive Little to the lanky and awkward Chiron to the hardened and muscular Black. And in

---

[6]Wayfinding is a term of art in the fields of architecture, design, geography, and psychology, comprising four basic elements: orientation, route decision, route monitoring, and destination recognition. Planners take such elements into account when imagining how best to analyze, facilitate and prevent the movement, gathering, distribution and dispersal of populations across public and private spaces of the natural and built environment (Gibson 2009; Kitchin and Freundschuh 2000).

that silence his mind seems absorbed not so much in longing or reflection as in mystery.[7]

From one angle, his moments of contemplation might resemble daydreaming or even dissociation, two of the most notable examples being his blank stare in Mr. Pierce's high school classroom at the start of the second act (which is interrupted politely by the teacher and then derisively chalked up by an all-too-eager Terrel to Chiron's "woman problems") and his lingering gaze at his lieutenant, Travis (Stephon Bron), negotiating a drug transaction in the alley at the start of the third act (which is interrupted by the escalating tensions and rising voices between Travis and the two men he confronts). But the lack or surplus of meaning in each case is established formally by the fact that we have no access to the protagonist's thoughts at the time and the narrative elements that would lend coherence to the shot are edited out. The gaps in audience understanding, then, leave us wondering as well: we know that Mr. Pierce is teaching a lesson on the biochemistry of autoimmunity and Travis is collecting debts from delinquent customers, but what are they, or any of us, doing *really* when we make the grade or make money, when we make plans or make promises, or meaning or love? Chiron registers, again, the strangeness of our existence, of all existence, in a way that we might call radical; from the cellular structure of life to the elementary structures of kinship to the organizing principles of society to the basic contours of the natural world and the cosmological movement of the celestial bodies (Fig. 6.7).

"In the moonlight, black boys look blue": the observation sits at the crux of Juan's seaside parable, illuminating has paternal advice about the imperative of self-naming. He relays this tale to Little for several reasons: (1) at the level of phylogeny—to reveal that black people are diverse and can be found all over the world, due not only to the recent historical production of Diaspora (including the inauguration of racial slavery to the New World in and around the colonization of Cuba by the Catholic Monarchs of a newly unified Spain), but also to the larger evolutionary fact of human origination on the African continent; (2) at the level of ontogeny—to introduce

---

[7]This distinction corresponds to the three expressions of prayer in the Catechism of the Catholic Church: longing would be the hallmark of vocal prayer (in which one ritualistically embodies one's faith through recitation), reflection the hallmark of meditation (in which one evaluates the alignment between one's principles and practices), and mystery the hallmark of contemplation (in which one directly shares in an experience of God's ineffability).

Fig. 6.7 Chiron (Ashton Sanders) meets Kevin on the beach. Image reproduced under terms of fair use

the possibility of individual transformation and growth, and of migration to other locales; and (3) at the level of sociogeny—to establish the idea of tradition as selective inheritance and application of received wisdom among and across the generations that mediates between the other two levels. On this score, Juan passes on to Little a many-layered conception of *poiesis*: production, formation, invention.[8] But, the *optical* effects of the titular moonlight described by the old Afro-Cuban woman are left conspicuously unremarked in both the film's dialogue and its critical reception to date.[9] Yes, the cinematography makes great use of filtered lenses that enhance the blue hues and tints of the color palette, especially in those cool tonal scenes shot in or near the ocean. By day, the aquamarine of tropical waters plays subtly off the azure sky; by night, where the artificial light of advanced civilization reaches its limit, the dark ocean blurs without horizon into the blackness above, and only the shimmering of the moonlight across opaque surfaces admits of any distinction whatsoever. But what does this tell us about the effect of staging *this* story as properly nocturnal, as other than or outside of the diurnal states of conscious awareness and enlightenment?

---

[8] On the complex relations between phylogeny, ontogeny, and sociogeny and the concept of *poiesis* in the thought of Sigmund Freud, Frantz Fanon and Sylvia Wynter, see Marriott (2011).

[9] Much has been made of the symbolism of water in the film, from the ocean to the bath. See, for instance, Gilber (2016).

> I have always found something attractively perverse about artistic works that portray the hours of darkness, something that seems contrary to a universal guiding principle. [...] After all, moonlight does not *reveal*, in the straight-ahead, visual sense; it transforms, changing colors and contours in its shape-shifting light. (Attlee 2011, 5)

So writes James Attlee in his compelling travelogue, *Nocturne*. Moonlight does not reveal, it does not illuminate in the usual meaning of the word; it transforms, playing tricks on the eyes, confusing the mind. How so? Physicist Tony Philips offers the short answer: We don't know. The lunar blueshift remains unexplained for contemporary scientific research. We can only describe its effects and speculate about its causes. Black boys, like everyone and everything else, look blue because: "(1) moonlight steals color from whatever it touches, (2) if you stare at the gray landscape long enough, it turns blue, and (3) moonlight won't let you read" (Philips 2006). Given even this preliminary outline of the moon's deceptive luminescence, how could anyone fail to see the film as anything but an audiovisual poem about the beauty in the breakdown and failure of our powers of perception and apperception; or, rather, of their aesthetic deconstruction?

Chiron gives the lie to the fictions of narrative coherence, a point that is only highlighted by the visual disjuncture of his performance by three actors of rather varied stature, comportment and bearing. And for the good reason that his story is drawn from a life, or lives, that reckon privately and publicly with the inherent difficulty of understanding and the pronounced limits of any knowledge whatsoever.

> Playwright Tarell Alvin McCraney wrote *In Moonlight Black Boys Look Blue*, on which *Moonlight* is based, in the summer of 2003, in the midst of graduating from Chicago's DePaul University and losing his mother to AIDS-related complications. At a crossroads, McCraney was filled with questions—about himself, about life, about going out into the world—that he could not turn to his mother to answer. Neither a traditional stage or screen play, *In Moonlight* served as a "circular map" for McCraney, a way to locate himself, socially and historically. (Brathwaite 2017)

When Les Fabian Brathwaite interviewed McCraney for *Out* magazine, he framed the project that became a cinematic landmark a bit more hopefully than the author himself. Which is to say the generic conventions of the coming-of-age story imputed to *Moonlight* seep into the space of the interview itself. McCrary's circular map was straightened out into a linear narrative by Jenkins's adaptation, and the uncertainty, the worry and the wonder that mark the earlier text are domesticated, as it were, into the schema of an open ending. "I was very afraid of what my life would look like," McCrary tells Brathwaite. "I was very lonely. I still feel very alone most of the time and so I tried to figure out and put down as much of the memory that I could. I think it was an experiment in what life could look like" (Brathwaite 2017). An experiment, we must add, that the young writer inhabits in the present tense: "I was very lonely. I still feel very alone…" Elsewhere, in an interview for the *Guardian*, McCrary responds to Benjamin Lee's question—"Was it a difficult experience finally watching the film?"—as follows:

> The first time, no. I think I was just so excited to see something that looked exactly like memories to me. *Then the glee of that wore off*—and I did remember feeling very depressed and very heartbroken about a lot of it. Mostly because these are not things that I have found the answers to and understand how they work. I actually ended up feeling that these are still looming questions in my life, questions about my own identity and my own self-worth that I'm still trying to figure out. Then seeing the film again, I was like shit, *these are still here and they're not going anywhere*. (Lee 2016b)

"Looking blue" is not, then, simply a visual impression of pigment and complexion in altered state. It is also a reference to the existence and experience of the blues and to those "blues people" whose creative genius McCrary participates in and renews, an acknowledgement that such work allows one to keep on keeping on, but does not, for all that, heal what ails (Davis 1998; Davis 2003; Floyd 1996; Jones 1999). This much would seem to be as evident as the visual significance of the film's title, or, as we'll see, the symbolism of the protagonist's name; but, yet again, the wide enthusiasm for an ultimately uplifting cultural event has overshadowed much of what is most moving, and most productively disturbing, about the enterprise. Chiron borrows his namesake from the oldest and most distinguished of the Centaurs of ancient Greek mythology, a Thessalian tribe of half-human, half-horse creatures. Chiron (pronounced *Kai*-Ron) was the son of the Titan Cronus, god of the harvest and seasons, and the Oceanid (or sea nymph) Philyra. Cronus was the son of Uranus, primordial god of the heavens, and Gaia, primordial god of the earth. Philyra was the daughter of the Titans Oceanus, god of the sea, and Tethys, goddess of fresh water. So Chiron

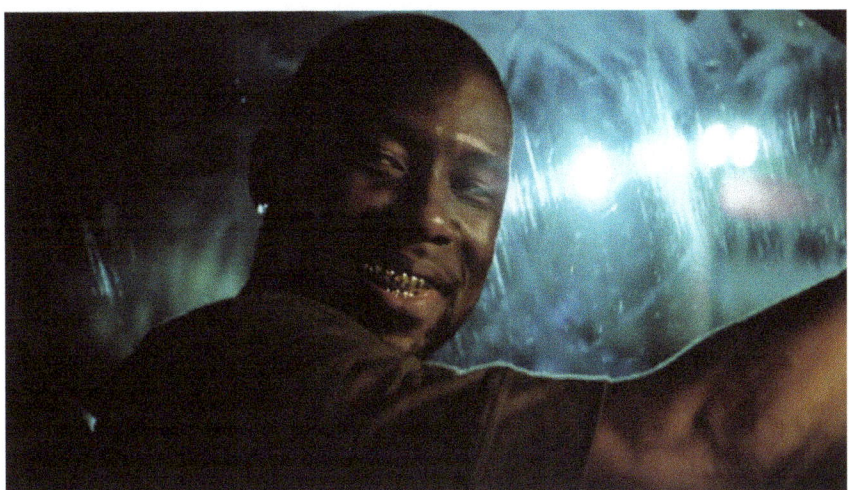

Fig. 6.8 Black (Trevante Rhodes) drives to Kevin's place after their reunion at the diner. Image reproduced under terms of fair use

inherits, on his mother's side, a profound connection to all of the waters of the world and, on his father's side, to the lands and the skies as well.[10]

Chiron's descent was, like all of the Greek myths, not without complication. Philyra had a son with Cronus while the latter assumed the form of a stallion, so that he might pursue her incognito and escape discovery by his wife (and sister) Rhea. This explains Chiron's hybrid embodiment (the other Centaurs were born from the mating of Centaurus with Magnesian mares). Philyra found Chiron's form to be repulsive and so sought distance from him. She begged the gods to spare her the shame of association and, as a result, was turned into a linden tree. The mother's repudiation seems resonant here, as does the graphic slippage between Philyra and Paula (which also means 'modest' or 'humble' or, better, 'small'). As Chiron was effectively abandoned by his mother, Philyra, and was never raised by his wayward father, Cronus, he was taken in by surrogate parents, Apollo—the god of light, truth, and prophecy, of art, music and poetry, and of healing—and his sister, Artemis—the goddess of the moon, of the wilderness, animals and hunting, of virginity and childbirth. Apollo and Artemis tutored Chiron in a range of skills, raising him to be a fabled teacher and healer in turn. So, beneath the above association of Juan and Teresa with Christian

---

[10]This account of Chiron et al. is drawn largely from Lamberton (1988). Accounts vary significantly across the vast literature, of course, but this narration should suffice for present purposes.

hagiography, we should cite these older mythological sources as additional inflection points (Fig. 6.8).

Chiron, due in part to his unique parentage, but more directly to his noble upbringing, was differentiated from the rest of the Centaurs, who were notorious for their lustfulness and ribaldry, and for their propensity for violence. Chiron was known to be wise and just, gifted in a myriad of ways, and eventually was credited with the discovery of ancient medicine based in botany, herbalism, and pharmacology. As fate would have it, Chiron's goodwill and good works were repaid with tragedy: he was injured by an errant missile, today's equivalent of a stray bullet. The mighty Hercules, in the course of executing the fourth of his legendary Twelve Labors, came into conflict with a group of Centaurs, some of whom sought refuge with their leader Chiron. One of the arrows Hercules shot into the group mistakenly struck Chiron instead and, because it had been dipped in the poisonous blood of the vanquished Hydra, a dreaded serpentine water monster dwelling in the passage to the underworld, caused Chiron intolerable pain. Not only intolerable, but also interminable, as Chiron's immortality prevented him from meeting what would otherwise be certain death. He was destined instead to an eternal suffering. Chiron prayed to Zeus for mercy and Hercules, anguished over his blunder against his mentor, negotiated an exchange in which Chiron would forfeit his immortality and die in the place of the Titan Prometheus, who had been punished by Zeus with a different manner of perpetual torture for bestowing fire without permission to humankind—shackled to a rock on Mount Caucasus, each day a giant eagle came and ate Prometheus's liver, only for the organ to regenerate each night, over and over again. Hercules thus liberated Prometheus from his imprisonment, the latter's sentence was commuted and his status restored. Zeus then memorialized the departed Chiron as the constellation Sagittarius, the Archer.

Chiron is, in this sense, the vanishing mediator between divine and human being, as well as between human and non-human animals. He is the great martyr whose sacrifice, brought about by another's zealous quest to redeem heroic manhood, consolidates the emergence of humanity as a break from or delinquency against the divine, rather than a simple reproduction of its image and likeness. Humanity is characterized here not by submission to or faith in the divine realm, however much worship of the gods and goddesses becomes institutional practice, but rather by resistance and rebellion, where, according to art historian Olga Raggio (1958), the "independence of human reason" is set in opposition to "the order of Zeus," the divine father. Reason, understood more capaciously as "divination, mathematics, the alphabet, agriculture—every science and every art" as well as "the virtues of reverence and justice" becomes the gift of a precocious and disobedient son who veers off the path of the straight and narrow, against the patriarchy (Raggio 1958, 45). And he is aided and abetted by the first immortal to relinquish his greatest power, to *choose* the limitations and finitude of mortality, that is, a fundamental vulnerability and a radical openness to the contingencies of existence. The gift of *poeisis*, again, is enabled by a combination of practical knowledge (*techne*) and practical action (*praxis*) illuminated by thinking at the limit (*theoria*).

There is something melancholic about this choice and one is put in mind of the competing moods and attitudes swirling about in the fictional lifeworld of *Moonlight* on that note. Chiron battles against the inheritance of unnamed and unnamable loss, try as he might not to fall fully into the cruelty of depression. We could think of this melancholia clinically, of course, since it is entirely understandable that Chiron would betray symptoms of the condition. "Melancholics," writes psychoanalyst Jacques Hassoun, "come smack up against a radical absence, a withdrawal from time, a necrosis that attacks the body, from which life has withdrawn before it even was inscribed there." He continues: "To pretend to live, a simulacrum facing a mere semblance of life, is the wearying task that rivets them to their inability to desire: what has been given them has immediately eluded them from the moment they entered existence" (Hassoun 1997, 54). How can we not see this semblance of life in the frailty of Chiron's halting and unsuccessful attempts to gain agency (not to be confused with control or stability per se), his pantomime impersonation of the various roles he's assigned in the stages of his development? This much appears congruent with the final query that Kevin poses to Black, after all these years apart, in the penultimate scene: "Who is you Chiron?" Chiron's response is tepid and unconvincing: "I'm me, man, ain't tryna be nothin' else." And his pivot to a confession of celibacy, while poignant, does no more to address the question, except to indicate that his focus and energies are elsewhere, withdrawn into himself when not employed half-heartedly in the underground economy. All Kevin concedes, finally, is that Black is not what he expected. Indeed (Fig. 6.9).

But perhaps it is better, given our protagonist's Hellenistic cast, to think of this melancholia in a more ancient, pre-psychological sense, as related to the old theory of humors handed down by the system of Hippocratic medicine (Arikha 2007). Sickness, on this account, is brought on by an imbalance in or corruption of one or more of the four primary bodily fluids, or humors: blood, yellow bile, black bile, and phlegm. Any such problems would result in the four major tempers. Do we not see, in the drama

Fig. 6.9 Kevin (André Holland) stands in the kitchen and asks Black, "Who is you, Chiron?" Image reproduced under terms of fair use

among black men struggling with and against the creative power of sexuality, these four humors represented in succession: Kevin, the sanguine (represented by spring, childhood, and air); Terrel, the choleric (represented by summer, youth, and fire); Juan, the phlegmatic (represented by winter, old age, and water); and Chiron, the melancholic (represented by autumn, adulthood, and earth)? Juan comes into Little's life as a figure of wisdom, an old man or at least an OG (original gangster), who brings him to the healing water to feel its soothing qualities. Kevin befriends Little in his earliest years, laying the seeds for their later encounter, during which they bond over a common pleasure in the respite of the ocean breeze. Terrel comes to the fore in Chiron's youth, ablaze with incendiary comments and searing criticism. And Black fully assumes his melancholic temper as an adult, rebuilding himself from the ground up, solid as the earth he walks on. The point is not to suggest that one position is better than another, or even that the positions are all equally bad, providing their own benefits and drawbacks. Rather, the lesson, if we can call it that, is in the constellation as it is assembled, the tension that obtains in the space outlined by connecting the dots. Temperament, after all, is not simply an index of the dominance of one of the humors over the others—or, as it happens, one pairing over the others. It signifies the attempt, always incomplete, always impossible, to find some creative way to balance oneself along the lines running between them.

Many have read Chiron's search for *an ars vitae* suitable to the circumstances as a matter of self-affirmation, and then asserted that such affirmation is, in this case, best found in the genuine acceptance and celebration of same sexuality, and of homoerotic desire more generally, as a means for greater connection within and beyond black communities. Crawley's meditation is exemplary:

> *Moonlight* reminds me that black life is about a life touched and held, and that there is joy therein, that the touch I have sought and still seek is one that many of us desire, and that such desire is worthy of its pursuit. And *Moonlight* reminds me that we should seek out and find delight in black life, and that this joy and delight can be found in the general spaces, the regular places. That we can desire and find touch that frees; touch that makes us remember and makes us forget; touch that holds us close until we lovingly and intentionally embrace those parts of ourselves that we dared not speak into existence. Crawley (2017)

The reading is compelling as far as it goes. But Chiron's oracular message is not only or even most importantly concerned with whether we can and should be able to be ourselves, if you will, without apology or compunction. He demonstrates in the enigma of his own living that the question—who is you?—remains strictly unanswerable insofar as it is a claim to self-knowledge. In this respect, Chiron is foregrounding a certain Socratic insight, seen from awry, that is well stated by Rosemarie Waldrop in her poem, "All Greek to Some Greeks": "And Socrates knew that he / knew 'nothing.' And allowed the fact to split his 'I' into he who knows and he / who is known (yet cannot be known) to know nothing. And he oscillated between/them without ever finding rest" (Waldrop 2010, 118).

Chiron, the mythical Centaur, found rest only in the larger cosmos, converted to the light of a hundred stars at the center of our galaxy, and who's brilliance reflects, however faintly, upon the surface of our moon as well. The final tableau, wherein Kevin holds Black's head gently against his shoulder, invokes something of the look of the heavenly constellations, points of light amid the sumptuous darkness. "I think the ending we have is true to the experience of the characters, not myself," Jenkins said of his film. "I love happy endings, and even *obviously* happy endings. But I can't force one upon my characters" (Tate 2016). And so he refrained from that imposition and allowed something else to linger in those last moments, something other than a happy ending, something too ambiguous to be sad either. Were it not for Kevin's unexpected call in the night, as inexplicable to him as it was unexplained to Black, the protagonist would have carried on in his life of wonder and dream, astonished at the fact of his own existence, his arrival

Fig. 6.10 Little looks out over the ocean at dusk. Image reproduced under terms of fair use

and his journey, living in the aftermath of a miracle crossed indelibly by a scandal for the ages. Though we noted earlier that moonlight does not allow us to read, in general, there is one final 'caveat lunar' from the good scientists that seems relevant at this late hour: "Some people can read by moonlight," we are told. "These people have 'moonvision'" (Philips 2006). Chiron's deeply affecting *solitude*, the one characteristic that seems to unite all of the policed and pursued figures of black masculinity addressed in this study, solicits the feel of the devastating, merciful truth expressed in one perfectly elegant line: "All isolation isn't loneliness, or yearning" (Henry-Smith 2016).

We can thank the stars for that (Fig. 6.10).

References

Als, Hinton. 2016. *Moonlight* Undoes Our Expectations. *New Yorker*, October 24. Accessed May 28, 2017. http://www.newyorker.com/magazine/2016/10/24/moonlight-undoes-our-expectations.

Anderson, Melissa. 2016. "The Sensuous Moonlight Dares to Let Black Men Love." *LA Weekly*, October 18. Accessed May 28, 2017. http://www.laweekly.com/film/the-sensuous-moonlight-dares-to-let-black-men-love-7497012.

Arikha, Noga. 2007. *Passions and Tempers: A History of the Humors*. New York: Harpers.

Attlee, James. 2011. *Nocturne: A Journey in Search of Moonlight*. Chicago: University of Chicago Press.

Bataille, Georges. 1991. Reflections on the Executioner and the Victim, trans. Elizabeth Rottenberg. *Yale French Studies* 79: 15–19.

Bradshaw, Peter. 2017. A Visually Ravishing Portrait of Masculinity. *Guardian*, February 16. Accessed May 28, 2017. https://www.theguardian.com/film/2017/feb/16/moonlight-review-masculinity-naomie-harris.

Brathwaite, Les Fabian. 2017. A *Moonlight* Revolution: The Black Queer Experience Comes of Age in America. Out, January 31. Accessed May 28, 2017. http://www.out.com/out-exclusives/2017/1/31/moonlight-revolution-black-queer-experience-comes-age-america.

Brody, Richard. 2016. The Unbearable Intimacy of *Moonlight*. *New Yorker*, October 28. Accessed May 28, 2017. http://www.newyorker.com/culture/richard-brody/the-unbearable-intimacy-of-moonlight.

Brown, Effie. 2001. *Stranger Inside*. DVD. Directed by Cheryl Dunye. New York: HBO Films.

Crawley, Ashon. 2017. To Be Held by *Moonlight*. *The Root*, February 27. Accessed May 28, 2017. http://www.theroot.com/to-be-held-by-moonlight-1792774994.

Davis, Angela Y. 1998. *Blues Legacies and Black Feminism: Gertrude 'Ma' Rainey, Bessie Smith, and Billie Holliday*. New York: Vintage.

Davis, Francis. 2003. *The History of the Blues: The Roots, The Music, The People*, New York: Da Capo Press, 2003.

Derrida, Jacques. 1987. *The Post-Card: From Socrates to Freud and Beyond*, trans. Alan Bass. Chicago: University of Chicago Press.

Dest, Stephen. 2017. *I Am Shakespeare: The Henry Green Story*. DVD. Directed by Stephen Dest. Los Angeles: Indie Rights.

Floyd, Samuel A. Jr. 1996. *The Power of Black Music: Interpreting Its History From Africa to the United States*. New York: Oxford University Press.

Gardener, Dede. 2016. *Moonlight*. DVD. Directed by Barry Jenkins. New York: A24.

Gibson, David. 2009. *The Wayfinding Handbook: Information Design for Public Places*. Princeton, NJ: Princeton Architectural Press.

Gilber, Sophie. 2016. And, Scene: Moonlight. *The Atlantic*, December 26. Accessed May 28, 2017. https://www.theatlantic.com/entertainment/archive/2016/12/the-power-of-water-in-moonlight/511547/.

Hall, Stephen. 2017. Man-Child Under the Moonlight: Black Masculinity in the Promised Land. *Black Perspectives*, February 28. Accessed May 28, 2017. http://www.aaihs.org/man-child-under-the-moonlight-black-masculinity-in-the-promised-land/.

Hartman, Saidiya. 2007. *Lose Your Mother: A Journey Along the Atlantic Slave Route*. New York: Farrar, Straus and Giroux.

Hassoun, Jacques. 1997. *The Cruelty of Depression*, trans. David Jacobson. Reading, MA: Addison Wesley.

Henry-Smith, Sean D. 2016. *Body Text*. Baton Rouge, LA: New Delta Review.

Hornaday, Ann. 2016. *Moonlight* is Both a Tough Coming-of-Age Tale and a Tender Testament to Love. *Washington Post*, October 27. Accessed May 28, 2017. https://www.washingtonpost.com/goingoutguide/movies/moonlight-is-both-a-tough-coming-of-age-tale-and-a-tender-testament-to-love/2016/10/27/45d88eea-9b80-11e6-9980-50913d68eacb_story.html.

Jones, Leroi. 1999. *Blues People: Negro Music in White America.* New York: HarperCollins.
Keeling, Kara. 2009. Looking for M-: Queer Temporality, Black Political Possibility, and Poetry From the Future. *GLQ: A Journal of Lesbian and Gay Studies* 15: 565–582.
Kermode, Mark. 2017. A Five-Star Symphony of Love. *Guardian*, Febraury 19. Accessed May 28, 2017. https://www.theguardian.com/film/2017/feb/19/moonlight-review-five-star.
Kitchin, Rob, and Scott Freundschuh (eds.). 2000. *Cognitive Mapping: Past, Present, and Future.* New York: Routledge.
Lacan, Jacques. 1991. *Seminar I: Freud's Papers on Technique, 1953–1954*, trans. John Forrester. New York: W. W. Norton & Company.
Lamberton, Robert. 1988. *Hesiod.* New Haven, CT: Yale University Press.
Lang, Nico. 2017. *Moonlight* is the First LGBT Movie to Win Best Picture. Here's Why It Matters. *Salon*, Febraury 28. Accessed May 28, 2017. http://www.salon.com/2017/02/28/moonlight-is-the-first-lgbt-movie-to-win-best-picture-heres-why-it-matters/.
Lee, Benjamin. 2016. "'It's Impossible to Be Vulnerable': How Moonlight Reflects Being a Black Gay Man in the US." *Guardian*, September 15. Accessed May 28, 2017. https://www.theguardian.com/film/2016/sep/15/itsimpossible-to-be-vulnerable-how-moonlight-reflects-being-a-black-gay-man-in-the-us.
Lee, Benjamin. 2016a. Devastating Drama is Vital Portrait of Black Gay Masculinity in America. *Guardian*, September 3. Accessed May 28, 2017. https://www.theguardian.com/film/2016/sep/03/moonlight-review-devastating-drama-is-vital-portrait-of-black-gay-masculinity-in-america.
Lee, Benjamin. 2016b. Moonlight's Tarell Alvin McCraney: 'I Never Had a Coming Out Moment'. *Guardian*, October 21. Accessed May 28, 2017. https://www.theguardian.com/film/2016/oct/21/moonlight-film-tarell-alvin-mccraney-interview.
Marriott, David. 2011. Inventions of Existence: Sylvia Wynter, Frantz Fanon, Sociogeny and 'the Damned'. *CR: The New Centennial Review* 11: 45–89.
Mujica, Barbara. 2009. *Teresa of Ávila: Lettered Woman.* Nashville, TN: Vanderbilt University Press.
Orr, Deborah. It's Painful Watching the Male Crisis Onscreen—More Painful in Real Life. *Guardian*, Feb 18. Accessed May 28, 2017. https://www.theguardian.com/commentisfree/2017/feb/18/film-therapy-masculinity-manchester-by-the-sea-moonlight.
Phillips, Tony. 2006. Strange Moonlight. Science @ NASA, September 28. Accessed May 28, 2017. https://science.nasa.gov/science-news/science-at-nasa/2006/28sep_strangemoonlight.
Raggio, Olga. 1958. The Myth of Prometheus: Its Survival and Metamorphosis up to the Eighteenth Century. *Journal of the Warburg and Courtauld Institutes* 21: 44–62.

Richardson, Matt. 2003. No More Secrets, No More Lies: African American History and Compulsory Heterosexuality. *Journal of Women's History* 15: 63–76.

Scott, A.O. 2016. *Moonlight*: Is This The Year's Best Movie? *New York Times*, October 20. Accessed May 28, 2017. https://www.nytimes.com/2016/10/21/movies/moonlight-review.html.

Shapiro, Ari. 2017. Moonlight Composer Describes Process. *National Public Radio*, Febraury 20. Accessed May 28, 2017. http://www.npr.org/2017/02/20/516292253/song-exploder-moonlight-composer-describes-process.

Smith, Valerie. 1992. The Documentary Impulse in Contemporary African American Film. In *Black Popular Culture: A Project by Michelle Wallace*, ed. Gina Dent, 56–64. New York: Dia Center for the Arts.

St. John, Maria, and Cheryl Dunye. 2004. Making Home/Making *Stranger*: An Interview with Cheryl Dunye. *Feminist Studies* 30: 325–338.

Summer, Robert. 2007. *Choral Masterworks from Bach to Britten: Reflections of a Conductor*. Lanham, MD: Scarecrow Press.

Tate, Greg. 2016. How Barry Jenkins Turned the Misery and Beauty of the Queer Black Experience Into the Year's Best Movie. *Village Voice*, December 21. Accessed May 28, 2017. http://www.villagevoice.com/film/how-barry-jenkins-turned-the-misery-and-beauty-of-the-queer-black-experience-into-the-years-best-movie-9478791.

Vesey, Alyx. 2011. Bechdel Test Canon: *Watermelon Woman*. *Bitch Media*, December 12. Accessed May 28, 2017. https://www.bitchmedia.org/post/bechdel-test-canon-the-watermelon-woman-feminist-film-review.

Waldrop, Rosemarie. 2010. *Driven to Abstraction*. New York: New Directions Publishing.

White, Armond. 2016. *Moonlight*: A Plea for Pity for a Black, Gay Statistic. *National Review*, October 22. Accessed May 28, 2017. http://www.national-review.com/article/441280/moonlight-barry-jenkins-intersectionality-black-gay-character.

Wigley, Mark. 1995. *The Architecture of Deconstruction: Derrida's Haunt*. Cambridge, MA: MIT Press.

Winokur, Mark. 2001. Body and Soul: Identifying (with) the Black Lesbian Body in Cheryl Dunye's *Watermelon Woman*. In *Recovering the Black Female Body: Self-Representations by African American Women*, ed. Michael Bennett and Vanessa D. Dickerson, 231–252. New Brunswick, NJ: Rutgers University Press.

Index

0-9

48 Hours 37
9/11 4, 13, 85

A

Aaron, Quinton 93, 97. *See also The Blind Side*
Abolition 25, 128
Academy Awards
 2002 Academy Awards 4
Afterlife of slavery 121, 142
Aggressives, The 170
Akinship, racialized 98
Ali, Muhammad 48
All in the Family 133, 134
Als, Hinton 174, 175
Antiblackness 4, 17, 26, 51, 80, 156
 gendered viii
 in culture industry 4
Athletic Industrial Complex 93
Attlee, James 183

B

Bait 16, 30
Baldwin, James 7, 8, 12
 The Devil Finds Work 7

Barnett, Ross 113, 114
Beard, Carlena 126. *See also* Buckwheat
Bennett, William 140, 141
Berg, Peter 67. *See also Friday Night Lights*
Bernstein, Robin 130–132. *See also* Pickaninny image
Berry, Halle
 2002 Academy Awards 4
 Monster's Ball 5
Binder, Guyora ix
Birth of a Nation, The (1915) 28
Birth of a Nation, The (2016) xii
Bissinger, H.G. 67. *See also Friday Night Lights*
Black athlete 48, 72, 98, 102, 121
Black competitive swimmers 38, 47. *See also Pride*
Black complicity, institutionalized 4
Black criminalization 29, 57, 60
 as perceived sexual threat 21
Black freedom struggle 38, 124, 131, 134
Black independent cinema movement 13
Black kinship 168, 169

© The Editor(s) (if applicable) and The Author(s) 2017
J. Sexton, *Black Masculinity and the Cinema of Policing*,
DOI 10.1007/978-3-319-66170-4

195

Black Lives Matter movement vii
Black male coming-of-age story 174
Black male cop character 6, 7
Black masculinity 3, 30, 56, 57, 85, 126, 145, 161, 168, 169, 190
  Black female masculinity 168
Black maternity 166, 168
Blackness and gender 30
Black Panther Party 59
Black patriarchy 79
Black power 55–57, 91, 123, 124, 133, 141, 148
Black radicalism 10, 60, 74
Black "rascals" 121, 126, 130, 131
"Blacks in officialdom" 4
Black state violence 26
Black-white buddy films 9
Black women 5, 14, 21, 23, 26, 110, 141, 148
Black women filmmakers 14
Blaxploitation 13
Blind Side, The 93–96, 99, 102, 110, 117, 121, 162
Buckwheat 122, 125, 126, 129–132, 145, 162. *See also* Black "rascals" and *Our Gang*
Burnett, Charles 13
Bush, George W. vii
  administration 4

C

Campanis, Al 38
Carrington, Ben 102
Carter, Ken 68, 74
  as depicted in *Coach Carter* 68. *See also Coach Carter*
Carter, Nell 38
Carter, Thomas 67. *See also Coach Carter*
Child welfare 137–140, 148
Chiron, Greek mythology 184, 185
Civil Rights Movement, modern 1

Civil War U.S. 91
Clinton Administration 68
Coach Carter 67–69, 73–74, 76–79, 81, 83, 85, 86, 121, 162
  character of Ty Crane 72, 81, 162
Coleman, Gary 125, 131, 132, 136, 137, 143. *See also Diff'rent Strokes*
Colorblindness, neoconservative 4
Coogler, Ryan 2. *See also Fruitvale Station*
Coppola, Francis Ford
  Apocalypse Now 28
Crawley, Ashon 174, 189

D

Dangerous Minds 81
Dash, Julie 14
Dawson, Kevin 41–43
Dest, Stephen 170. *See also I Am Shakespeare: The Henry Green Story*
Diff'rent Strokes 121, 125, 132, 133, 136, 142, 144, 146, 148, 149, 156
  character of Arnold 125, 132
Dunye, Cheryl 14, 162, 166, 168, 172
DuVernay, Ava 14

E

Ellis, Jim 38, 43, 46, 48–50, 52, 54, 58, 61
  as depicted in *Pride* 46, 60. *See also Pride*
Emancipation 142
Emancipation Proclamation 1
Evers, Medgar 113

F

Fanon, Frantz 23, 102
Farley, Anthony x, xi
Foner, Eric 1
Foster, Marcus 53, 58, 60, 61

Friday Night Lights 67–72, 76, 79, 82, 83, 85, 121, 162
   character of Coach Gary Gaines 68
Fruitvale Station 2. *See also* Grant, Oscar
Fuqua, Antoine 4, 5, 13–16, 18, 28, 30, 31. *See also Training Day*

G

Gardner, Chris 94, 95. *See also The Pursuit of Happyness*
Gerima, Haile 13
Ghosts of Ole Miss, The 115, 117
Goldberg, Whoopi 4
Gonera, Sunu 46, 60. *See also Pride*
Gordon, Lewis 17, 86
Grant, Oscar 2
Griffith, D.W. xii. *See also The Birth of a Nation* (1915)
Guerrero, Ed 9, 13–15

H

Hamamoto, Darrell 134, 135
Hancock, John Lee 93. *See also The Blind Side*
Harris, Jeff 144. *See also Diff'rent Strokes*
Harris, Leslie 14
Hartman, Saidiya 142, 168
Holder, Eric 1
Hollywood 4–6, 11–16, 21, 28, 46, 48, 67, 86, 93, 97, 110, 134, 162, 168, 169
Hoop Dreams 68
Hoosiers 76, 82, 83
Hughey, Matthew 93. *See also The White Savior Film*
Hunter-Lattany, Kristin 122, 123, 125, 126

I

I Am Shakespeare: The Henry Green Story 170

Interracial adoption 110, 121, 137, 141, 150, 152, 156, 158
In the Heat of the Night 6, 8, 10
   character of Detective Virgil Tibbs 6

J

Jackson, Samuel L. 6, 15, 68
Jacoby, Joe 101, 102
Jeffersons, The 133, 136
Jenkins, Barry 170, 172, 174, 179, 184, 189. *See also Moonlight*
Jim Crow 44, 56, 91, 92, 113
Judy, R.A. 50, 56

K

Keeling, Kara 170
King Kong (1933) 28–30, 106
King Kong as allegory 29–31
King, Martin Luther, Jr. 74
King, Steve 141. *See also* Wilders, Geert
Kinte, Kunta 136
Ku Klux Klan xii
Kukoff, Bernie 144. *See also Diff'rent Strokes*

L

Landlord, The 122
Latinos 19, 23, 26
Lean On Me 81
Lear, Norman 133, 134, 136
Lee, Spike 5, 12, 13
   Malcolm X 5
Lemieux, Jamilah 3
Lewis, Emmanuel 133. *See also Webster*
Lewis, Michael 93, 96, 100. *See also The Blind Side*

M

Malcolm X 5, 30
Malcolm X Grassroots Movement 3
Mandela, Nelson 38, 74, 75, 77

March on Washington for Jobs and Freedom, 1963 1
Martin, Darnell 14
Martin, Trayvon 2
McCraney, Tarell Alvin 174, 183. *See also Moonlight*
Mehserle, Johannes 2. *See also* Grant, Oscar
Men in Black 161
Meredith, James 112, 114, 116
Miles, Boobie 69, 71, 81, 162
  as depicted in *Friday Night Lights* 162. *See also Friday Night Lights*
Mitchell, Fritz 115. *See also The Ghosts of Ole Miss*
Monster's Ball 5
Mooney, Paul 39
Moonlight 11, 75, 172–174, 177–183, 187, 189, 190
  character of Chiron 172, 178, 179, 187
  reviews of 174
Morris, Wesley, review of *Pride* 49
Moynihan report 141
Multiculturalism, neoliberal 4
Murphy, Eddie 6, 37, 125, 131
My Baby's Daddy 162

N

Natal alienation 127, 150, 166
National Association of Black Social Workers 137
National Football League 89
New American Century 4
New Negro ix
Nixon Administration 2, 133
No Child Left Behind Act xii
Nyong'o, Tavia 127, 129, 131

O

Obama, Barack 1, 4, 44
  2008 election 4, 44

My Brother's Keeper xi
Oher, Michael 93, 95, 96, 99, 100, 102–104, 112, 116, 162
  as depicted in *The Blind Side* 93, 95, 99, 162
  as described in the book *The Blind Side* 93, 96. *See also The Blind Side*
Open Society Foundations Campaign for Black Male Achievement xii
Our Gang 121, 126, 130–132

P

Parker, Nate xii
Parting the Waters 47
Philadelphia Department of Recreation Swim Team 43. *See also* Ellis, Jim and *Pride*
Pickaninny image 130, 145
Poitier, Sidney
  2002 Academy Awards 5
  Guess Who's Coming to Dinner? 8
  In The Heat of the Night 6, 8
  Lilies of the Field 6
Policing 4, 7, 19, 25, 31, 40, 80, 121, 122, 161, 170
Pride 46, 49, 51, 60, 61, 121, 162
Prison 2, 12, 17, 31, 73, 76, 79, 91, 92, 166, 168, 172
Pursuit of Happyness, The 94, 95

R

Race to the Top xii
Racial allocation of guilt 23
Racial capitalism 90, 93
Racial wealth gap 1, 39, 95, 139
Reagan Administration 125, 140
Reagan-Bush Era 85, 134
Richardson, Matt 164
Roberts, Dorothy 139, 140
Robeson, Paul 48
Roots 136
Rothman, Barbara 142

Index

S

Said, Edward 99
Second Reconstruction 1
Shelby County v. Holder 1. *See also* Voting Rights Act of 1965
Silver, Stu 153. *See also Webster*
Sinha, Manisha ix
Slavery 29, 31, 38, 42, 91, 92, 97, 98, 100, 121, 127–130, 136, 141, 162, 168, 181
    allegory of the slave trade 30
    maritime 162
Slaves ix, x, xi, 30, 42, 128, 129, 131
    desire for equality x
    dream-work x, xi
Smith, Will 6, 15, 94
    The Pursuit of Happyness 94
Sociogeny 182
Spillers, Hortense 42, 99, 141, 142
Squires, Catherine 136, 137, 142
Stand your ground laws 3
Stanley-Jones, Aiyana 2
Stowe, Harriet Beecher 122, 127–129, 143. *See also Uncle Tom's Cabin*
Stranger Inside 162, 165, 166, 168, 170, 172
    character of Treasure Lee 166. *See also* Dunye, Cheryl
Symbionese Liberation Army 59. *See also* Foster, Marcus

T

Tate, Greg 169, 173, 174, 189
Taylor, Lawrence 100
Tea Party vii
Tears of the Sun 16
Thirteenth Amendment ix
Thomas, Billie 125, 126. *See also* Buckwheat
Topsy 122, 127–131, 140, 145, 162. *See also* Black "rascals" and *Uncle Tom's Cabin*
Townsend, Robert 13
Training Day 4, 5, 7, 12, 15–19, 21, 23, 29–31, 37, 73, 121
    character of Detective Alonzo Harris 19
Trump, Donald vii
    Administration 4
Tubman, Harriet 30
Turner, Nat insurrection xii

U

Uncle Tom's Cabin 122, 127, 129, 140
University of Mississippi 93, 107, 112, 113
    Ole Miss Riot of 1962 114

V

Voting Rights Act of 1965 1

W

Wacquant, Loïc 7, 91, 92
War on Drugs 2
War on Terror 13
Washington, Denzel 4–6, 11, 12, 15, 19, 161
    2002 Academy Awards 4
    Training Day 5, 12, 19
Watermelon Woman 162–166
    Fae Richards 162–164. *See also* Dunye, Cheryl
Webster 121–158, 162
    character of Webster 150
Weekley, Joseph 2, 3. *See also* Stanley-Jones, Aiyana
White Savior Film, The 93
Wilders, Geert 141
Wilderson, Frank B., III 81
Williamson, Marianne 75. *See also Coach Carter*
Wiltse, Jeff 40, 43–45, 54

Z

Zimmerman, George 2, 3. *See also* Martin, Trayvon

GPSR Compliance

The European Union's (EU) General Product Safety Regulation (GPSR) is a set of rules that requires consumer products to be safe and our obligations to ensure this.

If you have any concerns about our products, you can contact us on

ProductSafety@springernature.com

In case Publisher is established outside the EU, the EU authorized representative is:

Springer Nature Customer Service Center GmbH
Europaplatz 3
69115 Heidelberg, Germany

www.ingramcontent.com/pod-product-compliance
Ingram Content Group UK Ltd.
Pitfield, Milton Keynes, MK11 3LW, UK
UKHW021257180426
11947UKWH00011B/816